ASSESSMENT OF DIVING
MEDICAL FITNESS
FOR
SCUBA DIVERS AND INSTRUCTORS

Best Publishing Company

ASSESSMENT OF DIVING MEDICAL FITNESS FOR SCUBA DIVERS AND INSTRUCTORS

MEDICAL • PHYSICAL • PHYSIOLOGICAL • PSYCHOLOGICAL

by

Peter B. Bennett, Ph.D., D.Sc.
Frans J. Cronjé, M.D., M.Sc.
Ernest S. Campbell, M.D., FACS.

With contributions by:
Alessandro Marroni, M.D. and Neal W. Pollock, Ph.D.

Cover Design by Rick Melvin

First Printing, 2006
Printed in Canada

Layout and Graphic Design by Rebecca Henestofel
Editing by James T. Joiner and Joel Russell

ISBN-13: 978-1-930536-31-9
ISBN-10: 1-930536-31-3

Library of Congress Control Number: 2006925655

Published by Best Publishing Company
2355 North Steves Blvd.
P.O. Box 30100
Flagstaff, AZ 86003-0100

Tel: (928) 527-1055
Fax: (928) 526-0370
divebooks@bestpub.com
www.bestpub.com

TABLE OF CONTENTS

ABOUT THE AUTHORS

Peter B. Bennett, Ph.D., D.Sc.

Dr. Bennett, Professor of Anesthesiology, Senior Director, Center for Hyperbaric Medicine and Environmental Physiology, Duke University Medical Center, has published over 200 papers and 6 books in all aspects of diving medicine and physiology. He also provided the vision and guidance necessary to found and develop the world's largest diving medical, health, and safety organization—Divers Alert Network—in 1980. After 20 years with the British RN Scientific Service and two at DCIEM Toronto, Dr. Bennett was invited to Duke Medical Center in 1972.

Dr. Bennett has been responsible for conducting and initiating international research in areas that have benefited both the recreational, commercial, and military diving fields over the past 50 years. This includes such areas as nitrogen narcosis, oxygen toxicity, submarine escape, deep diving (high pressure nervous syndrome—HPNS), decompression illness, ascent rates, and flying after diving.

International recognition for Dr. Bennett's research and endeavors has come from many parts of the world. The first Prince Tomohito of Mikasa (Japan) Prize was awarded to him in 1990 to honor his "great accomplishments and to record his name in the annals of *Fédération Japonaise des Activités Subaquatiques*."

Following this, in 1994, he was recognized as one of only 21 foreigners to be elected to the 300-year-old Russian Academy of Science. He joined such notables as Charles Darwin and Louis Pasteur in the past, and Michael DeBakey and John West more recently.

This international recognition continued in 2001, when Dr. Bennett's research was recognized by his receiving an honorary degree, the Doctor Honoris Causa from the Université de la Meditérranée at Marseille, France. For several decades, he has had close ties with diving researchers in the south of France, such as Henri Delauze, Jean Claude Rostain, and Xavier Fructus.

Also in that same year, the Russian Academy of Sciences presented him with the Pavlov Award, which recognized his 50 years of accomplishments in dive physiology and dive medicine, including the development of Trimix. This was confirmed by deep dive studies to 2250 fsw conducted at Duke University and in Germany at GKSS.

Two more outstanding awards for Dr. Bennett were presented in 2002. He received the Carolinas' Ernst and Young Entrepreneur of the Year award for contributions to business in the life sciences. This award recognized the unique, rapid growth of DAN, a dive safety, health, and membership-driven non-profit organization. Also, the Diving Equipment and Marketing Association honored Dr. Bennett with its highest award, the "Reaching Out Award." This award is intended to recognize individuals who have made significant contributions to the diving community by "reaching out" to bring diving to people throughout the world.

Frans Cronje, M.D., M.Sc.

Frans Cronje is the Executive & Medical Director of Divers Alert Network Southern Africa. He is specialized in Aerospace and Hyperbaric Medicine and runs a private Diving and Hyperbaric Medical and Recompression Facility at the Eugene Marais Hospital in Pretoria, South Africa. He is the President of the Southern African Undersea and Hyperbaric Medical Association (SAUHMA) and serves as a medical advisor to the International Marine Contractors Association (IMCA). He is a trained Commercial Diver, Recreational Diving Instructor and DAN Instructor Trainer Examiner. He serves as the Course Director of one of five UHMS-designated introductory courses in Diving and Hyperbaric Medicine. He lectures regularly and internationally on diving medicine and fitness and supports a variety of academic programs for physicians, nurses, paramedics, and divers. He was the 1999 recipient of the DAN America Award. He has dedicated his professional career and much of his personal life to the health and safety of divers and the advancement of diving medicine and physiology.

Ernest S. Campbell, M.D., FACS.

Dr. Campbell, a retired Board Certified general surgeon, is an experienced sport diver who has used his combination of medical and diving knowledge to develop a web site, *Diving Medicine Online*, now in its ninth year, located at www.scuba-doc.com. He is the author and webmaster of the widely visited and quoted site which is a free source of diving medical information for divers, instructors, and diving medical professionals. In addition, he writes the diving medicine newsletter, *Ten Foot Stop*, which is read by some 5500 divers over the world.

A diver since 1967, initially certified by SSI and now a PADI certified Advanced & Rescue Diver, Dr. Campbell has had over 1500 sport dives in all kinds of conditions all over the world while attending many diving medical courses and seminars by DAN and Medical Seminars. An avid sailor, Dr. Campbell has earned his USCG Master's license, with a 50-ton sailing attachment.

Dr. Campbell, who has been Medical Editor for the diving magazines *Scuba Times Online* and *Scuba Diving*, has also written diving medical articles for DAN's *Alert Diver* and for the Internet medical web site, *Medscape*. In addition, he participated in physician workshops with Medical Seminars resulting in the earlier editions of the publication, *Medical Examination of Sport Scuba Divers*, now edited by Bove.

Prior to his retirement, he had been President of the Medical staff, Chairman of the Department of Surgery, and a member of the Board of Directors at Brookwood Medical Center in Birmingham, Alabama. A Fellow of the American College of Surgery, his memberships included the American Medical Association, American College of Physician Executives, Southern Medical Association, Medical Association of the State of Alabama, Southeastern Surgical Congress, Birmingham Clinical Club, Birmingham Academy of Medicine, Birmingham Surgical Society, and the UHMS.

Dr. Campbell, a Divers Alert Network referral physician and a member of the Divers Alert Network Strategic Education & Training Team, resides in Orange Beach, Alabama.

Alessandro Marroni, M.D.

Dr Marroni, a Specialist in Diving and Hyperbaric Medicine, Occupational Medicine, and Anesthesiology and Intensive Care, has published over 150 scientific papers and several books on different aspects of diving and hyperbaric medicine.

An avid skin-diver since his early years, he learned scuba diving at the age of 13 and became a Certified Diver with CMAS in 1964 and a scuba instructor in 1966, and he is still active as such.

During high school and University years he was an active athlete in Underwater Orienteering and Fin Swimming from 1964 to 1968 and was a member of the Italian National Team in 1964–1965.

During the University Medical Studies, he became progressively involved in diving medicine, starting experimental and (for the time) innovative studies on physiological monitoring of the submerged diver.

In 1973 he assisted, as the diving medical officer, Jacques Mayol's breath hold diving record (-86 meters), performing extensive physiological monitoring during the training period and the actual record dive.

In 1980, Dr. Marroni was called as a member of the steering group of the first European Post Graduate Specialization School in Underwater and Hyperbaric Medicine, at the University of Chieti, Italy.

In 1982 Dr. Marroni founded IDA—International Diving Assistance—the first not-for-profit organization in Europe and the second in the world to provide 24-hour emergency diving medical advice, transport, and hyperbaric treatment to injured divers worldwide.

The organization grew rapidly until, in 1988, a process of unification was started with the Divers Alert Network in the USA, and IDA transformed into DAN Europe and became part of the present International DAN group.

Dr. Marroni has been particularly active in pursuing the goal of harmonizing underwater and hyperbaric medicine and safety, internationally in general and in Europe in particular, and promoted the European Committee for Hyperbaric Medicine in 1989.

Dr. Marroni is currently President and Medical Director of DAN Europe, Chairman of the Board of Directors of the International DAN, Vice President of the European Committee for Hyperbaric Medicine, President of the European Foundation for the Education in Baromedicine, and Secretary General of the European College of Baromedicine.

He has also been President of the Foundation for the International Congress on Hyperbaric Medicine, and of the European Underwater and Baromedical Society.

Dr. Marroni has served as Associate Professor of Underwater and Hyperbaric Medicine at the Underwater and Hyperbaric Medicine Post Graduate School of the University of Chieti and at the Post Graduate School of Anesthesiology and Intensive Care of the University of Ancona, between 1980 and 1997, and is the International Faculty Coordinator and Professor of Hyperbaric Medicine at the International Post-Graduate School of Baromedicine of the University of Belgrade Medical School, Serbia and Montenegro, since 1997.

Neal W. Pollock, Ph.D.

Neal Pollock is a Research Associate in the Center for Hyperbaric Medicine and Environmental Physiology, Department of Anesthesiology, Duke University Medical Center, Durham, North Carolina, USA. His research interests focus on human health and safety in extreme environments.

Active and recent projects of the Duke group include: use of exercise to optimize oxygen pre-breathe and decompression procedures for astronauts preparing for extravehicular activity, determination of safe limits for flying after diving (civilian and military applications), development of oxygen breathing systems for medical and high altitude use, and comparison of end-tidal and arterial concentrations of carbon dioxide during hyperbaric exercise.

Dr. Pollock maintains an interest in field work as well as laboratory studies. He has participated in five Antarctic diving expeditions since 1990.

He received his bachelor degree in zoology (University of Alberta), master's degree in exercise physiology (University of British Columbia) and doctoral degree in exercise and environmental physiology (Florida State University).

ACKNOWLEDGMENTS

We would like to acknowledge the additional help in the production of this book by Captain Frank Butler, MC, USN, who helped with much of the material related to the eye. Sherry Strickland has labored hard over the manuscript collation and editing by the authors to produce a final book ready for publication and has been a singular asset to this book's preparation.

PREFACE

Whether you realize it or not, you as a dive instructor may be the first person to form an opinion as to the necessary general health and diving medical fitness for a prospective or certified diver to dive. This may be by way of evaluating a completed medical questionnaire, or more informally, through the practical, performance-based assessment of diving fitness during dive training. With some individuals, the problems are obvious. There are those who seem unlikely to survive the exertion of putting on a wetsuit, let alone go diving. Others, however, may be present in more subtle ways. The diver with a history of heart disease may not appear to pose a problem at first glance. Yet 40% of diving-related fatalities are related to cardiac problems. We realize that as a non-medical person you may feel a little out of your depth in dealing with these matters. Indeed, it is very difficult for an instructor to explain to an enthusiastic student why their uncontrolled epilepsy may present problems for them under water and precludes them from diving. It is for this purpose that this book was developed.

It is designed to provide the principles behind the medical considerations and decisions on diving fitness. Behind the "unfit to dive," seemingly casually scribbled on the report from the dive physician, lies a whole host of medical principles and risk/benefit considerations. We hope that this book will better allow you to explain to your dive students that, although diving is a safe sport, it may not be safe for them as individuals. It should help to make them realize that they have a social responsibility to their buddies and their families not to put their lives and health at risk by diving with a serious medical problem. This should hopefully discourage divers with serious medical conditions from succumbing to the temptation of simply doctor-shopping until they happen upon a physician ignorant enough to sign them off. It may help to reduce liability for instructors in taking divers with medical problems where they should not venture, and ultimately allow students to better enjoy their underwater excursions with greater safety.

Nothing can replace the role of a face-to-face discussion with the prospective diver and physical examination by a physician trained in diving medicine. However, we believe that this book will empower the instructor to determine when the input from a diving physician is mandatory or strongly recommended, how to avoid pitfalls in diving fitness, how to sensibly screen your prospective divers or dive students for medical problems, what to do if you discover a problem, and ultimately how to improve their health in general.

This book should also be of value to the prospective divers themselves who are considering diving and to the already trained diver with medical questions relating to their continued fitness to dive as various medical conditions arise during their lifetime.

We hope that you will enjoy reading this book as much as we enjoyed writing it.

Safe diving,

Frans J. Cronjé
Peter B. Bennett
Ernest Campbell

HOW TO USE THIS BOOK

Assessment of diving fitness is not merely the exclusion of disease; it is the thoughtful risk-analysis of the abilities and disabilities of a given individual within the context of the demands of the diving environment. This assessment includes its physical, physiological, and psychological components.

The diving instructor plays an invaluable part in this assessment. Indeed, many prospective divers—regardless of the status of their medical questionnaire or even their formal diving medical fitness evaluations—are eventually eliminated from the sport by the canny instructor as unable to master the necessary skills and abilities to dive safely. The danger is that business pressures may interfere with common sense and good judgment, thereby introducing an individual to the sport who may ultimately endanger his or her own life or those of their dive buddies. In the first part of the book we address how instructors can sharpen their senses to identify those individuals who might be at risk while diving.

A second aspect of diving fitness is often forgotten: ongoing diving fitness. Upon completion of the first dive course, there is no further requirement for periodic diving fitness assessment. Unless a diver undertakes further training, he or she may enter the sport at age 14, or even earlier today, and never receive another diving medical assessment prior to retiring from diving or from this earth! Here again, the instructor can play an invaluable role in explaining the concept of "dynamic dive medical fitness" to divers. Health is a dynamic phenomenon. It is punctuated by episodes of injury, infection, disability, and dependence on medication. Divers must know that their diving fitness is therefore also dynamic. They are ultimately responsible for their diving fitness for the major part of their lives, and they also must be empowered to assess whether or not they are fit to dive. The second part of the book is therefore dedicated to the principles of preservation of health and diver health education. In addition, many divers will from time to time be confronted with illnesses or symptoms related to their diving activities. Middle ear barotrauma, external ear infections, sea sickness, and headache are some obvious examples. We have therefore included these common nuisances and afflictions of divers and have provided advice on how to avoid or manage them.

Finally, it is never an easy task to refuse entry to diving, to a potential diver or an already trained diver, on the basis of a medical condition. There is enormous sensitivity about so-called medical "labels." People with asthma, epilepsy, or diabetes resent being called "asthmatics," "epileptics," or "diabetics"—as though these titles are a surrogate for their real name or personal identity. Accordingly, it requires much sensitivity and a careful scientific explanation to convince such individuals to not only declare these illnesses, but also to accept the fact that diving may have extra risks for them. Part Three of this book addresses the various common or important medical conditions and diseases that may impact on diving; we have listed them alphabetically for ease of reference. Each condition is explained briefly. This is followed by a brief factual overview of the impact of the condition on diving safety, the principles of diving fitness evaluation that may apply, and the generic recommendations to individuals suffering from them.

In the final analysis it is the diver him- or herself who is ultimately responsible for the decision as to whether to dive. This book, therefore, is designed to provide advice in relatively simple non-medical language to help make that decision.

PART ONE

THE ROLE OF THE INSTRUCTOR IN EVALUATING DIVING FITNESS

THE ROLE OF THE INSTRUCTOR IN EVALUATING DIVING FITNESS

INTRODUCTION

INTRODUCTION

Before we immerse you in the many useful ways in which an instructor may evaluate diving fitness in a dive student, we would like to dispel a myth of oversimplification that divers are medically disqualified on the simple basis of disease or diagnosis. Kindly allow us to drag you through the cobwebs into the deep corners of the mind of the diving physician for a brief glimpse of how aspects of a diver's medical history are analyzed and "weighed" in terms of the potential impact on diving safety.

To begin with, it is true that certain disorders—like uncontrolled epilepsy—are absolute contraindications to diving. This is not due to the diagnostic label; it is due to the inability to exclude the very real possibility that such individuals will drown while diving. For most other conditions, there is a risk analysis. This involves a determination whether pressure may have harmful effects and whether the individual is able to respond to and exercise within the environment without undue risk.

Although by no means exhaustive, for each of these two elements, we have listed a limited number of diseases that would jeopardize this fundamental aspect of diving fitness and thereby render an individual suffering from them to a variable degree of extra risk under water.

PRESSURE
- Middle Ear Infections
- Sinusitis
- Pneumothorax
- Asthma
- Bronchitis
- Upper Respiratory Tract Allergies And Hay Fever
- Poor Dental Fillings
- Ear Plugs
- Hollow False Eyes

RESPONSIVENESS TO AND EXERCISE TOLERANCE WITHIN THE DIVING ENVIRONMENT

- Epilepsy
- Fainting
- Cardiac Arrhythmias
- Hypertrophic Obstructive Cardiomyopathy (Thickened Heart Muscle)
- Aortic Valve Stenosis
- Coronary Artery Disease
- Cardiovascular Fitness
- Anti-hypertensive Medication
- Obesity
- Asthma
- Peripheral Vascular Disease
- Muscular Dystrophy
- Mitral Valve Stenosis
- Thyroid Disease (Hypothermia)
- Diabetes
- Psychiatric Disturbances
- Medication
- Physical Disabilities
- Extreme Motion Sickness
- Balance and Coordination Problems
- Neuromuscular Dysfunctions
- Adrenal Disease
- Physical Disabilities and Equipment Misfit
- Reynaud's Disease, Peripheral Vascular Disease, Vasculopathies (Blood Vessel Disorders)
- Balance and Coordination Problems including Meniere's Disease
- Thermal Adaptability Problems, including Thyroid Disease

PRESSURE AND THE BODY

INTRODUCTION

From a very broad point of view, nearly all diving accidents are related to being in a non-breathable environment with consequent effects of increased pressure on the body at depth. This is not to understate the importance of initiating factors such as poor physical conditioning, inadequate training, underlying medical conditions incompatible with diving, a panic attack, or poor planning with an out-of-air situation. The final outcome of fatal diving accidents is often written off as drowning, but the underlying cause of the drowning is the result of a progression of events related to pressure, i.e., nitrogen narcosis, gas embolism, decompression illness, or oxygen toxicity.

TERMINOLOGY AND DEFINITIONS

- **Compression**—That part of a dive that increases pressure upon a diver. The deeper a diver goes, the more the pressure.
- **Decompression**—That part of a dive when the diver ascends toward the surface, decreasing the pressure. In a chamber dive, that part of a dive when the pressure is being decreased.
- **Recompression**—A return to compression after ascent to the surface on a water dive; a return to surface pressure from altitude; a term used to describe medical treatment of decompression sickness.
- **Hyperbaric**—A word used to describe increased pressure over the pressure of one atmosphere (surface).

PRESSURE CONCEPTS

- **Pressure**—A force acting on a unit of area: Pressure = Force divided by Area
- **Atmospheric pressure**—Pressure exerted by the weight of the atmosphere; this varies with the altitude. (The higher the altitude, the lower the pressure).

- **Barometric pressure**—A measurement of atmospheric pressure; one atmosphere of pressure is equal to 760 mm Hg or 1.03 kg/cm^2 or 14.7 psi (pounds per square inch).
- **Hydrostatic pressure**—The force of a column of water acting upon a body immersed in the water, equal in all directions at a specific depth. During descent, pressure increases 0.445 psi per foot of depth in salt water or one atmosphere per 33 feet of salt water (fsw). The pressure increases by 0.432 psi per foot of depth in freshwater or one atmosphere per 34 ffw.
- **Gauge pressure**—The difference between absolute pressure and atmospheric pressure. This can be converted to absolute pressure by adding 14.7 psi or 1.03 kg/cm^2. Absolute pressure—this is the sum of all pressures acting on an object. In diving this is the sum of the atmospheric pressure (14.7 psi) + the hydrostatic pressure.

Some Characteristics of Gases

Carbon dioxide is a direct product of metabolism and is found at a maximum level of 1.5% at the surface. It is the gas that determines our rate of ventilation and is implicated in hypoxia of ascent (sometimes also called shallow water blackout) with consequent drowning. The concentration of carbon dioxide determines fresh gas ventilation schedules in diving systems and hyperbaric chambers.

Carbon monoxide is the product of incomplete combustion of fuel, usually caused by faulty compressors or faulty filtration during compression. Its toxicity is caused by its affinity for hemoglobin and the poisonous effect on our cytochrome A3 system where oxygen is converted to energy. The maximum allowable level is 10 parts per million (10 ppm or 0.001%), which is about what we get on a city street.

Nitrogen is an inert gas consisting about 78% of the air we breathe. It produces nitrogen narcosis in humans at a depth of 100 fsw (30 msw) and causes decompression sickness on ascent due to bubbles that form on reduction of pressure. It is the gas and time that determines our decompression schedules.

Oxygen is the life sustaining gas that allows our bodies to create cell energy from the food that we eat. Because oxygen is consumed (removed) by the body it can be valuable as a decompression gas, because it does not accumulate and therefore may help to avoid supersaturation. Oxygen is also used as a therapy for decompression disorders, either at one atmosphere or under pressure.

Helium is an inert gas present in air in very small quantities (0.0005%) and is used to prevent nitrogen narcosis and to reduce the work of breathing at great depths. It results in body heat loss, creates communication difficulties (Donald

Duck sounds), and increases the chance of decompression sickness with brief exposures (i.e., bounce diving).

GAS LAWS AND THEIR PHYSIOLOGICAL SIGNIFICANCE

Boyle's Law
At a given temperature the volume of a given mass of gas will vary inversely with the absolute pressure:

$$PV = K$$

Boyle's law determines the volume of gases and accounts for the major portion of diving medical problems. Stated simply, the volume of gases are reduced when pressure is increased (diver descending) and the volume is increased on reduction of pressure (diver ascending). Bubbles are reduced in size when chamber pressures are increased and air-containing spaces (lungs, middle ears, sinuses) try to expand when chamber pressures are decreased or when the diver surfaces.

Charles' Law of Constant Volume (Gay Lussac's Law)
At a constant volume, the pressure of a mass of gas varies in proportion to the absolute temperature:

$$V1/T1 = V2/T2 \text{ or } P1/T1 = P2/T2$$
V=Volume T=Temperature P=Pressure

This explains why compressed gas cylinders pressurize when heated and visa versa. Cooling scuba tanks in water while filling lowers the pressure, making them easier to fill and avoids a large drop in pressure when they cool during a subsequent dive. This is a different phenomenon to the increase in the temperature of a gas during compression (e.g., when pumping a bicycle tire or scuba cylinder) or decompression (e.g., when releasing air from a scuba tank). In these examples the mass of gas changes; the associated temperature change is explained by the Joule Thomson effect.

Dalton's Law
Total pressure exerted by a mixture of gases is equal to the sum of the partial pressures that would be exerted by each gas alone as if it alone occupied the total volume. This "the-total-is-equal-to-the-sum-of-the-parts" law also works in reverse. If the total pressure of a mixture increases, it has a proportional effect on each of its components. This explains why—breathing air—we may ultimately suffer oxygen toxicity, nitrogen narcosis with increasing depth, and also the danger of even small quantities of contaminant gases, e.g., carbon monoxide.

Because the same number of molecules fill the same space (Avogadro's law) we are able to say that partial pressure is a function of the proportion of a gas in a mixture. For example, if a gas contains 20% oxygen molecules, then the oxygen will also make up 20% of the total pressure of the gas mixture. Dalton's law allows us to determine three critical aspects of diving with compressed gas: (1) at which depth the respective constituent gases of a mixture will become toxic, (2) what mixture may be safely breathed at a particular depth, (3) and what the partial pressure of constituent gases will be when breathing a given mixture at a certain depth.

Graham's Law
This states that gases flow to areas of lesser pressure (lower concentrations) and explains movement of oxygen and inert gas molecules in the tissues of the body.

Henry's Law
In fluid, gases dissolve in direct proportion to the partial pressure of the gas to which the fluid is exposed.

This law explains oxygen transport and inert gas uptake and elimination.

Pascal's Law

$$P = FORCE \div AREA$$

Pressure (P) applied to a confined liquid at any point is transmitted undiminished throughout the liquid in all directions and acts upon every part of the confining vessel at right angles to its interior surfaces and equally upon equal areas. Practical applications of the law are seen in hydraulic machines. This is why we are not transformed into amoebas when we dive—all pressures remain in balance. It is also the reason why deep tissue compartments and internal bubbles experience the same pressure changes that occur outside the body.

HOW GASES MOVE ABOUT
- **Perfusion**—the flow of liquids in the body (blood or lymph) through an organ or tissue, during which gases and/or chemical substances are exchanged and/or redistributed.
- **Absorption**—the process of moving a gas into the liquid phase in the body.
- **Solubility**—the tendency of a particular gas to dissolve in a given medium or solvent. It determines the amount of gas that will dissolve at any given partial pressure.
- **Diffusion**—the net movement of dissolved substances from higher concentrations to lower concentrations.

- **Gradient**—the relative difference in concentration of a particular substance or gas in a solution. Gas will diffuse along a gradient, from a higher concentration to a lesser one.

CONVERSION FACTORS

Pressure Conversion Factors for One Atmosphere (1 atm) of Pressure:
- 10.08 meters sea water (msw)
- 33 feet sea water (fsw)
- 101.3 kilopascals per square meter (kPa/m^2)
- 1.033 kilogram per square cm (kg/cm^2)
- 1.013 bar
- 760 millimeters of mercury (mm Hg or Torr)
- 1034 centimeters of water (cm H_2O)

1 atm = the pressure exerted by the weight of all the air in the atmosphere upon the surface of the earth = 33 feet sea water (fsw) = 14.7 pounds per square inch (psi) = 0.445 psi/fsw^{-1} = 2.25 fsw/psi^{-1} = 0.0303 atm/fsw^{-1}

- One pint of water = one pound of weight
- 1 liter (L) = 1 kilogram (kg)
- 1000 liters (L) = 1 cubic meter (m^3)
- 1 cubic foot (cf) = 28.3 liters (L)

GASES AND DECOMPRESSION

INTRODUCTION

The physiologic effects of gases are related to their partial pressure and change according to depth (pressure). The partial pressure of a gas is the product of a concentration of gas (%) and the surrounding or ambient pressure, e.g., the concentration of oxygen (O_2) in air is about 21%; at 1 atmosphere absolute (1 ATA), the partial pressure of oxygen in air is about 0.21 ATA. The concentration of oxygen in air remains the same—irrespective of depth—but the partial pressure increases as a function of increasing ambient pressure so, at 2 ATA, the number of oxygen molecules per unit volume is twice what it is at the surface, and the partial pressure is double.

As the partial pressure of oxygen increases, toxic effects appear. Pulmonary oxygen toxicity with lung damage occurs with extended exposure to a partial pressure of oxygen (PO_2) above 0.6 atmosphere, i.e., the equivalent of 60% O_2 at the surface, or 30% O_2 at 33 fsw (10 msw). Seizures may occur if the oxygen tissue tension approaches or exceeds 2 ATA, e.g., 100% O_2 at 33 fsw (10 msw) or 50% O_2 at 99 fsw (31 msw), especially in dives with exertion.

Increased partial pressures of nitrogen (N_2) produce nitrogen narcosis, a condition that may resemble alcohol intoxication. In divers breathing air, this effect becomes noticeable at 100 fsw (30 msw) and sometimes less. It is generally incapacitating at about 10 atm abs (300 fsw / 94 msw), where it produces an anesthetic effect resembling that of 30% nitrous oxide (N_2O or laughing gas) at sea level. Helium has very weak anesthetic properties and is used in place of nitrogen in deep diving.

Partial pressure of carbon dioxide (CO_2) in the body and lungs is modified by metabolic activity (CO_2 production in exchange for O_2) and the depth and frequency of breathing. It accumulates rapidly with breath-hold diving and in underwater swimming without breathing apparatus. The impulse to return to the surface and resume breathing depends largely upon accumulation of CO_2 in the body. A breath-holding diver may hyperventilate beforehand to "cheat" (postpone) the urge to breathe by artificially reducing the amount of CO_2 in the body. However, although this blows off carbon dioxide, it adds little to stores of oxygen. This may then cause unconsciousness from hypoxia without warning before the carbon dioxide increases enough to become an effective stimulus to breathe.

Diving to a significant depth during breath-hold diving complicates the situation by temporarily elevating the partial pressure of oxygen in the lungs due to compression. However, whatever the increase was during descent will be matched by a corresponding decrease on the way back to the surface. A diver who has "pushed the limits" under those circumstances may then lose consciousness on ascent when O_2 levels fall too low to sustain consciousness. This phenomenon (hypoxia of ascent) may be responsible for many unexplained drownings among spearfishing competitors and others who do extensive breath-hold diving. The term shallow-water blackout is sometimes applied, but is best reserved for its original meaning: unconsciousness from nitrogen buildup in rebreathing types of scuba.

NITROGEN NARCOSIS ("RAPTURE OF THE DEEP")

Nitrogen is an inert gas existing in largest quantity in the atmosphere—78% in air. It is inert because it does not take part in energy transformations in the body. It causes nitrogen narcosis through the effect of Dalton's law with increasing pressure while at depth, and it may cause decompression sickness with reduction of pressure on ascent from depth. Accordingly, nitrogen uptake determines decompression schedules (see Dalton's law, page 9).

Nitrogen narcosis describes the anesthetic effect of nitrogen on the brain and nervous system due to increased partial pressure of nitrogen at depths below 100 fsw (31 msw).

Some mental effects of nitrogen narcosis include a decrease in complex reasoning and manual dexterity. The condition causes loss of motor function and decision making ability and can be compared to becoming "drunk" in a similar way to alcoholic intoxication. The comparison to having had a number of martinis (sometimes called Martini's Law) is apt, and it has been stated that one should consider the narcotic effect of one martini for every 50 fsw (16 msw) of sea water. (Of course this depends on the strength of the martini and there is actually a difference between the strength of a martini in, e.g., the UK vs. the US!)

Nitrogen narcosis can be prevented by avoiding dives below 100 fsw (31 msw). Factors that increase the possibility of nitrogen narcosis include cold, stress, heavy work and fatigue, carbon dioxide build-up, and sedatives such as medication or alcohol. If diving significantly deeper than 130 fsw (41 msw), it is advisable to use helium and oxygen (heliox or bimix) or helium, nitrogen, oxygen mixtures (Trimix) to reduce the narcotic effects.

Nitrogen narcosis can be treated effectively by an immediate, controlled ascent to less than 100 fsw (30 msw) or to the surface if appropriate, with the buddy or divemaster observing the diver for any unsafe behavior. If there are residual effects on the surface, another cause should be sought, such as low blood sugar, carbon monoxide poisoning, medication, or decompression illness. In such cases the administration of oxygen is recommended, with cessation of diving until the cause is found and fully resolved. Prevention is the best treatment, with no diving below 100 fsw (31 msw). It is common for the diver not to remember the extent of their incapacitation and to deny the effects of nitrogen. However, everybody is affected, although there is a variation in the visible effect between individuals.

OXYGEN TOXICITY

Oxygen is a toxic gas. However, the body is able to exploit its beneficial properties while controlling its poisonous effects at 1 atmosphere. However, the toxic effects of oxygen are increased at depth and the body gradually loses the battle of controlling these effects over time. The higher the inspired oxygen partial pressure, the more quickly this point is reached. For short exposure diving, the maximum recommended limit is a PO_2 of 1.6 ATA[1] due to concerns that the elevated oxygen tissue tension may cause oxygen convulsions. This is the primary limiting factor in the use of nitrox (nitrogen-oxygen mixtures) for increasing the bottom time.

Other forms of oxygen toxicity include damage to the lung, which may occur with prolonged exposure to oxygen partial pressures >0.6 ATA. However, seizures pose the greatest immediate risk to divers. Nevertheless, concerns about lung toxicity should not deter the use of appropriate oxygen first aid for diving injuries.

Signs and symptoms of oxygen toxicity include some or all of the following: muscle twitching and spasm, nausea and vomiting, dizziness, vision (tunnel vision) and hearing difficulties (tinnitus), twitching of facial muscle, irritability, confusion and a sense of impending doom, difficulty breathing, anxiety, unusual fatigue, incoordination, or convulsions. Unfortunately, there may be no signs or symptoms before a convulsion.

---

1. Note that various recreational and commercial dive training agencies have different recommendations ranging from 1.2 to 1.6 ATA. As explained by Dalton's law, this is achieved by breathing air (21% O_2) at 218 fsw (68 msw), 32% O_2 (Nitrox 32 or NNI) at 132 fsw (40 msw), or 100% O_2 at 20 fsw (6 msw).

A convulsion or loss of consciousness in water, unless using a full face mask, usually results in drowning and/or arterial gas embolism during rescue or breath-hold ascent. It can be avoided by not using pure oxygen breathing with scuba deeper than 20 fsw (6 msw) and by using appropriate Nitrox mixtures at greater depths.

There are certain diving factors that increase the risk of oxygen toxicity. These are: increasing exposure time, increasing depth, increasing the percentage of inspired oxygen (as in nitrox mixtures), immersion itself, exercise that increased the metabolic rate, increased carbon dioxide in the tissues (which may be due to cerebral vasodilatation with greater delivery of toxic oxygen quantities to the brain), cold stress (shivering, like exercise, increases metabolic rate), fever and other systemic diseases that increase the metabolic rate (such as thyroid diseases), and sympathomimetic drugs (drugs that mimic adrenaline in effect).

There are some factors that have been shown to delay, reduce, or modify the possibility of oxygen toxicity, including intermittent reduction of high PO_2 (air breaks), medication, etc.[2] The damaging or toxic effects of oxygen therapy likely are related to the unbridled formation and release of so-called reactive oxygen species, such as superoxide, hydroxyl radical, and hydrogen peroxide. Usually, enzymes in the body, such as superoxide dismutase, catalase, glutathione, and glutathione reductase, keep the formation of these aggressive and damaging chemicals in check. There also are other so-called antioxidants that defend the body against oxygen toxicity, including vitamin C, vitamin E, beta kerotene, selenium, etc. However, if the oxygen load is excessive, e.g., due to prolonged exposure to high PO_2, the toxic substances accumulate and damage cell membranes, proteins, and normal chemical processes in the body.

Pulmonary oxygen toxicity (Lorraine Smith effect) is a direct time/dose relationship on the lungs caused by the direct effect of oxygen on the lungs, resulting in damage to lung tissues, blockage of airways, increased carbon dioxide, pulmonary surfactant (i.e., substances that make the lungs flexible and distensible) changes, and enzyme interference. The best treatment is prevention and removal of pure oxygen at the first signs of toxicity.[3] These include a pain or burning sensation in the throat and chest, dry cough, and breathlessness.

---

2. In Bove & Davis' *Diving Medicine*, 3rd Edition, p.135, the following mitigating agents are listed: (1) Acclimatization to hypoxia, (2) Adrenergic blocking drugs, (3) Antioxidants, (4) Chlorpromazine, (5) Gamma-aminobutyric acid, (6) Ganglionic blocking drugs, (7) Glutathione, (8) Hypothyroidism, (9) Reserpine, (10) Starvation, (11) Succinate, (12) Trisaminomethane, (13) Intermittent exposure, (14) Disulfiram, (15) Hypothermia, (16) Vitamin E. Most of these have very limited practical value.
3. Pulmonary oxygen toxicity is highly unlikely to develop in a first aid situation and should not discourage the use of surface oxygen for diving injuries. Most sources recommend that 100% O_2 can be administered safely for between 8 and 16 hours without undue cause for concern. This is far longer that oxygen supplies are likely to last or transport to a recompression chamber or medical facility would probably take. Never withhold surface oxygen first aid if it is indicated.

CARBON DIOXIDE (CO_2) RETENTION

Carbon dioxide retention with the attendant dangers of death from convulsions and hypoxia (low oxygen level) are primarily of concern to scuba divers who "skip breathe" (i.e., intentionally try to breathe less to conserve their compressed gas source and increase their time under water). Other sources of carbon dioxide retention are breath-hold diving, breathing in a sealed environment, faulty regulator, exercise at extreme depth, and using contaminated air.

Symptoms include rapid, deep respiration, rapid pulse rate, shortness of breath, and convulsions and unconsciousness.

The carbon dioxide level in the blood is unchanged by the ambient pressure (i.e., the depth) *per se*. The partial pressure of carbon dioxide in a scuba diver's blood and lungs is a function of the metabolic rate (i.e., activity) and the rate and depth of breathing (i.e., ventilation)—exactly the same factors that determine blood carbon dioxide concentration at 1 ATA on the surface.

Unlike other gases and contaminants that are delivered to the body from the compressed gas source and undergo an increase in partial pressure with increasing depth, most of the carbon dioxide is produced by the body and depends on breathing to eliminate it. It does not, therefore, increase with depth as do other gases such as nitrogen, oxygen, carbon monoxide (CO), and hydrocarbons. Abnormal carbon dioxide accumulation in the blood can occur from too high a level of metabolism (such as from exercise at depth) and/or inadequate breathing (usually not breathing deep enough or skip breathing). The medical term for high carbon dioxide in the blood is *hypercapnia*. When the level is high enough, it can cause "CO_2 toxicity," which can lead to shortness of breath, headache, confusion, and possibly drowning.

Elevated carbon dioxide levels also play a significant role in enhancing *oxygen toxicity* and *nitrogen narcosis*. The acceptable carbon dioxide level for diving operations is 1.5% surface equivalent (10.5 mm Hg).

With the increased usage of closed circuit scuba diving, mainly by the military—but recently by more and more civilian divers—there is the possibility of high carbon dioxide levels (also called *hypercarbia*) being increasingly more involved in diving injuries.

Signs and symptoms that may be observed are hyperventilation, shortness of breath and tachycardia (rapid heart beat), headache and excessive sweating, mental impairment, and finally, unconsciousness.

This hypercarbia is often due to malfunction of the carbon dioxide absorbent canisters and can be avoided by decreasing the exercise rate, being observant of the operating limits of the canister, checking for leaks at the start of the dive, and not reusing the absorbent.

SHALLOW WATER BLACKOUT / HYPOXIA OF ASCENT (LATENT HYPOXIA)

Latent Hypoxia (LH), *Shallow Water Blackout* (SWB), and *Hypoxia of ascent* (HOA) are overlapping and in some ways synonymous terms used to describe a sudden loss of consciousness caused by oxygen starvation while in water.

There are about 7000 drownings in the U.S. annually—many victims were good swimmers. Survivors of near drowning nearly all had hyperventilated prior to the swim, did not have an urge to breathe, and had no warning of the impending unconsciousness. This phenomenon is called Latent Hypoxia (LH).[4]

In breath-hold diving, unconsciousness strikes most commonly within 15 fsw (5 msw) below the surface, where the decreasing pressure on the lungs causes a drop in oxygen partial pressure and even a drawing of oxygen from the blood into the lungs. Once unconsciousness ensues, drowning is likely. The blackout occurs quickly, insidiously, and without warning. Divers die without any idea of their impending death.

Hyperventilation is used by free divers to reduce the concentration of carbon dioxide, thereby extending the length of breath-holding by delaying the "breakpoint".[5]

Novice breath-hold divers, because of their lack of adaptation, are not generally subject to this condition. It is the intermediate divers who are most at risk. They are in an accelerated phase of training, and their physical and mental adaptations allow them to dive deeper and longer each day—sometimes too deep and too long. However, advanced divers are not immune. HOA is a common cause of death amongst champion breath-hold divers and spear fisherman.

---

4. For the purpose of this section, the terms *Latent Hypoxia* (LH); *Shallow Water Blackout* (SWB) and *Hypoxia of Ascent* (HOA), are used synonymously. Strictly speaking, SWB is reserved to describe loss of consciousness on rebreather systems in shallow water due to dilution of oxygen by inert gas leaving the body and accumulating in the rebreather. However, it is often used synonymously for LH and HOA — a special form of hypoxia incurred during ascent from breath-hold diving. LH will be used throughout this section.

5. The "breakpoint" in breath-hold diving is when the process of breathing resumes (regardless of whether a person is above or below water). If this occurs under water, aspiration of water with drowning or near drowning results. Two breakpoints are distinguished: "psychological" and "physiological." The "psychological" breakpoint is important in novice breath-hold divers; it is related to the anxiety of being submerged and may range from 5 to 30 seconds. The "physiological" breakpoint is the result of build-up of carbon dioxide, forcing involuntary breathing to resume due to stimulation of the brain stem. This may be extended by artificially lowering carbon dioxide levels through hyperventilation and is the reason why experienced breath-hold divers continue to practice it.

Conditions that Produce Latent Hypoxia

Hyperventilation
Hyperventilation is the practice of excessive breathing with an increase in the rate or depth of respiration, or both. This does not increase significantly the delivery or storage of oxygen in the body. On the contrary, if practiced too vigorously, it may actually rob the body of oxygen. The benefit of hyperventilation is that it reduces the carbon dioxide levels that ultimately stimulate the need to breathe.

The beginning diver is very sensitive to carbon dioxide levels. The acclimated diver blows off large amounts of carbon dioxide with hyperventilation, thus tricking the brain's breathing center. Normal metabolism produces carbon dioxide at a regular rate, eventually building up to the point where breathing resumes. However, this may be at odds with the decrease in oxygen so that loss of consciousness may occur before developing the urge to breathe.

Hyperventilation—as such—also causes some dangerous central nervous system changes. Practiced to excess, it causes decreased cerebral blood flow, dizziness, and muscle cramping in the arms and legs, a condition called *tetany* (i.e., muscle spasm due to a reduction in available blood calcium with the carbon dioxide-induced changes in blood acidity). Moderate degrees of hyperventilation can also cause a state of euphoria (i.e., a sense of elation or well being), leading to over-confidence until reaching loss of consciousness.

An aggravating factor is the pressure-related changes in lung PO_2. During descent, the lung PO_2 is increased in proportion to the ambient pressure. However, it drops again on the way back to the surface. Accordingly, oxygen levels—able to sustain consciousness at depth—may rapidly become critically reduced during ascent. This explains why loss of consciousness often happens just prior to surfacing. This particular form of Latent Hypoxia is therefore called Hypoxia of Ascent because of the association with ascent at the end of a breath-hold dive. The effect is most pronounced in the last 10 to 15 fsw (3–4.7 msw) below the surface where the greatest relative lung expansion occurs. The blackout is instantaneous and without warning. It is the result of a critically low level of oxygen which, in effect, switches off the brain.

The Physiology of Breath-Hold Diving
In addition to the changes due to Dalton's law, there are other physiological changes that take effect during breath-hold or free diving.

Diving Reflex
The human body is capable of remarkable adaptations to the underwater environment. Even untrained divers will show a dramatic slowing of the

heartbeat when immersed. This is commonly referred to as the diving reflex. Immersion of the face in cold water causes the heart to slow automatically. Chest compression can also slow the heart. Untrained divers can experience up to a 40% drop in heart rate. Trained divers can produce an even lower heart rate; some can slow to an incredible 20 beats per minute.

Spleen Effects

Trained free divers develop several other physiological adaptations that lead to an ability to dive deeper and longer. The spleen, acting as a blood reservoir, assists trained divers in increasing their depth-time performance. Apparently their spleen shrinks while diving, causing a release of extra blood cells and blood.

This adaptation, similar to one observed in marine mammals (the Weddell seals' blood cell concentration increases by up to 65 percent), could increase the divers ability to take up oxygen at the surface. It could also increase oxygen delivery to critical tissues during the dive.

Interestingly, the spleen's contraction and the resultant release of red cells are not immediate; they start taking effect after a quarter-hour of sustained diving. This spleen adaptation, as well as other physiologic changes, probably take a half-hour for full effect. This might account for the increased performance trained free divers notice after their first half-hour of diving, and also may be one of the causes of unexplained heart failure in the diver with a border line heart condition.

Other Adaptations

There are other known adaptations. Blood vessels in the skin contract under conditions of low oxygen in order to leave more blood available for important organs, namely the heart, brain, and muscles. Changes in blood chemistry allow the body to carry and use oxygen more efficiently. These changes, in effect, squeeze the last molecule of available oxygen from nonessential organs. Most importantly, the diver's mind adapts to longer periods of breath-holding. He can ignore, for longer periods of time, his internal voice that requires him to breathe.

Prevention of Latent Hypoxia

Several factors have been identified that can contribute to this condition. These include hyperventilation, exercise, a competitive personality, a focused mind-set, and youth.

The use of hyperventilation in preparation for free diving is controversial. No one disagrees that prolonged hyperventilation (i.e., several minutes of vigorous breathing accompanied by dizziness and tingling in the arms and legs) is dangerous. In fact some diving physicians believe that any hyperventilation is dangerous because of the variation in effects among individuals and in one person, from one time to another. The problem is that it works. For those in pursuit of longer bottom times, it is effective. The U.S. Navy Diving Manual (Volume 1, Air Diving), states, "Hyperventilation with air before a skin dive is almost standard procedure and is reasonably safe if it is not carried too far. Hyperventilation with air should not be continued beyond three to four breaths, and the diver should start to surface as soon as he notices a definite urge to resume breathing."

Medical researchers feel that many pool deaths, classified as drownings, are really the result of Latent Hypoxia. Most occur in male adolescents and young adults attempting competitive endurance breath-holding, frequently on a dare. Drowning victims, especially children, have been resuscitated from long periods of immersion in cold water for as long as 30 minutes or more. The same is not true for victims blacking out in warm-water swimming pools. Warm water hastens death by allowing tissues, especially brain tissues, to continue metabolizing rapidly. Without oxygen, irreversible cell damage occurs in minutes.

Summary
- Do not hyperventilate more than three or four breaths.
- Reduce exercise at depth.
- Recognize the danger of ignoring the urge to breathe.
- Don't hesitate to drop your weight belt.
- Avoid endurance dives.
- Adjust your weight belt so that you will float from 15 fsw (4.6 msw) to the surface if loss of consciousness occurs.
- Don't practice breath-holding in a swimming pool without having an observer standing by to assist.
- Learn the basics of CPR and think about adapting them to your diving arena, whether diving from shore, board, or boat.

HIGH PRESSURE NERVOUS SYNDROME

Helium
Because of the many risks of diving with nitrogen, other gases such as helium, neon, and argon have been used as substitute inert gases. Helium was found to be an almost perfect gas for diving. It is the second lightest element known to man—only hydrogen is lighter. Helium is one seventh as light as air, and our atmosphere only contains 5 parts per million of helium. Certain natural sources in the U.S. and Canada contain as much as 2% helium, and this is where much of this gas is collected.

Helium is chemically inert; it has no color, taste, or odor. However, helium has two disadvantages. First, helium is extremely expensive due to its rarity. Secondly, helium has high heat conductivity and will rob body heat from a diver at a rapid rate. There are also other major disadvantages to diving with helium mixes. It is more difficult to decompress, particularly in non-saturation diving. Deeper and longer stops are required as compared to air, and there is a greater risk of a serious case of decompression sickness if stops are not done as planned. Finally, in deep saturation diving, under rapid compression rates, divers may suffer from a phenomenon known as the High Pressure Nervous Syndrome (HPNS).

High Pressure Nervous Syndrome (HPNS)

Certain symptoms occur in divers at depths >600 fsw (183 msw) when diving with helium. Initially called helium tremors, the condition is now called HPNS (High Pressure Nervous Syndrome); the condition is characterized in humans by dizziness, nausea and vomiting, tremors, fatigue and sleepiness, myoclonic jerking, stomach cramps, decreases in cognition and psychomotor performance, poor sleep with nightmares, and abnormal brain wave activity in the EEG (electroencephalogram [used to record the electrical activity of the brain]).

Methods of preventing or ameliorating HPNS include using a slow and steady rate of compression to depth, stage compression with long pauses at selected intervals, employing exponential compression rates, adding other inert gases such as nitrogen or hydrogen to helium/oxygen mixtures, and selecting personnel carefully. At present, the data suggest that adding 5% nitrogen to a helium/oxygen mixture, combined with the use of a slow compression rate, and stages for adaptation, ameliorates many of the serious symptoms of HPNS.

HPNS can result from diving with mixtures that contain helium. There are three actions that you can take to avoid HPNS. They are:

- Don't dive oxygen/helium deeper than 600 fsw (188 msw).
  Note: Adding as little as 5% nitrogen to helium/oxygen mixes buffers the mix to the point that it can be used deeper than 600 fsw(188 msw) without experiencing HPNS, provided attention is given to an adequately slow descent.
- Use slow descent rates. Descending slower than one foot (0.3 msw) per minute beyond 400 fsw (125 msw) on heliox and 600 fsw (188 msw) on trimix helps keep HPNS at bay. Unfortunately, this slow rate of descent is only practical in commercial diving and is of little use in technical diving.

DECOMPRESSION SICKNESS

First described by Robert Boyle, who noted decompression induced bubbles in the eye of a snake in 1670, decompression sickness (DCS) has gradually become better understood. The popularity of sport scuba diving has caused a corresponding increase in DCS cases, allowing us to better understand the illness in its many forms. It's safe to say that DCS is caused by the production of nitrogen bubbles in the circulation and tissues, and this is related to the depth, time at depth, and to the rate and way in which the diver ascends from depth.

Called "bends" by early investigators, DCS is classically divided into Type I, Type II, and Type III. Type I DCS includes cutaneous manifestations and minor joint pain, or "pain only" bends and malaise; Type II includes severe symptoms related to the cardiopulmonary, neurological, and inner ear systems; and Type III is a combination of arterial gas embolism (AGE) and DCS with neurologic symptoms. In fact it is now realized that DCS and AGE may have overlapping causes and presentations. This has popularized the catch-all terms "decompression illness," "dysbarism," and more recently "gas bubble disorders" for clinical situations in which the distinction between DCS and AGE cannot be made confidently.

Pain syndromes primarily affect the limbs, not the central skeleton. It frequently presents as a deep ache that is difficult to characterize and pinpoint and affects the shoulders, elbows, and hands in recreational divers. Compressed air workers and commercial divers more regularly appear to have pain in their lower extremities. The cause of pain is not completely understood, but it is thought to be related to blockage of specialized blood vessels in the fatty marrow of limb bones. Left untreated, it may be the cause of dysbaric osteonecrosis (bone rot or bone death) as a long term effect.

Neurologic decompression syndromes are the most common form of DCS in sport divers. The spinal cord appears to be particularly vulnerable. Symptoms include abdominal, low back, or lower extremity pain, weakness, and loss of feeling and function. Cerebral involvement is much more common than previously thought, while lesions in peripheral nerves (nerves outside the substance of the brain and spinal cord) may also be involved in causing numbness, limb pains, and weakness.

Management and Treatment of DCS

Recognition

The first step in managing DCS is realizing it exists. DCS can present in a large variety of ways ranging from mild to life-threatening. Therefore, any unexplained sign or symptom following a dive—particularly if this involves the nervous system—should be suspected as possibly being DCS.[6] Manifestations usually appear between 15 minutes and 12 hours after surfacing.[7]

Signs
- Blotchy rash
- Paralysis or weakness
- Coughing spasms
- Staggering or instability
- Unconsciousness

Symptoms
- Tired feeling
- Itching
- Pain in arms, legs, or trunk
- Dizziness
- Numbness, tingling, or paralysis
- Chest tightness and shortness of breath

Early Management
- Provide 100% oxygen:
  - For breathing persons: via a demand valve or non-rebreather (reservoir) mask
  - For non-breathing persons: Use a pocket mask or bag-valve-mask (if trained) with oxygen supplementation
- This should be continued until professional medical assessment has been obtained, even if the diver seems cured
- Prevent inhalation of stomach contents in breathing divers by placing them on their side (i.e., recovery position)
- Transport the diver to the nearest emergency medical facility for stabilization and confirmation of the diagnosis, after which they can be moved to a recompression facility if appropriate

---

6. *Signs* and *symptoms* are often used synonymously or may be combined to avoid ambiguity. Strictly speaking, a symptom is a complaint that is *invisible* to others – such as headache, tiredness, or loss of appetite. A sign, on the other hand, is *visible* to others, such as weakness, paralysis, bleeding, etc. On the whole, signs are more serious than symptoms. A final distinction is that symptoms are usually confirmed by careful *questioning*, whereas signs are discovered on careful *examination*. The term *manifestation* avoids these subtleties and allows for a discussion of both visible and invisible features of a medical condition.
7. DCS manifestations may present under water or take as long as 48 hours to become noticeable, especially with subsequent altitude exposure. However, in most cases symptoms are detected within 6 hours, while it becomes less likely to develop symptoms for the first time after 24 hours.

Prevention of DCS

Some important diving-related factors that increase significantly the chances of developing DCS include:

- Repetitive diving (particularly deep dives)
- Diving on the edge or exceeding no-decompression stop limits
- Running out of air and/or rapid ascents
- Deep or repetitive dives using a computer (particularly if no-decompression stop limits are exceeded)
- Flying after diving as well as diving at altitude (without adjusting decompression schedules accordingly)
- Underestimated depth
- Table "fudging" (i.e., approximations of depth and time or table switching that introduce leniencies in decompression scheduling)

There are also certain physical and physiological factors that may affect the chances of getting DCS. Although there is little hard evidence to confirm or quantify these risks, they include in alphabetical order:

- Adaptation, conditioning, or recent diving history
- Age (risk for DCS increases in proportion to increase in age)
- Alcohol and hangover states (related to dehydration)
- Asthma (treated or untreated)
- Dehydration (due to any cause including caffeine, oral diuretics, alcohol, vomiting and diarrhea states, failure to drink adequate non-alcoholic liquids)
- Failure to do decompression or safety stops
- Fatigue, chilling (hypothermia), and hard physical work
- Gender (there is limited evidence that suggests that females may have variations in risk associated with the menstrual cycle)
- Injury to muscle, bone, or joint (due to increased blood flow to inflamed area)
- Medical problems increasing the viscosity of the blood (sickle cell anemia and trait)
- Obesity (although it is unknown if this is due to increased body weight or fat content or decreased fitness)
- Patent foramen ovale (opening between the two atria of the heart)
- Rate of ascent
- Repetitive, multi-day dives—particularly after a long lay-off, deep prolonged air diving
- Smoking
- Vigorous exercise before or after a dive

RISK OF INCAPACITATION
AND LOSS OF CONSCIOUSNESS

LOSS OF CONSCIOUSNESS UNDER WATER (LOCU)

Humans are not designed for survival under water. Diving is and remains an unnatural activity. The only way to engage in and return safely from prolonged submersion is by learning and following certain procedures and by mastering the use of complex equipment. All this requires alertness and the capacity to adapt to a hostile, alien environment and the ability to react quickly and appropriately to potentially life-threatening emergencies logically and with clear and effective patterns of action. From the classroom to confined water and ultimately to the open sea there is a continuum of learning and response that requires both intelligence and constant situational awareness. This is exemplified by the golden rule taught in virtually all diver training programs: "**stop, think, breathe, plan, act**." To do so, a diver must be in complete control of both body and mind.

It stands to reason, therefore, that any condition that may impair attention, awareness, or the proper evaluation of risk, let alone consciousness itself while scuba diving, may have catastrophic results and the prospect of death by drowning. One could even say that loss of consciousness under water equals death unless very, very lucky. This could also apply to situations where only self-control or effective decision-making is lost—a form of functional unconsciousness—leading to uncontrolled behavior and dangerous, impulsive actions by the diver. This is most poignantly observed during panic, when a diver might make a frantic ascent to the surface in search of "air," forgetting that in scuba diving a better, safer remedy can usually be found in the assistance of a buddy, rather than in a hazardous flight to the surface where barotrauma, decompression illness, and death may await them. To illustrate the very real and practical ways in which mental impairment may affect a diver's safety, here are some real-life examples:

- A diver suffering from *petit mal* epilepsy, leading to moments of "mental absence," performed a dive to 100 fsw (30 msw). As a result of an episode of "absence" the diver omitted several minutes of decompression and made an uncontrolled ascent due to an over-inflated BC to which he was oblivious at the time. The result was that he suffered serious decompression illness.

- Another diver, suffering from diabetes for which he was taking insulin, developed a seizure under water due to hypoglycemia (low blood sugar). Miraculously, fortunately, the diver was rescued and taken to the surface, but because he had not disclosed the fact that he was a diabetic for fear of being precluded from diving, this was not suspected as a cause. The diver was taken to a chamber for presumed decompression illness and suffered permanent brain damage as a result of the prolonged and uncorrected low blood sugar.

- A double fatality resulted from a serious case of nitrogen narcosis: two divers performed an air-dive to 220 fsw (66 msw). One became completely disorientated and started swimming towards the ocean floor. The other, also presumably affected by nitrogen narcosis, tried to retrieve his buddy. Both lost consciousness and drowned with more than 1000 psi (70 bar) in their scuba tanks.

- Another fatality occurred recently in a diver on a rebreather. As a result of a relatively rapid ascent from a 290 fsw (90 msw) dive, the diver experienced dilution hypoxia at 60 fsw (18 msw). As the diluted gas he was breathing at depth became unable to sustain consciousness closer to the surface, the device was unable to adequately enrich the breathing mixture with oxygen due to an over-inflated counterlung. He was discovered hours later dead on the ocean floor.

These are but some examples to illustrate that loss or even a lapse in consciousness under water may result in injury or death. As much as we may fantasize about liquid breathing, inhalation of water is usually the precursor to death. Unlike unconsciousness on land, where we are at least able to continue breathing, water does not afford us the same luxury.

IMPORTANT CAUSES OF LOSS OF CONSCIOUSNESS UNDER WATER (LOCU)

Among the many possible causes for LOCU, the following are the most likely and frequent:

H: Hypos & Hypers (i.e., lows and highs): Hypoglycemia, Hypotension, Hypoxia, Hypocarbia, Hypercarbia, HPNS

E: Epilepsy, Electrolytes

A: Apoplexy, Arrhythmias, Animals

D: DCI, Drugs, Damage

H:

- *Hypoglycemia* (low blood sugar): a possible complication of insufficiently controlled diabetes
- *Hypotension* (low blood pressure): can lead to insufficient oxygenation of the brain, with sudden LOCU. This is unlikely during immersion for a number of reasons, including an increased oxygen partial pressure in the breathing gases at depth and the anti-gravity effect of immersion, which prevents blood from "going to our feet." However, a hypotensive individual may suffer from the consequences of low blood pressure when exiting the water.
- *Hypoxia* (low oxygen concentration/partial pressure): leads to sudden blackout and can occur during ascent from a deep free dive, due to malfunction in a rebreather, or due to accidental gas switching during technical diving
- *Hypocarbia* (low carbon dioxide): although infrequent under water, may be caused by excessive ventilation (e.g., due to panic) and, at its extremes, can lead to reflex compensatory breath-holding, with possible LOCU.
- *Hypercarbia* (high carbon dioxide): may occur with excessive skip-breathing or as a side effect of insufficient gas exchange at depth due to greater gas density and possibly combined with nitrogen narcosis. Eventual consequences may include precipitating panic or LOCU.
- *HPNS (High Pressure Nervous Syndrome)*: is primarily associated with deep commercial or military diving, but it may well affect the modern extreme recreational technical divers. Its extreme results are tremors of the hands, muscle jerking, nausea, vomiting, dizziness, hallucinations, bouts of somnolence, and deterioration of mental and motor performance.

E:

- *Epilepsy* and seizures in general (due to oxygen toxicity, hypoglycemia, or many other causes) result in loss of control and consciousness under water
- *Electrolytes* (body salts): illnesses cause changes in body salts or electrolytes in the body. These various salts and ions in our blood and body fluids determine the proper function of our cells. Our bodies are particularly vulnerable to changes in sodium, potassium, and calcium concentrations, each of which can lead to LOCU situations, frequently complicated by cardiac dysfunction. Diseases, conditions, and even medication that may cause changes in electrolyte equilibrium should be carefully considered when assessing fitness to dive.

A:

- *Apoplexy (stroke)* is a term used to indicate sudden cerebral vascular accidents (i.e., stroke), which obviously causes immediate and serious cerebral consequences. Although loss of consciousness during stroke is relatively rare, it may occur. More commonly, sudden weakness or paralysis from a stroke may jeopardize a diver's safety. High cerebrovascular risk individuals should consider their fitness to dive very seriously.
- *Arrhythmias* are alterations of the cardiac rhythm (heart rate). Some of them may cause unpleasant sensations of a pounding pulse, anxiety, and even panic. Occasionally certain arrhythmias may result in an immediate loss of consciousness. Any condition affecting heart rate or rhythm should be evaluated prior to diving. Some arrhythmias are innocent and may even indicate health. Bradycardia (i.e., a slow heart rate) may occur in highly trained individuals or runners. Dramatic slowing of the heart may also occur due to stimulation of certain areas within the body such as the neck below the angle of the jaw and behind the eyes. Manual pressure or tight fitting equipment may cause extreme bradycardia with LOCU and even cardiac arrest in particularly susceptible individuals (vaso-vagal reactions). These individuals are normally disqualified from diving.
- *Animals*: Certain marine animal lesions can cause immediate strong pain, fear reaction, panic, and even rapid LOCU, due to serious trauma (sharks, sting-rays), envenomation (coelenterates, jelly-fish, sea-snakes, stone-fish, etc.), or anaphylaxis (a severe form of allergic reaction).

D:

- *Decompression Illness* (DCI): in its most serious forms can cause LOCU both during ascent and at surface.
- *Drugs*: the use of certain drugs, such as sedatives or recreational drugs, can cause loss of mental acuity, drowsiness, enhancement of nitrogen narcosis, and even LOCU when used during diving activities.
- *Damage/Trauma*: Finally, physical damage, such as head trauma (e.g.,

bumping the head on the bottom of the boat or being hit by the cylinder of a diver rolling off a boat), even when not immediately causing LOCU, can precipitate anxiety, panic, loss of control, uncontrolled ascent, pulmonary barotraumas, DCI, or drowning.

MINIMIZING THE RISK OF LOCU

Apart from the obvious causes listed above, there are many other conditions that may pose a risk of LOCU. Previous head trauma with loss of consciousness or memory for more than 30 minutes carries a significant risk of epilepsy, even months later. Similar risks are incurred following brain surgery. Even minor head injuries should prompt a delay of six weeks before returning to diving.

Epilepsy is generally considered an absolute contraindication to diving. While under water a diver may be exposed to possible triggering stimuli for seizures, including glare, flickering lights, sensory deprivation, hyperventilation, and increased oxygen partial pressure. Having a convulsion under water often involves breath-holding during the fit, making pulmonary barotrauma a high risk, as well as drowning. These are some existing recommendations on the subject.

British Sub Aqua Club Medical Committee: "an epileptic can be permitted to dive after five years free from fits and off medication. Where the fits were exclusively nocturnal, this can be reduced to three years."

Undersea and Hyperbaric Medical Society—Diving Committee: "individuals with epilepsy, who have been seizure-free for five years and take no medication, who choose to dive should be advised to avoid hyperventilation and cautioned that elevated pressures of oxygen may precipitate seizures. Individuals with controlled epilepsy (taking medication, seizure free for two years) are advised not to dive."

Even individuals who may meet these recommendations should bear in mind that they may still be at a significantly higher risk for developing seizures. They should advise their buddies to this effect and keep within close contact during diving.

Diabetic divers who are well controlled can usually dive without seriously increased risks. However they should bear in mind that they remain at risk for hypoglycemia (low blood sugar) and therefore also to LOCU. Attention should be given to minimizing the risk, for example, by eating before diving. The planned elevation of blood sugar should be modest, however, to avoid possible complications of hyperglycemia.

Second only to loss of consciousness, panic remains the most common cause of diving fatalities. In a review of 12,149 recreational divers by David Colvard consisting of 2916 females and 9233 males, he discovered that 45% of the males and 57% of the females who reported an episode of panic under water had experienced prior episodes of panic on land. The authors concluded that a history of prior panic corresponded to a two-fold increased relative risk of panic while diving.

MANAGING AN UNCONSCIOUS DIVER AND MINIMIZING RISKS FOR THE RESCUER

When providing emergency first aid or assistance, always remember that the first attention should go to the safety of the rescuer. It is undesirable to increase the number of victims further. Yet the urge to help often blinds rescuers to the dangers, and this also becomes a form of functional loss of consciousness. A frequently ignored factor is the risk of developing decompression illness (DCI). In fact, it is not uncommon to end up treating the rescuer for DCI after an heroic retrieval of their dead buddy from the ocean floor. While contentious in all its aspects, a victim found on the ocean floor after an unwitnessed descent, with the regulator out of the mouth, is likely to be beyond hope of recovery. In this situation, the victim, if this can be undertaken safely, should probably be allowed to make an independent, buoyant ascent to the surface. At the surface, their chances are at least marginally better than remaining under water. Otherwise, the body should be attached to a buoy line or have the air removed from the BC to limit drifting and thereby improve the chances of recovery during a subsequent search. Clearly this situation is different from being confronted by a breathing but anxious or incapacitated diver. For the rescuer this then becomes a moral decision. Their health for the sake of the other's life; risk today or guilt tomorrow—a Hobson's choice at best. For the victim, the risk of developing DCI is certainly more acceptable than the prospect of death by drowning.

Loss of consciousness, whether real or functional, remains one of the biggest threats to a diver's safety under water. It is incumbent upon instructors and dive leaders to be attuned to these risks. They need to be vigilant and wary of those who may be particularly susceptible, to identify them in advance, and—hopefully—to protect them from harm.

DYNAMIC DIVING FITNESS—
YESTERDAY, TODAY, AND TOMORROW

INTRODUCTION

How effective medical fitness assessments are remains controversial. Many specialists in any medical area firmly believe in the preventive value of them, while others claim that there is little significant evidence in their support.

Anecdotes are often quoted of people having a full cardiovascular assessment one day, with absolutely normal results, and suffering a heart attack the day after!

One could then argue:
- Are diving medicals really necessary?
- Can they prevent diving accidents?

Some data from the published comments emphasize the controversy. For example, it has been stated:

Arguments in favor:
- Medical conditions have been reported as the cause of 74% of fatalities.
- Pre-participation examinations are valid, as they permit an informed choice.

Arguments against:
- Self-administered checklists have been reported as efficient as medical examination to identify unfit candidate.
- The majority of DCI cases stem from human error.
- Most doctors, even if trained, are unable to make a correct decision on unfitness to dive.

The underwater environment implies physiological, psychological, and environmental stresses that are different from those encountered on land. This requires both correct information and awareness by the examining doctor and the diver who, arguably, should have the final right to choose whether to dive or not.

However, this should be an informed choice, based on correct information, since the rights of the individual are not protected if he or she is allowed to dive in ignorance of the risk superimposed by his or her medical condition.

Why is diving fitness necessary in recreational diving? Because it:
- Permits greater enjoyment of the sport by avoiding ear pain or other problems
- May prevent injury or death due to a medical condition
- Will minimize the risk to buddies, rescuers, or emergency services by avoiding the need for assisting a diver with a medical fitness problem
- Protects the right of a trainee diver to be in the hands of an individual who is not likely to become incapacitated under water due to a pre-existing medical condition incompatible with diving
- Allows a diver to perform his or her civil obligation as a buddy without physical impairment
- Avoids aggravation of existing illness

The University of Rhode Island National Underwater Accident Data Center and the Divers Alert Network have, over the last 30 years, recorded data on over 3000 scuba fatalities. In addition, other international DAN organizations have contributed data. DAN Europe's statistics, for example, show that around 28% of preventable injuries and deaths are related to pre-existing medical problems. In 25% of diving fatalities, there were obvious pre-existing problems that specifically contributed to the fatality;[8] if the diver had either received a medical or—as in some cases—listened to the advice they were given, the deaths may have been avoided (Table 1).

---

8. It is difficult to make accurate assessments on the effectiveness of measures in the prevention of deaths. The value of diving medicals has been assessed as being between 25% and 75% in preventing disease-related deaths while diving. The dilemma is that divers do not have regular assessments; in many cases they continue diving after only a single entry-level medical assessment. So the dive medical is not an infallible solution. Far more important and readily available is the intuition of the diveleader and instructor. In spite of commercial pressures, they need to find ways to assess divers continually—both formally and informally—and have the courage to recommend that a particular diver refrains from diving until they are in better health.

Table I. Diving Fitness Factors vs. Diving Fatalities (DAN Europe Accident Data)

Diabetes	1%
Epilepsy	1%
Ear Problems	2%
Severe Disability	3%
Physically very unfit	4%
Taking unsuitable prescription medications	7%
Other pulmonary pathology	7%
Asthma	8%
Gross Obesity	8%
Hypertension	8%
Advised that they were unfit to dive	9%
Pre-existing cardiac disease	12%
Age > 50[9]	18%

Why does it seem as though diving medicals may be somewhat disappointing in their ability to prevent injury and death? Well, there are many reasons. Firstly, all that can be said after performing a diving medical is that an individual—at that moment only—does not appear to have a medical condition incompatible with safe diving. Of course many divers never have another medical, have changes in health never reported to a diving physician, and usually suffer the consequences of their own choices and actions rather than any medical conditions under water. On the side of the physician, there are also limitations. Current questionnaires and examination systems may fail to adequately identify high risk individuals. The demands of the underwater environment may not be fully appreciated; standards may be applied variably due to ignorance; most medical professionals focus on the exclusion of disease rather than the confirmation of health; psychological factors are difficult to assess objectively, and are usually overlooked. Ultimately, for recreational divers, it is the divers themselves who determine their readiness and willingness to dive. So, besides taking into account lists of specific diseases and conditions "classically" considered a contraindication to diving, *all divers* should be able to perform a *self-evaluation*, based on the knowledge of a few simple concepts given below.

GENERAL FITNESS AND HEALTH
Common sense should not be overlooked in favor of pursuit for greater expertise or the rationalization of risk! Recreational diving is a leisure activity that should be relaxing and enjoyable. Health impairment brings greater risk and erodes the enjoyment of the diving experience.

---

9. As the diving population continues to age, the implications of diving fitness will become increasingly important.

"FUNCTIONAL" FITNESS

Certain organs and body systems are primarily involved in diving. They are the "vital organs of diving" and include the:

- Lungs
- Heart
- Ears and paranasal sinuses

Accordingly, any condition compromising the function or reliability of these organs, even if temporary and apparently trivial, may become a life threatening problem once under water.

"DYNAMIC" FITNESS

Our health and fitness status is ever changing and it even oscillates from day to day. Lack of sleep, hangovers, transitory ailments, a common cold, fever, a seasonal viral infection, etc., all significantly affect our performance under water (as well as on the surface).

A single favorable diving medical assessment does not immunize a diver to future disease and contraindications to diving. There is no "permanently fit to dive" certificate. Divers therefore have to take into account the variability of the human condition and how this can affect safety under water on the day of the dive. This concept should already be introduced during initial dive training, and instructors and dive leaders would do well to lead by example. An allegory to this (which may be useful when explaining this concept to students): You do not get injured or die every time you decide to drive without a seat belt, but we all realize it is both unwise and unsafe to do so. Therefore, we wear them all the time (or at least most of us do). Why then do we not apply this same principle to diving fitness?

THE EXTRAORDINARY ENVIRONMENT OF DIVING

Diving is performed in an unnatural environment. It is only by virtue of special techniques, equipment, procedures, awareness, and knowledge that we are able to survive, let alone enjoy, the experience.

Divers should never underestimate the specific hazards and restrictions related to the diving environment, nor the impact of the aquatic realm on their health and fitness:

- You cannot breathe water
- Water restricts the speed and effort of movement
- Immersion and submersions may cause disorientation motion sickness and panic due to loss of the sense of gravity and limited visibility

- Being in the water, especially if deep with no visible bottom, can induce uncontrollable anxiety and panic, even in expert swimmers/divers
- The ability to breathe under water is done at the expense of the greater partial pressure of the gases we breathe. With this come toxicities and risks of effervescence and over-expansion injuries. Only by continually respecting these factors and bearing these in mind in what we do can we avoid the dangers they hold.

PRESSURE-DEPENDENT PHYSIOLOGICAL VARIABLES

When embarking on a dive medical assessment, both divers and physicians should realize and consider the specific laws of physics and their effects on human physiology. Rather than a mere evaluation of health or the search for some invisible disease, a diving medical should consider:

Organs and conditions that may be affected by the variations of ambient pressure:
- Are gas-filled cavities, natural or artificial, normal and freely communicating with the external environment (i.e., able to equalize)?

Conditions that may jeopardize survival in the extraordinary diving environment:
- Are there any conditions (neurological, cardiac, metabolic, psychological) that may cause sudden incapacitation, loss of consciousness, or loss of control?

Conditions affected by your aerobic performance:
- Is there any impairment in the ability to exercise if required during the dive? Consider special diving environmental conditions, such as strong currents, high seas, and distant diving boats, particularly if it is known that these are the conditions for which the individual is preparing.

Conditions affecting strength and agility in water/ nautical environments:
- Are the individual's age, maturity, physique, strength (i.e., the ability to cope with the size and weight of diving equipment), psychological make-up, swimming skills, motor co-ordination and balance (i.e., the ability to cope with unstable platforms such as boats) compatible with the ability to dive safely?

FITNESS STANDARDS

In the past, diving medical standards have frequently been imposed in a parochial, presumptive, and arbitrary way. However, unlike working divers, recreational divers have no compulsory need to undergo a diving medical. Only if this is specifically imposed by the dive operator or training establishment may they end up getting an examination. Even then they have a choice to shop for a more lenient dive school or physician or to simply avoid disclosing the medical condition which previously prompted further scrutiny or censure. For these reasons it is so important for instructors and diving physicians to explain clearly and specifically why a particular condition may impose a partial or unacceptable risk on diving.

Many diving fitness standards remain empirical. There is limited scientific data to support them and even less to determine the relative probabilities of risk. Even the International Jury of the 6th European Consensus Conference of the European Committee for Hyperbaric Medicine on the Prevention of Dysbaric Injuries in Diving and Hyperbaric work (Geneva, 2003) stated:

> *The method of assessment for compliance with these fitness recommendations may vary. For example, different categories of diving may select a greater or lesser dependence on the use of self-administered questionnaires. It is considered that at present there is insufficient evidence to make a final decision on this and the Jury recommends that the ECHM-EDTC conducts a future review on the basis of validated evidence.*

and:

> *The Jury recommends that periodic re-assessment be required for all and that re-assessment is also required occasionally in between such periodic assessments. This may be the result of some illness or accident whether it occurs while diving or when at the surface. It is recommended by the Jury that the diver or worker at raised environmental pressure be instructed on their personal responsibility for initiating this process.*

Ultimately the diver is the most variable but ultimately the most fundamental link in this safety chain. Valid information, knowledge, experience, and awareness can only improve the ability for making better decisions. In this, the dive leader can make all the difference, sometimes a vital difference.

PSYCHOLOGICAL ASPECTS OF DIVING

INTRODUCTION

Diversity is one of the most stimulating and challenging aspects of dealing with people. In addition to different genders, ethnicities, nationalities, and languages, our integration into and interaction with society is a function of our unique personalities. Our personalities develop within a complex evolutionary tug of war between inherited potential, psychosocial imprinting, and personal choice. In addition to our private persona, we also have a public personality that is affected by the immediate environment and the group we interact with. All this comes into the mix when learning to dive. Here a process of learning introduces us to the foreign and inevitably stressful experience of submergence and the acquired ability to breathe under water. This conditioning process is colored by our personalities. It adds a further layer of complexity as we are guided by an instructor while participating within a group of individuals—usually predominantly strangers.

Instructors and Divemasters quickly develop a sixth sense in anticipating problems during dive training or open water diving. Although obviously problematic, individuals are quickly flagged as "highly strung," anxious, nervous, "squirrely," or "jumpy;" every now and then there is an individual who catches you unaware—one who suddenly and unexpectedly panics and bolts to the surface. The question is: are there ways to identify these individuals in advance, or even better, prevent them from panicking in the first place? In addition, can one somehow use the uniqueness of an individual's personality to their own advantage? Can we use our knowledge of personality to guide the way we relate to the people and how we train and guide them under water? This section explores the possibility of doing just that.

PERSONALITY TYPES

The history of psychology has seen many attempts at categorizing people according to personality traits. Various systems have emerged, including Cattell's Factor-Analytic Trait Theory, Goldberg's Five-Factor Model of Personality, and Eysenck's Trait Dimensional Theory. Most psychoanalytical systems are too complicated for lay people to apply and it is always dangerous to "label" people. However, certain fundamental observations have great utility in managing people.

The two dimensional system, elaborated by Eysenck (Fig. 1), divides people into four basic personality types, based on how outgoing (extroverted vs. introverted) and emotional (unemotional vs. emotional) they are. Hippocrates originally attributed these traits to the presumed contents of the circulatory system (blood, yellow bile, black bile, or phlegm). Of course this is overly simplistic, but it goes a long way towards gaining a fundamental understanding of people and even predicting their behavior.

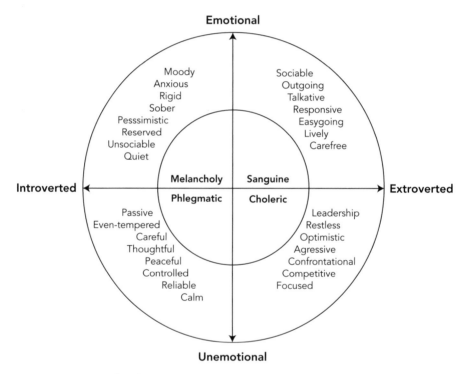

Figure 1 Modified from Eysenck's Two-Dimensional Classification of Personality

- Emotional & extroverted (sanguine—red blooded): *The party animal*
- Unemotional & extroverted (choleric—yellow bile): *The go-getter*
- Emotional & introverted (melancholic—black bile): *The cynic*
- Unemotional & introverted (phlegmatic—phlegm blooded): *Old-faithful*

PERSONALITY-BASED TRAINING

For training to be successful, learning needs to occur. As diving is primarily a practical endeavor, students need to absorb the information being presented, integrate it within their mental library of prior knowledge and associations, remember it, and ultimately master the appropriate practical skills to dive safely and care for themselves under water.

We all learn in different ways. We have sensory preferences too. Some learn what they see, others what they hear, and others what they experience, feel, and touch. On top of all this are our unique personalities, which color this process and may facilitate or obstruct it. Understanding that nature of people—their personality—improves our ability to stylize the presentation of educational material and experiences in such a way that it is more acceptable to the recipient, and accordingly, learning is more likely to occur.

Although there are many exceptions, it is relatively easy to "peg" people according to their "instinctive" responses:

When faced with a challenge, adversity, or the need to master a new skill:
- The Sanguine will make light of it or be enthusiastic. The challenge is therefore to get them to focus on the job, while emphasizing the fun element that appeals to them.
- The Choleric will storm challenges head on. Here one needs to curb impatience and over-ambitiousness with sensitivity and wisdom, by providing recognition and rewarding good efforts.
- The Melancholics will tend to doubt themselves. They need to be told that their concerns are understandable but that they should not feel intimidated; the task is actually quite simple and manageable.
- The Phlegmatic will plod through it. They only need to be mobilized and informed that it will not take too much effort.

When faced with authority or instruction:
- The Sanguine may undermine the instructor with humor and teasing. Accept the humor and redirect the energy towards gaining cooperation. Invite participation and fence with enthusiasm.
- The Choleric may confront you. Acknowledge their intelligence and skills and make them feel part of the effort. Ask for their help.
- The Melancholic may outwardly conform, but may privately resent being instructed and become obstructive in passive ways—being late, etc. Show appreciation and sympathy.
- The Phlegmatic will follow instructions, but may need to understand exactly what is involved. Careful explanation is the best approach.

When mildly anxious or concerned:
- The Sanguine will chatter or joke.
- The Choleric may become testy.
- The Melancholic will mope.
- The Phlegmatic will grind to a halt.

When approaching near-panic levels, a personality inversion may occur and paradoxical behavior may manifest. Be careful when this is observed.

In most situations, a good broad-brushed approach is to tell the:

- Sanguine that it will be fun
- Choleric that it will be a challenge
- Melancholic that all will be OK
- Phlegmatic that it will not be inconvenient.

Try this out on your next course or diving experience. If nothing else it will add fun to the experience, be a challenge, not cause difficulties, and not require too much effort!

TIPS ON DEALING WITH ENTRY LEVEL DIVERS
Certain sections of entry level training are routinely approached with dread. They are notorious for yielding course dropouts and inducing panic attacks. However, with some preventative strategies, individuals who are likely to struggle can be identified and the problems overcome before they occur.

There are at least three ways in which to identify and counter an individual's "panic potential" during entry level training.

1) Squeamishness to Clear the Ears and "Ear Fear"
Most novice divers find the fullness associated with ear clearing "unnatural." In anxious individuals or those who have had problems with their ears in childhood, this may present as fear and even panic. It is quite difficult to explain to someone what it feels like to clear the ears or exactly how hard to blow. Two practical hints that have served very well are as follows:

a. Explain that ear clearing may not be obvious and sound more like clicking your nails together or the soft squishing sound when separating your thumb and index finger next to your ear after wetting them.
b. There is usually an associated feeling of fullness or blocked-ness, but often the only noticeable change may be a change in hearing—this may be either better or slightly worse with ear clearing depending on the position of the ear drum prior to equalizing.

c. For those who battle to equalize, it is helpful to obtain a device called the Otovent® (http://www.invotec.net). This simple combination of a nozzle and a balloon allows the prospective student to understand how hard they should blow to equalize. In addition, the process of inflating the balloon distracts the attention so that the fear of equalizing is transiently lost. By the time the balloon has deflated itself, the lesson is learned and the process becomes so much easier.

2) Difficulty Breathing Through the Mouth With the Nose Closed

As trivial as this may seem, people who are unaccustomed to being in water or swimming find it very uncomfortable to breathe through the mouth with the nose closed (as happens when wearing a face mask). In extreme cases this alone may lead to panic. By explaining the adjustment process to them, and having them practice at home—preferably snorkeling in their own bath (where no one is likely to be anxious) with their dive mask on their face—much of this anxiety can be overcome before being confronted by a cold swimming pool surrounded by other dive students.

3) Difficulty Clearing the Mask

Once ear equalizing is mastered, the three most challenging skills for a diver to learn are mask clearing, demand valve recovery, and buoyancy control. Of these, mask clearing is most likely to send them to the surface choking and in sudden fear of drowning. Again, much can be gained by having an individual practice breathing through a snorkel, lying prone in their own bath, while closing the eyes and pinching the nose. Once this is mastered, the diver can practice releasing the nose and using the soft palate to prevent the entry of water into the nose. As a further step, the mask can be worn and gradually removed as confidence is gained. One of the greatest reassurances an instructor can offer a student is that it is acceptable, initially, to pinch the nose after getting water into the mask—at least until they have regained their breathing rhythm. In time this will no longer be required and, by then, confidence will have overcome their "bolting potential."

Despite all these and other strategies, some people simply do not belong in the water and the wise instructor will allow a person who really "wants out" to leave the course with their egos intact. Opportunity to return later and other gentle "let downs" can go a long way towards avoiding dive training becoming a chapter in their "Life's Worst Experiences" book!

TIPS ON DEALING WITH OPEN WATER DIVING

A unique feature of open water diving is that an Instructor or Divemaster may not necessarily have the benefit of getting to know their aquatic partners in advance. However, a combination of subtle questioning, careful observation, wise partnering, and careful surveillance can avoid healthy excitement from becoming lethal fear. In addition, to knowing something about personality types (see the section on Personality-based Training page 39), it is important to observe and interpret behavior. A person's body rarely lies and much can be learned about the contents of a person's mind by observing their movement of their limbs.

Eighty percent of all communication is non-verbal. Accordingly, paying attention to body language and movements may reveal a person's true feelings. Behavior often contradicts a person's words. In case of a discrepancy—believe their bodies.

There are four basic behavior patterns to look out for: defensiveness, over-attentiveness, erratic movements, and withdrawal.

   1) Defensiveness

   This behavior type includes all forms of limb crossing, ranging from simple leg crossing to arms folding. The tighter the posture, the tighter the tension. Respond with open gestures and friendly, calming words; it is rare to find (with the possible exception of someone who is trying to stay warm) that an individual will remain physically "clenched."

   2) Over-attentiveness

   This can be recognized in someone who keeps checking their equipment, is forever looking for personal belongings, or obsessively fidgets with something without an apparent objective. Reassurance about equipment or careful enquiries about concerns may be helpful. Don't reveal your observation, as this may add further tension, simply address its subtext: worry!

   3) Erratic Movements

   This is especially obvious under water. Four-limb swimming, treading water with an inflated BC, frequent changes in direction and posture, all hint at latent discomfort. Distraction is often useful to unwind a person's mind, e.g., pointing out a beautiful marine creature or involving them. As a Divemaster, in such situations, it is best to try to stay in one area with everyone close together until the nervous individual settles and is able to catch their emotional and physical "breath."

4) Withdrawal

This is an ominous sign and generally indicates that a person is so uncomfortable that they are bracing themselves for the worst. Unlike the other forms of behavior that may be harbingers of panic, these divers may just quietly disappear or stray from the group. Pay close attention to these individuals and try to engage them in conversation. Buddy them with responsible and attentive partners if possible.

The human psyche is far too complex to be reduced to a few simple observations. However if these principles are observed, many problems can be spotted before they result in injury, and your ability to add to other's enjoyment of diving will increase dramatically.

NOTES

PART TWO

DIVING FITNESS
THE DIVER'S RESPONSIBILITIES

DIVING FITNESS
THE DIVER'S RESPONSIBILITIES

HEALTH MAINTENANCE

FITNESS TO DIVE—INTEGRATED FOR ALL SYSTEMS

Fitness to dive is based upon a number of factors that can be categorized as foundation, capacity, and readiness elements (Figure 2). The foundation is established by sound fundamental medical, psychological, and physical fitness. Capacity is established by adequate knowledge and physical skills—adequate to meet both the normal demands of the type of diving being considered and the exceptional demands that may arise in emergent situations. Readiness is established by sound acute medical, psychological, and physical fitness and nutritional status.

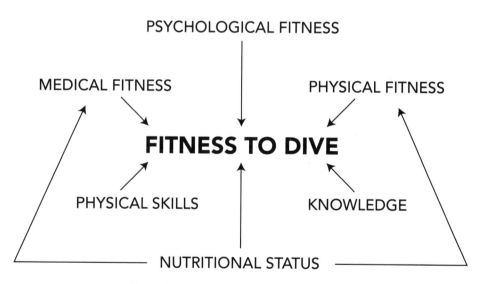

Figure 2 Factors contributing to fitness to dive

The most practical strategy to maintain good health and, by extension, good diving health and safety, is to control the risks of living. An honest appraisal of each of the factors contributing to fitness to dive is an excellent start.

Assessment of Readiness and Fitness to Dive

The Diving Medium—Water and Immersion

The aqueous environment provides some wonderful freedoms. Perhaps the most significant of becoming submerged is the sudden relative loss of gravity, the opportunity to get some sense of what operating in an environment without gravity feels like. Our self-powered horizons are suddenly increased from two primary dimensions to three.

However, water immersion also has some physical costs. It has both a greater density and a greater specific heat than air (i.e., the amount of heat required to increase the temperature of a unit of mass). The heat capacity of water (i.e., density multiplied by specific heat) is approximately 3500 times greater than that of air. Effectively, water that is cooler than body temperature will conduct heat energy away from the body at a rate 20–27 times faster than still air. Thermal protection is required in even relatively warm water to maintain comfort. Unless protected, an immersed body will continue losing heat energy. A reference threshold exists between 29°C–33°C (84°F–91°F) for a semi-naked, resting subject. This is called "critical water temperature" and is defined as the lowest temperature at which maximal vasoconstriction can maintain core temperature without shivering or exercise. There is some individual variability depending on body size, shape, and composition.

The high density of water generates much higher resistance and drag forces that must be overcome to move through the water. The energy efficiency of swimming typically ranges from 2%–9%. The efficiency of a diver is even less due to the additional drag caused by the equipment. The variables that can be most easily altered to reduce the effort of swimming in dive gear are frontal surface area and speed:

Frontal Surface Area:

While the frontal surface area of a diver will always be greater than that of a swimmer because of the extra equipment worn, it can be improved by maintaining the most streamlined position possible. Divers should also avoid pivoting into a more vertical position—often caused by excess weight on a weight belt. Overweighting *per se* also requires additional air in the buoyancy compensator, which tends to shift the diver upright, thereby increasing frontal surface area. Divers should be encouraged to re-evaluate neutral buoyancy on a regular basis. Many divers fail to appreciate that they will need less weight once they become more comfortable in the water. Many divers continue having buoyancy problems and even develop lower back discomfort before realizing that they have outgrown the need for all the weight they carry.[10] Similarly, divers who have problems with their feet "floating up" may resort to ankle weights. Ankle weights do help to keep the ankles down—a common concern of novice divers. What they may fail to realize is that a relative "feet high" position is generally the best to look at things on the bottom without disturbing them. Ankle weights may also exaggerate the force pushing a diver into an upright position, thereby again increasing frontal surface area and decreasing efficiency. More importantly, they add a "cost" to each kick stroke. Even a relatively small amount of mass placed so far away from the center of mass (i.e., making a long moment arm) has a substantial effect on each effort to move it. Increasing, the work of finning makes little sense unless a diver wants to work harder than necessary. A final argument for ankle weights often comes from novice drysuit divers who are worried about air traveling to their feet and blowing off their fins. First, it should not be a significant risk if the suit fits and the diver is properly weighted and trained. If fin blow-off remains a concern, wearing straps alone at the ankle would be a better choice than adding weight there.

Swim Speed:
The second easily modifiable factor is swim speed. The drag of water increases with the cube of the speed. This means, for example, that doubling swim speed will increase drag eightfold (i.e., 2 x 2 x 2). Experiment with finning speed to find the best combination of greatest underwater travel for the least amount of effort.

Exercise Capacity and the Demands of Diving
Measuring Exercise Capacity
Exercise capacity can be evaluated in a variety of ways. Laboratory tests are objective but the conditions they employ may be quite different from those experienced during real world activities. Field evaluations can be designed to test performance under closer-to-real-world conditions, but interpretation of the results can still be difficult. The results of a test developed under a specific set of conditions may not apply equally to a different set of conditions or with a different type of subject. While the adoption of standard, validated tests is convenient, the limitations of any test must be considered. This is most important when the results may be used to qualify or disqualify an individual from participating in any activity. The use of multiple, complementary methods of evaluation may then be more appropriate. Limitations on the availability of testing options also make it important to have a sense of how the results of different tests may compare.

---

10. Transient lower back discomfort can be reduced by having the diver grab his or her knees and contract the back muscles to hold a stretch in a forward flexed position for a few seconds. This is easier to do when supported by water than in any other circumstance.

Laboratory Testing

The laboratory or clinical test that is closest to a "gold standard" for determining general exercise capacity is the test of aerobic fitness (or aerobic capacity or $VO_{2\,max}$). While it is certainly not the only measure, it is highly objective and a reasonable predictor of overall performance. $VO_{2\,max}$ is defined as the maximum amount of oxygen that an individual can consume per unit time. An analogy would be to measure the peak gas consumption of an automobile to determine its performance capability. While not entirely flawless in principle, it is one of the best biological yardsticks we have. $VO_{2\,max}$ is most accurately measured with a progressive, staged exercise test that ends when the subject can no longer continue. The exercise employed is typically treadmill running or stationary cycling, but a few laboratories have developed specialty test systems for swimming, kayaking, or other specific sports as required.

The subject's expired breath is measured throughout the progressive test and the content of oxygen and carbon dioxide compared against room air. The test does not evaluate specific muscles, but provides a whole body measure of the person's metabolic capability. It is temporarily exhausting, but a relatively efficient and non-invasive means of evaluating an important standard for physical fitness. An electrocardiogram can be monitored during the test to identify cardiac abnormalities that may become evident during physiological stress.

$VO_{2\,max}$ performance is normally reported as either whole body oxygen utilization (liters of oxygen consumed per minute at maximal effort, i.e., $L \cdot min^{-1}$) or as utilization indexed to body mass (milliliters of oxygen per kilogram body mass per minute, i.e., $mL \cdot kg^{-1} \cdot min^{-1}$). The latter form is more useful since it allows direct comparison between individuals of different size. Consumption can also be indexed to lean body mass (LBM or fat free mass, i.e., $mL \cdot kg^{-1} \cdot min^{-1}$ LBM) if substantial differences exist in body composition. Since fat tissue is metabolically inactive, the effort of working muscle is underestimated in simple weight-indexed measures for individuals with large percentages of fat. Unless specified, the more standard measure of indexing oxygen consumption to whole body mass will be used in this discussion.

The normal range of $VO_{2\,max}$ values in the healthy population is 17 to >85 $mL \cdot kg^{-1} \cdot min^{-1}$. Unfortunately, the numbers and units associated with $VO_{2\,max}$ results can seem unnecessarily complicated to the lay person. A simpler way to present the results is in terms of metabolic equivalents (MET). The MET is a dimensionless value that equates to the standard assumed metabolic rate at rest (3.5 $mL \cdot kg^{-1} \cdot min^{-1}$). Maximal aerobic capacity in MET units (MET_{max}) is determined by dividing the value for $VO_{2\,max}$ in $mL \cdot kg^{-1} \cdot min^{-1}$ by 3.5. For example, an individual with a $VO_{2\,max}$ of 35 $mL \cdot kg^{-1} \cdot min^{-1}$ would have a MET capacity of 10 (i.e., 35 $mL \cdot kg^{-1} \cdot min^{-1}$ ÷ 3.5 $mL \cdot kg^{-1} \cdot min^{-1}$).

The use of a single standard MET value for both genders puts women at a disadvantage since on average they have a higher percentage of body fat (the healthy, normal range is 12%–18% for males and 22%–29% for females). The higher percentage of body fat is reflected in a lower metabolic rate at rest. While not commonly done, it is reasonable to compute MET_{max} values for women using a standard of 3.2 $mL \cdot kg^{-1} \cdot min^{-1}$.

The normal range of MET_{max} values in the healthy population is 5–25. Table 2 below characterizes expected physical performance patterns with various MET_{max} capacities and the corresponding $VO_{2\ max}$ values for both genders.

Table 2. Predicted Fitness Capacity Based on Lifestyle

Fitness Capacity Description	$VO_{2\ max}$ $(mL \cdot kg^{-1} \cdot min^{-1})$ Males	MET_{max}	$VO_{2\ max}$ $(mL \cdot kg^{-1} \cdot min^{-1})$ Females
Reasonable for inactive lifestyle	>25	>7	>22
Reasonable for modestly active lifestyle	>35	>10	>32
Optimal for lifetime fitness	>50	>14	>45
Athletically competitive	>60	>17	>54
Sub-elite to elite (sport-specific)	>70	>20	>64

Predictive Tests

Laboratory-based maximal tests are undoubtedly powerful, but often also unavailable or impractical. The tests are expensive and require specialized equipment and specially trained personnel to conduct them. One alternative is the so-called predictive or armchair test. Predictive tests can be used to provide an estimate of an individual's fitness based on answers to a few simple questions. Some of these tests are surprisingly accurate, able to produce valid results despite a modest degree of violation of the assumptions or standards established for the test. Caution must be used in interpreting the results of predictive tests, but they can be useful as an initial screening tool. Individuals with questionable fitness as indicated by predictive tests may be more likely to perform at substandard levels in subsequent evaluations.

While a number of predictive tests have been produced, none have proven to be so effective as to become a true standard. Accepting that no predictive test would be perfect, the priorities are to use one that, in addition to being easy to apply, considers as many of the key variables as possible and was designed to evaluate a fitness range reasonably typical for the population of interest.

University of Houston Non-Exercise Estimate of VO$_2$ $_{max}$

The University of Houston Non-Exercise Test is a method used to estimate aerobic capacity (VO$_2$ $_{max}$) without involving any form of exercise. It is well established that aerobic capacity is negatively related to age and body composition, but positively related to exercise habits. The test is suitable for both men and women, and the equations are listed below:

Conversion from Imperial to Metric Units

weight in lb ÷ 2.2 = weight in kg (kilograms)
(height in inches x 2.54) ÷ 100 = height in m (meters)

Body Mass Index (BMI)

BMI = body weight in kg ÷ (height in m)^2
BMI = _____ ÷ (_____)^2
BMI = _____ kg·m^{-2}

Activity Codes

Use the appropriate number (0-7) which best describes your general activity level for the previous month

- *Do Not Participate Regularly in Programmed Recreational Sport or Heavy Physical Activity*
    - 0–Avoid walking or exertion, e.g., always use elevator, drive whenever possible instead of walking
    - 1–Walk for pleasure, routinely use stairs, occasionally exercise sufficiently to cause heavy breathing or perspiration
- *Participate Regularly in Recreation or Work Requiring Modest Physical Activity, Such as Golf, Horseback Riding, Bowling or Yard Work*
    - 2–10 to 60 minutes per week
    - 3–Over one hour per week
- *Participate Regularly in Heavy Physical Exercise Such as Running or Jogging, Swimming, Cycling, or Engage in Vigorous Aerobic Activity such as Tennis, Basketball, or Soccer*
    - 4–Run less than one mile per week or spend less than 30 minutes per week in comparable physical activity
    - 5–Run 1 to 5 miles per week or spend 30 to 60 minutes per week in comparable physical activity
    - 6–Run 5 to 10 miles per week or spend 1 to 3 hours per week in comparable physical activity
    - 7–Run over 10 miles per week or spend over 3 hours per week in comparable physical activity

Houston VO₂ max Estimate for Men

$VO_{2\ max}$ = 67.350 - BMI (0.754) - age (0.381) + activity code (1.921)
$VO_{2\ max}$ = 67.350 - ＿＿＿ (0.754) - ＿＿ (0.381) + ＿＿＿＿＿ (1.921)
$VO_{2\ max}$ = 67.350 - ＿＿＿＿＿ - ＿＿＿＿＿ + ＿＿＿＿＿
$VO_{2\ max}$ = ＿＿＿＿＿＿＿ $mL \cdot kg^{-1}min^{-1}$

Houston VO₂ max Estimate for Women

$VO_{2\ max}$ = 56.363 - BMI (0.754) - age (0.381) + activity code (1.921)
$VO_{2\ max}$ = 56.363 - ＿＿＿ (0.754) - ＿＿ (0.381) + ＿＿＿＿＿ (1.921)
$VO_{2\ max}$ = 56.363 - ＿＿＿＿＿ - ＿＿＿＿＿ + ＿＿＿＿＿
$VO_{2\ max}$ = ＿＿＿＿＿＿＿ $mL \cdot kg^{-1}min^{-1}$

The Houston Non-Exercise test is not the only one available but it reasonably targets the group of interest. The Houston test is used by the Center for Hyperbaric Medicine and Environmental Physiology at Duke University to pre-screen individuals expressing interest in participating in diving, altitude, and other studies. The correlation between Houston results and laboratory maximal testing results is reasonably high (r=~0.80; Pollock, unpublished data). The test can underpredict the aerobic capacity of extremely active individuals, but it does a good job with the moderately active individuals whose abilities may be more important to question. As a rule of thumb, any individual who provides an activity code score of 0–2 is targeted for follow up. The first step is to make sure that the score code they provided is a reasonable reflection of their physical activity. If so, low scores should trigger concern over adequate fitness level. It is important that all individuals base their activity code on recent activity patterns. Aerobic fitness can decline rapidly if regular exercise is not maintained. One must guard against the reporting of wishful activity levels, i.e., more indicative of past or planned activity patterns than realistic or current ones.

Field Tests

Diving certification agencies have swimming requirements that are to be met by candidates at various levels of training. Most instructors will have students complete swim tests in the early phase of dive training. The level of scrutiny is variable, however, and candidates are rarely "failed" due to weak swimming ability. The attitude demonstrated by the instructor often reflects his or her own swimming background. Instructors who are strong swimmers tend to value these tests as a useful assessment of both fundamental aquatic skills and as an index of physical fitness. Such instructors will likely spend more time encouraging students to achieve more than just passing performance. Instructors with weaker swimming ability may downplay the importance of swimming skills, sometimes actively taking the position that divers do not have to be strong swimmers to be able to dive. While a picture-perfect freestyle may not be a requirement to dive, strong watermanship tends to translate into greater comfort and competence in all water activities. Instructors who do not value and promote swimming skills are doing a disservice to their students. Encouraging the development and/or maintenance of strong swimming skills may have a great positive long-term impact on those same students.

Encouraging students to improve their swimming ability does not have to take a lot of class time. Starting each pool training session with a short swim will cut the chill of the cool water. It will also reinforce the importance of fitness, highlight areas of weakness, and possibly provide workout examples for students to follow outside of dive training sessions. Direction and encouragement often come best from example and interest.

The most powerful fitness evaluation combination for divers is undoubtedly a laboratory maximal test and swim test, whereas the Houston predictive test and swim tests are probably the most practical.

Fitness for Diving

MET_{max} scores can be used to establish guidelines for physical fitness to dive that complement medical evaluations and tests of swimming ability. It has been previously proposed that candidates should have a 13 MET capacity to be allowed to dive. This threshold fits well with the results of a U.S. Navy study that determined that the maximum work rate that could be sustained by a fully equipped diver was 13 METs (or, essentially, the ability to swim at 1.3 knots [1.5 miles per hour] in still water). However, it should be remembered that the required effort goes up dramatically as speed increases. The typical recreational diver probably rarely sustains a swim speed of > 0.5 knot in still water (requiring an approximate 3 MET effort).

Good physical fitness is important to meet the demands of both everyday situations and emergencies. The higher the fitness level the greater the physical reserves to handle challenges. At the same time, setting too high a threshold for fitness may inappropriately discourage participation or lead individuals to ignore fitness standards altogether. The most appropriate strategy is to set reasonable goals that consider the variable demands of diving.

The highest level of fitness is only required for physically demanding diving activities. These would include military, commercial, or other diving conducted in severe operational conditions. For these, a 13+ MET fitness capacity would be appropriate.

Recreational diving, conducted under more favorable conditions, does not require the same degree of fitness. For this, a 10 MET capacity is probably more reasonable. While students may begin their dive training with slightly lower fitness levels, they should be encouraged to achieve a 10 MET capacity by the time they reach the open water phase of their training. Novice divers usually experience a greater degree of physical and psychological stress than more experienced divers under similar conditions and will benefit from the reserve capacity.

Energy Consumption of Diving
The actual energy consumption for a given dive depends on a host of factors including size, efficiency, thermal stress, and swim speed.

Size is a basic determinant of caloric cost, with the cost increasing as a function of size. However, while total body weight is important during weight-bearing activities such as running, body composition modifies the influence of size during non-weight-bearing aquatic activities. The density of water (1.00 g·cc^{-1}) is approximately midway between the densities of lean tissue (i.e., muscle) (1.1 g·cc^{-1}) and fat tissue (0.9 g·cc^{-1}). The "average" person comes fairly close to being neutrally buoyant in water. Individuals with more body fat float more easily. Those with less body fat sink more readily. In practical terms, increased density means that the legs tend to sink and the swimmer/diver will have to work harder to maintain a streamlined body position.

A streamlined body position, as discussed previously, is important to minimize the frontal surface area that has to be pushed through the water. Adding frontal surface area dramatically boosts the work required, particularly as forward speed increases. Fortunately, experience and skill allow divers to minimize the impact of these factors. An experienced, competent diver is able to reduce his or her workload in many ways: maintaining good neutral buoyancy to minimize the effort required to hold or change levels in the water column, streamlining body position to reduce water resistance (drag), optimizing fin strokes to improve thrust, using water currents to get a less expensive ride, minimizing unnecessary movements that can reduce efficiency, and optimizing orientation to facilitate buddy monitoring with minimal maneuvering. Superior skill and relaxation allow a diver to become a much more comfortable element in the environment.

Thermal stress can also have a dramatic effect on the caloric cost of diving. Water temperature is obviously important, but its effect is modified significantly by the thermal protection the diver wears and the duration of the exposure. A diver wearing a drysuit and thick undergarments will usually experience a very different degree of thermal stress than a wetsuited diver under the same conditions.

Complicating the picture is the fact that the insulation provided by different suit configurations can also vary as a function of depth. The compressible neoprene found in most wetsuits may lose more than 50% of its surface insulation capability at 50 feet sea water (15 msw). Unfortunately, the decrease in thermal protection coincides with the more thermally stressful zone of many diving environments. Drysuits may or may not lose insulating ability depending on the material. The ability to add air to the drysuit during descent can make the insulation provided by the undergarments more stable throughout the depth range, although the migration of gas to the highest point can compromise this effectiveness. Protective suits do add an energy cost for their use. Foremost, they add a degree of resistance to movement. The resistance can increase dramatically as the thickness and inflexibility of the layers increases. Additionally, the frontal surface area will increase as suit configurations become bulkier. Ultimately, the severity of the thermal stress will determine the choice of suit and the acceptability of any associated increase in required work.

Thermal stress issues are not limited to equipment. Surface area is directly related to heat flow and decreases relative to an increasing size of the individual. This means that larger individuals will have relatively less surface area across which to lose heat. The case is worst for the tall, slender body shape (called ectomorphic) that has a much greater surface area than the short and stocky body shape (endomorphic).[11] Body composition also plays a role in this discussion. Skinfold thickness is largely determined by subcutaneous fat stores, and skinfold thickness is inversely related to heat flow across the skin. Thus, the thicker the skinfold, the less the heat flow (or the greater the insulation). While fat makes an excellent passive insulator, the human form has little ability to generate heat. Shivering is a phenomenon of muscle tissue, one that produces a substantial amount of heat energy. The best thermal protection would be found in someone with an endomorphic shape, with good skinfold thickness to provide passive insulation and good muscle mass to generate heat energy from shivering. The metabolic cost would be low as long as the body shape and passive insulation were adequate. Metabolic rate can increase three- to four-fold above resting levels once shivering begins. Given the same thermal protection, an experienced diver who is more efficient and working less may cool more quickly and begin to shiver sooner. The final area of thermal stress is respiratory heat loss. Each breath of inspired gas is actively warmed. The amount of energy required increases as the inspired gas temperature falls and/or as the gas density increases as a function of depth. Fortunately, the increase in heat loss due to increased gas density becomes important only at deeper depths, typically in excess of 300 fsw (94 msw).

---

11. The terms ecto-, endo-, or mesomorph are descriptions of body type. They refer to the three primary layers in the developing human embryo called ecto, endo, and mesoderm. Ectoderm eventually forms skin, and so an ectomorphic individual is "skinny." Mesoderm forms muscle, and so mesomorphs are well built. Endoderm forms the gut and so endomorphs are typically somewhat stocky or obese.

Swim speed can have a tremendous influence on the caloric cost of a dive. The effort will be approximately the same irrespective of whether a diver is actually moving forward or maintaining their position in a current. As discussed previously, U.S. Navy studies have indicated that a fit, fully suited diver may be able to sustain a swim speed of approximately 1.3 knots (1.5 miles per hour) in still water. It was also pointed out that this involved a more than four-fold increase in metabolic effort than swimming at a 0.5 knot speed. The slowest speeds will minimize the diver's energetic requirement.

Caloric Cost Estimation

Data have been gathered, primarily from the 1940s through 1960s, which document the energetic cost of a wide range of activities under neutral environmental conditions. While some of the estimates have been invalidated by the evolution of equipment and techniques, many are still sound. We can use some of the most straightforward estimates to make reference to the diving experience.

Caloric cost is conveniently computed as a weight-indexed value per unit time (thus standardizing for differences in body weight). The units are *kilocalories* of energy per kilogram body weight per minute of activity (kcal·kg^{-1}·min^{-1}).[12] The only conversion factor to remember is that 2.2 lb = 1.0 kg. To estimate caloric cost, you multiply the estimate of caloric cost per unit of activity by your body weight in kg and multiply the product by the number of minutes the activity will be sustained. For example, an activity with a unit caloric cost of 0.10 kcal·kg^{-1}·min^{-1}, a 154 lb body weight and a 30 minute duration:

Caloric Cost = caloric cost per unit of activity x body weight in kg x duration of activity
Caloric Cost = 0.1 kcal·kg^{-1}·min^{-1} x (154 lb ÷ 2.2) x 30 min
Caloric Cost = 0.1 kcal·kg^{-1}·min^{-1} x (70 kg) x 30 min
Caloric Cost = 210 kcal

The caloric cost of skin diving activity has been measured at 0.21 and 0.28 kcal·kg^{-1}·min^{-1} for "moderate" and "considerable" motion, respectively. A 30 minute duration would produce a caloric cost range of 310–420 kcal for a 110 lb individual and 480–640 kcal for a 170 lb individual. Such intensity, however, would probably not be sustained for such a long period. A more realistic average energy expenditure over the course of a recreational scuba

---

12. The excellent nutrition labeling standards helped to make us familiar with the term "calorie." The only problem is that the actual unit discussed on the nutrition labels is the "kilocalorie," or 1000 calories. The "kilo"portion was dropped to keep the term familiar (historically, "Calorie" with a capital "C" denoted the kilocalorie, while the lower case referred to the true calorie—hence the confusion). A kilocalorie is a unit of heat energy—one kilocalorie equals the amount of heat energy required to raise the temperature of one kilogram (kg) of distilled water one degree Celsius (°C) from 15° to 16°C. A calorie is the unit of heat energy required to raise the temperature of one gram (g) of water by the same amount. For those who prefer pounds (lb) and Fahrenheit (°F) scales, a kilocalorie will make 2.2 pounds of water increase 1.8 degrees Fahrenheit (from 59°F to 60.8°F).

dive for an experienced diver might fall between the effort of walking at a normal pace on a paved surface (0.08 kcal·kg⁻¹·min⁻¹) and a fast front crawl stroke (0.16 kcal·kg⁻¹·min⁻¹). A 30 minute dive time with these intensity brackets would produce a caloric cost range of 120–240 kcal for a 110 lb individual and 185–360 kcal for a 170 lb individual.

The most practical way to use this information is to compute the caloric cost estimate range for your own body weight and dive duration and then mentally factor in the unmeasured variables to get a sense for where your caloric cost might fall in the range. A realistic evaluation of the contributing factors will give you both a thumbnail estimate of caloric cost and a better appreciation of the subtleties that can affect diving performance.

FITNESS FOR LIFE

Poor physical fitness is a major problem in North America. The 2003 U.S. Surgeon General Report indicated that more than 60% of adult Americans do not engage in the recommended amount of regular physical activity. Approximately 25% of the adult population is classified as completely inactive. Similarly, approximately 63% of adult Canadians are described as not being physically active enough to achieve health benefits.

The argument that divers represent a more fit subsection of the population is not supported by fatality reports. According to diving fatality records collected by Divers Alert Network (DAN) for 1990–1995, cardiovascular disease was listed as either the cause of death or a major contributing factor in 12% (66/549) of cases. The incidence rose to 26% for victims greater than 35 years of age. Obesity was described as a contributing factor or "significant diagnosis" in 14% of the 77 fatal incidents reported to DAN for 2001. In addition, more than 15% of the victims were reported to be smokers.

The importance of fitness needs to be appreciated by divers and dive leaders before this picture is likely to change. Only when problems are identified will they have a chance of being remedied.

A 14 MET exercise capacity was described previously (Table 2) as "optimal for lifetime fitness." While this is a wonderful ideal, it is not realistic to expect that all individuals will be able to achieve this level. An important consideration is the decline in fitness associated with age. Unfortunately, this effect is not simply due to reduced effort. One longitudinal study revisited individuals at 40 years of age who had been elite athletes in their mid-20s. The investigators found that those who remained most active in the intervening years experienced an average aerobic fitness drop of 7% per decade, while those who were least active experienced an average drop of 16% per decade.

This observation is supported by more recent models of fitness, indicating an average one percent per year decline in aerobic fitness beyond age 25. Effectively, while some decrement may be inescapable due to a gradual loss of aerobic capacity and total mass of aging muscle, the rate can be slowed by adopting a lifestyle intended to sustain fitness.

The 14 MET (or higher) target is most useful as a target in early adult years. Not all individuals will be able to achieve it, but many can get close and some will be able to do substantially better. Attaining the highest fitness level possible is useful to develop a functional reserve adequate both for now and as aging continues. Achieving a high level of fitness early can help to establish habits that will encourage the maintenance of future fitness and provide a reserve capacity robust enough to tolerate age-related declines with minimal impact on activities of choice.

The Pursuit of Lifetime Fitness
Physical fitness will not compensate for all health problems, but it can take the edge off a number of them. The heart stays stronger or gets stronger, improving work capacity. Blood values of cholesterol tend to improve, reducing susceptibility to heart disease. Insulin sensitivity is improved, reducing the risk of developing diabetes. The ability to handle emotional as well as physical stress can improve, making daily stresses easier to manage.

Most individuals are aware that being fit can improve quality of life. The problem is that many also believe that the effort is incompatible with their lifestyles. Next week, next year, next life, perhaps. Not now. The goal is to help people see lifetime fitness as a pleasure instead of torture.

Two elements are of great practical importance in the pursuit of lifetime fitness: small changes and activities that help people embrace life.

Small changes, particularly when made in a variety of areas, can produce a substantial effect. This can be thought of as the "web" approach. A web is supported by strands running in all directions, each helping to support the structure. This can be an invaluable way to progress along the path to health and fitness.

The best strategy is to institute a series of small goals that are both achievable and that reinforce the effort. Small, positive changes in physical activity patterns might begin with taking the first available spot instead of cruising the parking lot. Taking the stairs instead of the elevators. Envision the web. The weight gain experienced by most North American adults does not occur overnight: the slow progression of weight gain can be slowed, stopped, and reversed by a series of small, committed changes. For example, eating habits can be altered by merely delaying a return for seconds. People often eat so quickly that they are overfull before the satiety message is disseminated through the brain. Postponing the second plate by 10 minutes can curb the appetite effectively. Perhaps more importantly, delaying rather than denying may make for less of a psychological barrier.

Long term changes are best made by finding enjoyable activities and like-minded people with whom they can be shared. Some peer groups may have to be changed if they discourage, rather than encourage, positive development. Opportunities that provide reminders of the joy of vitality and the pleasure that can be found in life should be seized. The goal of trying as many healthy activities as possible should be encouraged early. While anyone can fight the trend, it is less likely for new activities to be taken up after the mid-20s.

The specific choices for physical activity are far less important than the act of starting. Given a little time, the best part of physical activity and healthy lifestyle options is that they become self-perpetuating. It becomes easier and more attractive to do more.

Practical targets for lifetime fitness include inclusion of a significant amount of physical activity on a daily basis. The determination of "significant amount" will vary from individual to individual. An awareness of targets and honest self-appraisal will preclude the need for a more formal definition. Additionally, it is recommended that individuals complete a "training quality" activity three to four times per week. The training program can be independently generated or by following a formalized exercise prescription. Training activities will normally require 30–60 minutes per session. Employing different types of exercise—cross-training—can make workouts more interesting and minimize the risk of overuse or overtraining injury.

Exercise Prescription
Questions as to how much exercise is required to see a positive benefit vary from activity to activity and as a function of the fitness level of the participant. The basis for training recommendations is the exercise prescription.

The exercise prescription is based on the application of the "FITT" principle. This is a mnemonic which refers to the key elements of the prescription:

- Frequency (how often the exercise should be completed per week)
- Intensity (of the prescribed exercise)
- Time (or duration of the exercise per session)
- Type (or mode of exercise to be employed)

The key to an effective prescription is that it is appropriate for the individual. Differences in ability, limitations, interest, and goals must be taken into account to ensure optimal benefits.

While the FITT principle is conceptually simple, the application of the prescription does require further consideration. Any aerobic exercise bout should be divided into five phases: 1) static stretching, 2) warm-up, 3) target level, 4) cool-down, and 5) static stretching. Static stretching (slow and steady; no bouncing) should be used to increase flexibility and prepare the muscles and/or joints for the aerobic activity to follow. The stretching program should include the major muscle groups and body regions: neck, shoulders, arms, trunk, low back, quadriceps, hamstrings, calves and ankles. Stretching should be done cautiously to reduce the risk of injury, particularly in the novice. "Static" stretching is recommended, employing a slow, steady increase in intensity. "Ballistic" stretching, employing rapid bouncing movements, is more likely to cause injury. Each static stretch should be maintained for a period of 20–30 seconds. The initial stretch is taken to the limit of comfort (note: not to levels of significant discomfort or pain). Holding the stretch, a conscious effort is made to relax. When this makes the degree of stretch seem easier to hold, it should be increased again to the limit of comfort. The cycle of relaxation and increasing the stretch can be continued throughout the 20–30 second duration. The stretching conducted before exercise should be fairly light. The post-exercise stretching can be comprehensive, including three to five repetitions of each stretch after a short recovery period. Stretching programs can significantly improve flexibility over a fairly short period of time, but remember not to overdo it. Excessive stretching can cause injury and impair the ability to exercise.

The warm-up phase of an exercise bout allows the skeletal muscles and cardiorespiratory system to make gradual adjustments up to the target level of aerobic effort. The target level may be considered a steady-rate activity but, particularly for "real world" activities, it will likely be near-steady-rate with minor fluctuations up and down throughout the bout. An outdoor runner, for example, might be maintaining a nine minute mile pace, applying a little more effort on the uphill sections and a little less on the downhill sections. The need to recover from the brief bursts of increased effort during sustained exercise can be a potent training stimulus.

The most appropriate aerobic exercises will employ large muscle groups used rhythmically for a sustained period of time. Examples of exercises that fulfill these requirements include running/jogging, walking, hiking, swimming, skating, cycling, rowing, and rope skipping. The duration of the target level phase will depend upon the subject's current fitness level and physical skill, typically lasting 15–60 minutes. The physical skill component is more important in some activities than others. Swimming, for example, can be exhausting even for a very fit individual until skills improve. Both intensity and duration can increase as fitness and skill improve.

An often neglected part of an exercise bout is the cool-down phase. Immediately following the target level effort, an exerciser should engage in an active recovery by means of lower intensity effort. The active contractions of the muscles aid in the return of blood to the heart as well as helping in the removal of lactate from the muscles, which may otherwise contribute to soreness. The cool-down should be 5–10 minutes in duration. It should be continued for several minutes after heart and respiration rates have returned to near resting levels. Following the cool-down period, the static stretching described previously helps increase flexibility and eliminate muscular tightness and soreness.

An important element to consider is how the individual will evaluate his or her exercise intensity to ensure that they are operating in the target range. It must be remembered that as fitness increases, it will take a greater intensity to generate the same relative effort (i.e., usually described as a percentage of maximal ability). The simplest means of evaluating exercise intensity that is generally effective for healthy individuals is an evaluation of heart rate reserve (HRR—using the Karvonen formula) or the percentage of maximal heart rate (HR_{max}). Age-estimated maximum heart rate is used (220 minus age in years) if the individual's actual maximum heart rate is not known and a target range of exercise intensity is established (usually between 50%–85% [0.50–0.85] of HRR or 70%–90% of HR_{max}). Individuals are encouraged to maintain their exercise intensity at the low end of the range when they are starting out, gradually increasing as they become accustomed to the exercise. The top end of the range represents the maximal safe intensity for sustained exercise. Two methods of calculating target heart rate ranges follow:

Heart Rate Reserve (Karvonen) Method

1) Estimate HR_{max} (220 minus age [± 11])
2) Determine HR_{rest}
3) Calculate HRR ($HR_{max} - HR_{rest}$)
4) Calculate 50% and 85% of HRR
5) Add each to HR_{rest}

HR50 = HRrest + 0.50 · HRR
HR85 = HRrest + 0.85 · HRR

Note: a given percentage of HRR approximates the same percentage of $VO_{2\,max}$; for example, HR_{85} is roughly equivalent to 85% of $VO_{2\,max}$.

Percentage of Maximal Heart Rate Method
Calculate 70%–85% of age-estimated HR_{max}

> Note: this range corresponds to $\approx$55%–70% $VO_{2\ max}$ so, while the values are easier to compute than the Karvonen formula, the result cannot be correlated directly to $VO_{2\ max}$.

Effectiveness of Aerobic Training
Aerobic capacity is sensitive to training. $VO_{2\ max}$ can generally be increased by 25% relatively easily in untrained individuals with a reasonable training schedule. Additional gains can occur as body composition changes as the ratio of muscle mass to fat mass is improved. There are two primary stages of adaptation. The first comes in two to three weeks, primarily in the form of an increase in body fluid volume. The second begins after six weeks of training. At this point the regular exercise is stimulating the increase in metabolic potential within the muscle cells.

The primary adaptation to regular aerobic exercise is an increased work capacity. This increases the reserve potential to meet emergent needs and reduces the strain on the cardiorespiratory system from any submaximal work rate.

A similar pattern of detraining will be experienced if a training program is suspended. The fluid volume increase will be lost within the first two weeks and a decline in the metabolic readiness will follow. Fortunately, the same degree of effort required to improve aerobic fitness is not required to maintain it. Maintenance training that is of lesser duration but similar intensity can protect aerobic capacity.

Physical Activity Choices
The best comprehensive training program will include strength, aerobic, and dynamic/flexibility components. Programs can be traditional or idiosyncratic to best motivate the participant. Examples of strength activities include manual labor, weight lifting, kayaking, rowing, or climbing. Examples of aerobic activities include running, cycling, or swimming. Examples of dynamic/flexibility activities include volleyball, squash, racquetball, and yoga. In some cases, a single activity may contribute to more than one component. The key is to find options that keep training interesting and minimize the risk of injury. Low impact activities are better for lifetime enjoyment, particularly as aging bodies are more prone to injury and slower to recover from injury. Comparatively, cycling and swimming are easier on joints than running. Swimming is certainly the most relevant to diving, and front and back crawl tend to be the easiest on joints.

Health and Exercise Issues Specific to Diving

Regular aerobic exercise can produce many positive benefits. The major effects are well established. The physical demands of diving, both normal and exceptional, will be easier to meet. The susceptibility to chronic diseases that can limit future involvement will be reduced. Additionally, while the data specific to diving are preliminary, there is some evidence that elevated aerobic fitness can have more specific effects. For example, greater fitness levels may reduce bubble formation in animals and humans and reduce the incidence of serious decompression sickness in animals. A single bout of aerobic exercise conducted 20 hours prior to diving may also reduce the amount of bubble formation, a phenomenon not observed when the exercise was conducted much closer to the dive time. More work has to be completed to validate these findings, but the fundamental concept that high levels of fitness are beneficial for divers is uncontested.

AVOIDING HEART DISEASE

Heart disease has been noted to be the most frequently reported chronic health condition among persons who died while diving. DAN has reported almost 15% of the fatalities in 2002 were associated with high blood pressure and heart disease (2004 edition, DAN's Report on Decompression Illness, Diving Fatalities, and Project Dive Exploration). The percentage has remained about the same over the past several years. With this high percentage of association, it is important to have some tips to avoiding these conditions.

Most importantly, one should not smoke. It has been noted that as few as one to four cigarettes a day can double your heart disease risk. Keeping active also can cut the risk by 50%. A heart healthy diet will definitely be beneficial—make it a point to eat antioxidants, in brightly-colored fruits and vegetables, omega-3 fatty acids in oily fish and fiber in whole grains, beans, and fruits like apples, oranges, and grapefruit. As little as ten percent reduction in body weight can greatly cut your heart disease risk. And, finally, regular medical checkups and familiarization with your "numbers" and the optimal ranges—including blood pressure and cholesterol levels—can help you to stay on track.

In 2002, the American Heart Association revised its guidelines for preventing heart disease and strokes, which include the following:

> *Improve cholesterol*—People with at least two risk factors and a 10-year risk for heart disease or stroke of more than 20% should aim for LDL (harmful lipoprotein) levels of less than 100 mg·dL^{-1}. Dietary modifications of lowered intake of saturated fatty acids and cholesterol, eating plant stanols/sterols and dietary soluble fiber, weight reduction, and increased physical activity and drugs such as statins, niacin, and fibrate are now used in more cases.

Keep blood pressure low—People in normal health should aim for 120/80 mm Hg or less. Patients with certain health problems, such as renal insufficiency, heart failure, or diabetes, should aim lower. A healthy lifestyle modification should be promoted. Beneficial actions include weight reduction, reduction of sodium intake, consumption of fruits, vegetables, and low-fat dairy products, moderation of alcohol intake, and physical activity in persons with blood pressure of ≥130 mm Hg systolic or 80 mm Hg diastolic.

Exercise—Everyone in normal health should engage in at least moderate physical activity for a minimum of 30 minutes on most—if not all—days of the week. Moderate-intensity activities (40% to 60% of maximum capacity) are equivalent to a brisk walk (15–20 min per mile). Additional benefits are gained from vigorous-intensity activity (>60% of maximum capacity) for 20–40 min on 3–5 days per week. Recommended resistance training consists of 8–10 different exercises, 1–2 sets per exercise, and 10–15 repetitions at moderate intensity ≥2 days per week. Flexibility training and an increase in daily lifestyle activities should complement this regimen.

Healthy diet—Everyone should aim for a diet that contains a healthy balance of fruits, vegetables, grains, fish, nuts, legumes, poultry, lean meat, and low-fat dairy items. Avoid saturated fats and trans-fatty acids. Energy intake should be matched with energy needs and appropriate changes made to achieve weight loss when indicated. Reduction in saturated fats (<10% of calories), cholesterol (<300 mg · day^{-1}), and trans-fatty acids is accomplished by substituting grains and unsaturated fatty acids from fish, vegetables, legumes, and nuts. Limit salt intake to <6g per day. Limit alcohol intake (≤2 drinks per day in men, ≤1 drink per day in women) among those who drink.

Quit smoking—Also avoid exposure to second-hand smoke.

Maintain weight—People should aim for a BMI (body mass index) of 18.5 to 24.9 with a weight-management program through caloric restriction and increased caloric expenditure. For overweight/obese persons, reduce body weight by 10% in first year of therapy.

Taking aspirin—People whose risk for heart disease within ten years is 10% or more should take a low-dose aspirin every day, unless they have medical reasons to avoid aspirin. Benefits of cardiovascular risk reduction outweigh these risks in most patients at higher coronary risk. Doses of 75–160 mg per day are as effective as higher doses. Therefore, consider 75-160 mg aspirin per day for persons at higher risk (especially those with 10 year risk of CHD of ≥10%).

Diabetes management—Initiate appropriate hypoglycemic therapy to achieve near-normal fasting plasma glucose or as indicated by near-normal HbA_{1c} (glycemic hemoglobin). First step is diet and exercise. Second step therapy is usually oral hypoglycemic drugs: sulfonylureas and/or metformin with ancillary use of acarbose and thiazolidinediones. Third step therapy is insulin. Treat other risk factors more aggressively (e.g., change blood pressure goal to <130/80 mm Hg and LDL-C goal to <100 mg·dL⁻¹). Goals: normal fasting plasma glucose (<110 mg·dL⁻¹) and near normal HbA_{1c} (<7%).

Chronic atrial fibrillation—An irregular pulse should be verified by an electrocardiogram and conversion of appropriate individuals to normal sinus rhythm. For patients in chronic or intermittent atrial fibrillation, use Warfarin anticoagulants to INR 2.0–3.0 (target 2.5). Aspirin (325 mg·day⁻¹) can be used as an alternative in those with certain contraindications to oral anticoagulation. Patients <65 years of age without high risk may be treated with aspirin. Goals: normal sinus rhythm or, if chronic atrial fibrillation is present, anticoagulation with INR 2.0–3.0 (target 2.5).

AGE-RELATED PREVENTIVE MEDICINES

It is said that health is merely the slowest possible rate at which to die. While this is possibly a valid albeit cynical observation, health has important implications to divers. In addition to the conventional concerns related to life-expectancy and quality of life, certain health concerns may pose immediate risks within the diving environment and—as such—should be identified and managed in advance.

The transition from cradle to grave is usually punctuated by five groups of physical health-related challenges—infections, trauma, malignancy, and circulatory and degenerative changes. Depending on the stage of life, the prevalence for each of these tends to change. Of course there are no watertight compartments, but actuaries, for instance (i.e., people who gamble on other's misery to derive profits on insurance), are able to predict with a remarkable degree of accuracy how likely individuals are to be affected by disease or injury within a particular age group. Physicians use similar principles for developing screening strategies for disease with the objective of early detection and treatment.

In this section we will provide some basic principles for sustaining health for life, particularly as it may affect fitness to dive.

Infections

The most common infectious diseases are respiratory illnesses. Episodic infections affecting the skin, intestines, or blood are considered elsewhere.

Sexually acquired illnesses are common, but do not pose a specific risk to scuba diving unless associated with general immuno-suppression (e.g., HIV) or a possibility of cross-infection through the exchange of regulators (hepatitis B & C). Respiratory infections, on the other hand, are not only important to diving, they are also ubiquitous and almost unavoidable—we all get head colds and flu from time to time. For some people, this is a predictable, annual event. Fortunately, for those between five and sixty-five years old, respiratory illnesses are rarely life-threatening. Taking infected airways and lungs under water, however, may convert these mere health irritations into life-threatening risks. Obstructed airways—from whatever cause—introduce the distinct possibility of pulmonary barotrauma. So what are divers to do to prevent respiratory illness, and when may it be deemed safe to dive after suffering from one?

Preventing Respiratory Infections
Although many respiratory infections are spread through aerosolization of viruses and bacteria during coughing and sneezing, primary inhalation of these infective agents is not the most common means of transmission. Extensive research has shown that spread of infection via the hands seems to be most common. Two important principles that should therefore be observed are: (1) avoid contact between the hands and the mouth, nose, or eyes, and (2) wash your hands regularly—especially after touching objects that endure a lot of manual traffic (e.g., bank notes, railings, etc.), or the hands of individuals suffering from respiratory infections. Other obvious precautions include avoiding close proximity to infected individuals and crowding in general. Although research has yet to confirm the efficacy of immune boosters such as Echinoforce and vitamin C, there are many anecdotes of efficacy, and there is little risk to discourage their use. In short, if it works for you—it works for you.

When to Go Back to Diving
Following an acute respiratory illness, there is a period in which the lining of the airways recovers. During this time there may be increased mucous production and a tendency to cough or sneeze. Ears and sinuses may be "sticky" and there may be a feeling of pressure in the cheeks or between and behind the eyes, suggesting involvement of the sinuses. Although many divers have taken the chance to go diving during this period, it is not recommended. The ears and sinuses actually serve as a "safety net" for the lungs. If it is difficult to clear the ears, one should assume that it may be equally difficult to "equalize the lungs." As a rule of thumb, the after-effects of a respiratory illness are sufficiently resolved to continue diving when: (1) voluntary coughing does not produce phlegm (i.e., a wet cough); (2) there is no burning in the nose, throat, or chest; (3) there is no pain or discomfort in the ears and sinuses; (4) it is easy to equalize the ears.

Trauma

Accidents and violence remain one of the leading causes of death in the 15 to 40 year age group. Traffic-related injuries are particularly common and tourists are an endangered species. Common sense, vigilance, and responsible use of alcohol are basic but important considerations.

The one traumatic injury that requires specific mention relates to the lung. Even seemingly trivial injuries to the chest may cause partial collapse of the lung (i.e., a pneumothorax). Subsequent diving may be extremely dangerous as the ascent to the surface causes expansion of the trapped gas outside the lung which then starts to squash the heart and other lung (i.e., a tension pneumothorax). Individuals who have received blunt or sharp trauma to the chest, resulting in sustained pain and/or associated with breathing difficulties, should strongly consider being evaluated before returning to diving. Breathlessness is not always present with only a minor collapse of the lung, and the injury may be trivial, such as bumping the ribs on a table, falling off a chair (or bar stool!), or striking the steering column or dash board during a motor vehicle accident.

Another common concern with traumatic injuries is the risk for subsequent decompression illness. Although there are theoretical grounds and anecdotal cases of a traumatic injury subsequently seemingly predisposing someone to decompression sickness, there is little scientific evidence to support the association. As a general rule, however, return to regular activity (which includes diving) should usually be delayed for 4 to 6 weeks after any significant injury or fracture. The body follows a fairly predictable course when repairing uncomplicated wounds and injuries. The initial recovery process takes approximately 6 weeks. That is why this seeming empirical number commonly appears in dive medical advice notes. It is the minimum period in which the body is able to recover from any substantive insult.

Malignancy

Cancer remains a real and unsolved health threat. Although associated with increasing age, many malignancies manifest at a young age. While cancer is unlikely to affect diving fitness early on, it is important to adhere to published recommendations for screening—particularly for the common ones such as lung, breast, prostate, cervix, and colon cancer. Morning headaches, swelling of the testis, chronic fatigue, painless lumps and bumps, blood in the stool or urine, sudden change in bowel habits, breast lumps (especially if painless and unaffected by the menstrual cycle), and blood in the sputum (i.e., coughing up blood) should never be ignored.

Circulatory and Degenerative Changes

Although these are associated with aging, individuals develop them at varying rates. The most important complications are heart attack, stroke, and loss of exercise capacity and tolerance. Recommendations for healthy living and screening regimens for cardiac disease should be observed. The ability to climb two flights of stairs without stopping to rest is a good guide of a reasonable level of fitness.

THE PRE-DIVE HEALTH INVENTORY

People love checklists. Pilots use them all the time—fortunately! Prudent divers also use them when packing for a dive trip—especially a remote one. In short, we use checklists when there is a chance of forgetting something and where the implications of doing so are unacceptable.

Although we rarely think of health as something appropriate for checklisting, it actually is! We recommend a head-to-toe approach in reviewing your physical readiness to dive, whether months or just minutes before diving.

Begin with an ABC: Do you have:

    A. Aches & pains?
    B. Bleeding & wounds?
    C. Concerns or complaints?

Then go Head-to-toe:

Head:
- Alert, relaxed & ready (no hangover or fatigue)

Eyes:
- Corrective lenses
- Comfortable mask

Ears:
- Equalize easily
- Normal hearing
- Normal balance
- Motion sickness prophylaxis

Nose:
- Open (not congested)
- No sinus problems
- No bleeding

Teeth:
- No loose dentures
- No jaw (TMJ) pain
- Comfortable regulator mouthpiece

Throat:
- Adequately hydrated?

Neck:
- Mobile & relaxed

Arms:
- Range of movement OK/ pain-free

Hands:
- Thermal protection (gloves)

Chest:
- Unrestricted movement
- No burning or pain

Back:
- No Problems/pain (boat trip/equipment?)
- Comfortable fitting BC
- Tank positioned for comfort

Lungs:
- Cough?
- Wheeze?
- Physical fitness?

Heart:
- Physical fitness?
- Risk factors?

Guts:
- Indigestion/heartburn (note: this tends to gets worse with diving)?
- Hernias?

Waterworks:
- Gotta go (dry suit...)?

O-ring:
- Gotta go...?

Legs:
- Physical fitness?
- Cramps?

Feet:
- Thermal protection
- Comfortable fins

Although this seems very simple and is all but comprehensive, making a conscious effort to confirm your physical and mental readiness to dive is as important to your safety and enjoyment of diving as all your training and experience is. Don't neglect it.

DIVING NUISANCES

ATHLETE'S FOOT (See Dermatology)

EAR PROBLEMS
Of all the potential problems that affect divers, ear problems are not only the most common, but also most likely to keep divers out of the water, which for many is the grimmest prognosis of all!

In simple terms, diving problems affecting the ear are the result of immersion in water and exposure to pressure. Water affects the quality of hearing and our ability to localize sound. It exposes the external ear to water, with the risk of infection. Cold water exposure also may cause dizziness and exostoses (bony outgrowths in the external ear). Pressure, on the other hand, may result in trauma and may lead to absorption of inert gas with a risk of decompression sickness. It also may cause dizziness as a function of the extreme pressure itself—called the high pressure nervous syndrome. As problems of infection and barotrauma are the most common, and also primarily affect recreational divers, this section will be limited to a discussion of these conditions.

The ear consists of three parts: the external ear, a partly cartilaginous and partly bony canal, lined with skin that is exposed to water during diving; the middle ear, a isolated gas space through which sound waves are conducted to the inner ear, and which communicates to the outside world via the Eustachian tube; and the inner ear, where sound waves and balance stimuli are converted into electrical impulses and conducted to the brain. Each portion of the ear has its own unique features and problems which are described below.

The External Ear
The external ear begins with the visible auricular appendage called the pinna which also contains a fleshy protective lump, called the *trachus*. This tell-tale spot provides a valuable clue on the presence of external ear infections and it

becomes tender to any pressure early on. The external opening to the ear canal leads upwards, backwards, and inwards towards the ear drum. The skin over the external part of the ear contains hair and modified sweat glands that produce the *cerumen*, or ear wax. This wax is a natural barrier to water and infection and it is removed by continuous soaking during diving. Beyond the outer third of the ear follows an area of skin with no hairs and no wax glands. This smooth skin overlies bone and is very thin, very fragile, and very painful if infected or traumatized. This external ear canal ends at the ear drum, a pearly white, semi-translucent structure that is as thin as tissue paper, but surprisingly strong.

Exostoses

Divers and swimmers, especially those who spend a lot of time in cold water, sometimes develop bony outgrowths into the ear canal called *exostoses*. Theory has it that cold water irritates or damages the underlying bone, resulting in subsequent gradual overgrowth of bone. These bony outgrowths are not troublesome *per se*, but can eventually impair the natural removal of wax, water, and debris from the ear, or lead to a block of the canal. If this happens, surgery may be needed.

Otitis Externa

The most common problem with the external ear, and the second most common problem in all divers, is otitis externa, or swimmer's ear. It is the result of a combination of factors including the loss of protective cerumen, water-logging of the skin, colonization by water-loving bacteria or fungi, and sometimes trauma from divers using cotton buds or other foreign objects to dry or scratch an "itching" ear. The most important preventative strategy is not to fiddle with the ears and—for those who get these infections regularly—to replace the anti-bacterial effect of natural ear wax. Traditionally, various preparations have been used that contain vinegar (acetic acid). A combination of acetic acid/aluminium acetate/sodium acetate is marketed as Domeboro®, which is quite effective in preventing ear infections. Once an infection starts, a combination of antibiotics and anti-inflammatory medication is usually required on prescription. Ear ache due to external otitis can be severe, and once the ear canal has swollen shut it becomes more difficult to treat. Needless to say it can ruin a diving trip, so obtain medical assistance early—don't delay. Another remedy that has recently emerged is the ProEar® mask, which cups the ears in a way similar to a face mask and is connected to the mask to allow equalizing of the cups through two reinforced tubes. This mask keeps the ears dry, but ear equalizing is still required.

External Ear Barotrauma

Pressure damage of the external ear can result when a diver wears ear plugs, or when a tight fitting hood traps air in the external ear canal, or when the ear is completely blocked by wax. As the volume of gas decreases due to Boyle's law, the eardrum starts to bulge into the canal, and an ear plug may be forced deeper into the canal. Inappropriate attempts at ear equalizing only make matters worse. Fortunately it is rare for the ear drum to rupture in this way, and treatment of the after ache with simple analgesics is usually sufficient. Don't dive with ear plugs.

The Middle Ear

The middle ear starts at the inner side of the ear drum. It contains three miniature bones that form a chain—the malleus (hammer), the incus (anvil), and the stapes (stirrup)—which amplify sound waves from the ear drum to the inner ear. The middle ear communicates with the outside world via a collapsed tube called the Eustachian or auditory tube. This tube allows the oxygen that is continually absorbed by the mucus lining of the middle ear to be replaced, and permits pressure equilibration during changes in atmospheric pressure or while diving. When the diver equalizes, air is driven from the back of the throat through this tube into the middle ear. Because the space is semi-closed, there is a constant tendency to form a vacuum. The vacuum is usually broken, that is equalizing occurs, by yawning, swallowing, or chewing.

Most people can sense a pressure equivalent to a 30 cm column of water on the ear drum. However, if a diver descends much more than four feet (1.3 msw) from the surface, the increased pressure collapses the Eustachian tube, and it may be no longer possible to equalize—even with a forceful attempt. This is similar to trying to blow through a kinked straw. It can't be done. It needs to be unkinked first.

Barotrauma

Approximately 65% of all divers will suffer from this malady at some stage during their years of diving. Diving to a depth of as little as 3 to 6 fsw (1-2 msw) from the surface without equalizing will already cause some degree of barotrauma. If equalizing is still unsuccessful by the time the pressure on the ear drum reaches the equivalent of 6–33 fsw (2–10 msw) pressure, the eardrum will rupture. Many divers who have experienced ear drum rupture describe momentary relief of pain as the tension on the ear drum is relieved. An episode of extreme dizziness frequently follows as cold water rushes in and comes in contact with the bones surrounding the inner ear. Once the dizziness settles, as the water warms to body temperature, these divers may believe that their equalizing problems are over as the now fluid-filled middle ear has no need for equalization. However, there is usually significant deafness upon return to the surface, followed by severe pain some 2–5 hours later due to an inflammatory response to the water. Between minor irritation and perforation of the ear drum is a spectrum of gradual tearing and bleeding within and behind the ear drum. Middle ear barotrauma should be treated by a medical professional. Nasal and systemic decongestants are invariably prescribed in an effort to normalize Eustachian tube function—the key to a healthy middle ear. Return to diving should be delayed until pain has disappeared, signs of damage have resolved, perforations have closed, and the ability to equalize with ease has returned.

Prevention of Middle Ear Barotrauma—Ear Equalizing Techniques
Active ear equalizing is not a natural activity for humans. In fact, many people are "scared" of their ears. They describe the fullness of equalizing as uncomfortable or even painful. Further, the pain and memories of childhood ear infections may add to this fear, and such individuals are likely to equalize very slowly and carefully, ineffectively, or not at all. The confusion surrounding ear equalization is compounded by the fact that it is difficult to describe to someone how hard to blow (Valsalva technique) and what "successful" ear equalizing feels (or sounds) like. Divers should also be told specifically never to Valsalva during ascent—as this constitutes "breathholding." Instructors should bear in mind that divers that are particularly squeamish about their ears may not only have problems equalizing but may also be more prone to panic under water.

There are many techniques for equalizing the middle ear to ambient pressure. Only the most common and useful ones have been listed to provide divers with a number of options, as some people may respond better to one particular technique than to others. They include:

- Swallowing or yawning
- Voluntary Eustachian tube opening (beance tubaire voluntaire - BTV)
- Valsalva
- Toynbee
- Frenzel
- Twitching techniques.

Swallowing and yawning: These are the natural ways in which the middle ear is equilibrated, and the middle ear infections in childhood are largely the result of failure of these normal mechanisms. Even in sleep, equalizing occurs approximately every five minutes through swallowing, while it occurs every minute while awake.

BTV: Some individuals have the knack of opening their Eustachian tubes voluntarily by a kind of twitch in the throat. Many professional divers eventually master this technique.

Valsalva: Perhaps the most popular equalizing method is the technique described by Antonio Maria Valsalva in 1704. It involves blowing against a pinched, blocked nose so that air is forced up the Eustachian tubes, thereby equalizing the middle ear. It can unfortunately be performed too forcefully, leading to inner ear problems. Therefore, the safest recommendation to divers is blow harder than it would take to inflate a large balloon and to never perform an uninterrupted attempt of more than five seconds.

Toynbee: Joseph Toynbee described a technique of pinching the nose and swallowing simultaneously. The action of the soft palate and adjacent muscles then opens the Eustachian tube while a pressure wave in the nasopharynx moves air in and out of the middle ear. As a result, this is a very sensitive test for Eustachian tube dysfunction as only small pressures are involved.

Frenzel: A German flight surgeon, Herman Frenzel, described a technique for the benefit of Stuka pilots in WWII. It involves moving the tongue backwards quickly against the soft palate, thereby creating a pressure wave as well as positioning the muscles for easy equalization. The technique is even better when combined with pinching of the nose. The best way to teach this technique is to have the subject say "kick" in the back of the throat while pinching the nose. It is a very gentle and therefore a very safe technique. People who struggle with the Valsalva technique often find that this technique works for them.

Twitching: This is a good technique to get people started who are unfamiliar with equalizing. While pinching the nose, the subject swiftly turns the head to the side. The ear facing forward generally equalizes. The technique can be repeated for the other ear.

Head tilting: This technique is designed to correct asynchronous equalizing. Many divers find that one ear is more difficult to equalize than the other. The head is tilted sideways from the neck (so as to point the "bad ear" upwards) while keeping the shoulders horizontal. This stretches the folds around the Eustachian, making equalizing easier.

Edmonds: This technique exploits the effect of jutting the jaw forward. Again, this manoeuvre tends to open the Eustachian tube, and should be combined with other conventional equalizing techniques.

Lowry: Another combination technique described by Christopher Lowry may be useful to improve equalizing in general. It involves pinching the nose and blowing against a blocked nose while swallowing simultaneously.

Although this is impractical to do with a regulator in place, it can assist with the discovery and improvement of equalizing techniques.

Otovent®: A product distributed by Invotec International, the Otovent has been promoted for the prevention and treatment of otitis media by treating negative ear pressure caused by Eustachian tube dysfunction. This device—made up of a nozzle and a balloon—is very useful to train novice divers about the correct amount of pressure required to equalize. It also verifies effective attempts at autoinflation. Regular practice with the Otovent® may improve the ability to equalize.

In addition to equalizing techniques, several known factors may compromise Eustachian tube function and should be avoided or treated. Many people display a low-grade allergy towards dairy products. Avoidance of all dairy products two days prior to diving often provides some relief. Some people have very sensitive nasal linings. These are the people who, for instance, tend to sneeze immediately once their feet are in contact with a cold surface.

Preventative use of nasal decongestants with diving may be appropriate for this group of individuals. Physical obstructions are not uncommon in the nose and may include fleshy outgrowths called polyps or even a skewed nasal septum. Corrective surgery is a legitimate and effective remedy for these conditions. Inflammation of the nasal passages also clearly compromises the ability to equalize.

Smoking and head colds prevent effective drainage of mucus from the sinuses and may predispose to ear and sinus barotrauma. It should also be remembered that the ears are really a "safety net" for the lungs. Blockage of the nasal passages and ears is not an isolated phenomenon. Frequently there is some blockage and inflammation in the airways of the lungs as well. However, whereas blockage of the ears will only result in pain during diving, blockage of the airways may present fatal complications.

Finally, chronic use of nasal decongestants may result in the rebound congestion that will make equalizing problems worse. The two most commonly prescribed medications for equalizing problems or middle ear barotrauma are pseudoephedrine tablets and oxymetazoline nasal spray. Both are chemical relatives of adrenaline (epinephrine) and narrow blood vessels to reduce engorgement. The use of decongestants for the purpose of diving can only be justified if it is intended to improve an existing ability to equalize—not to make it possible—and even then it should be taken with caution, and for no more than five days. Prolonged use causes rhinitis medicamentosa—a chronic stuffy, running nose that is unresponsive to decongestion.

Finally, divers should know how to preserve and protect their ears. Upon discovering any equalizing problem or ear pain, further descent should be stopped immediately. The diver should then ascend three to six fsw (1–2 msw), to reverse the locked-blocked situation. Various techniques for ear equalizing may then be attempted, bearing in mind that the ear should never be forced, and no attempt at blowing should exceed five seconds. If all these measures fail, the dive should be ended.

HEADACHES

Headaches are one of the most common complaints in general medical practice. It therefore is not surprising that they are common in diving as well. Apart from the discomfort related to them, there is a concern that they may be the result of a more deep-seated or ominous problem. Therefore the management of diving-related headaches is done on three levels:

- Understanding what causes them—with the objective of prevention
- Knowing when a headache is serious—with the purpose of seeking professional medical assessment
- Knowing how minor diving-related headaches can be prevented or treated.

Understanding Headaches

Surprisingly, the centre of consciousness and all sensory input—the brain—is itself not particularly pain sensitive. There are only a limited number of areas within the brain, skull, and scalp that transmit pain impulses. This is helpful when trying to understand and unravel the causes of headache.

Pain around the head is particularly associated with four zones:

Zone I: The blood vessels of the meninges or membranes surrounding the brain. These blood vessels transmit pain impulses when they become dilated or irritated. The pain is usually throbbing in nature and may be associated with vomiting. If the meninges are also irritated, neck stiffness may be present.

Zone II: The scalp from the nape of the neck to the top of the head. This area, supplied by the uppermost nerves from the spinal cord, may be irritated as a result of persistent muscle contraction of the neck and associated scalp muscles. Irritation of this area usually results in a deep, band-like, constricting pain with or without scalp tenderness.

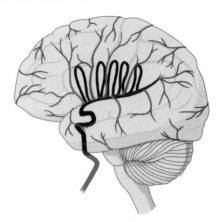

Figure 3 Zone 1

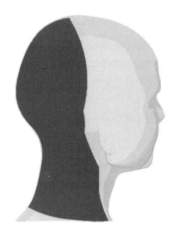

Figure 4 Zone II

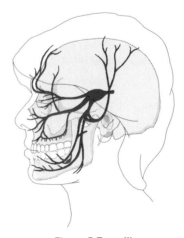

Figure 5 Zone III

Zone III: The scalp and facial structures of the face, forehead, and teeth. This area is supplied by the trigeminal nerve (5th cranial nerve), which is particularly sensitive to pain. Pain usually has a stinging, burning, or sharp, stabbing quality—like tooth ache. This area also contains the jaw muscles and jaw hinge joint—called the tempero-mandibular (TMJ) joint.

Zone IV: The sinus and middle ear cavities. These structures are sensitive to pressure and inflammation. Pain is usually experienced as a painful fullness or burning which is referred to the skin closest to the affected cavity. The pain is often exacerbated by lowering the head.

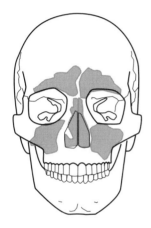 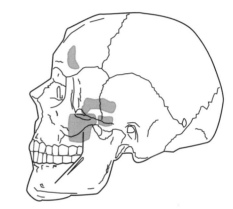

Figure 6 Zone IV

The purpose of this section is not to explore every day headaches (although they follow the same principles previously outlined). Our purpose is to list those specifically associated with diving. If you do suffer from regular or severe headaches, we recommend you have these assessed by a healthcare professional.

The most common causes of diving-related headaches are listed below according to the zones in which they are experienced.

Zone 1:
- Cold water
- Caffeine, alcohol, and other drugs
- Gas toxicity (especially high carbon dioxide)
- DCI (mostly in combination with other problems—weakness or numbness)

Zone 2:
- Hyperextension of the neck
- Anxiety/tension

Zone 3:
- Tooth, sinus, or ear barotrauma (acute)
- Tempero-mandibular joint (TMJ) pain (acute)

Zone 4:
- Sinus & ear infections
- Mask tension
- TMJ pain (chronic)

When Is a Headache Serious?

Headaches that are mild and have a gradual onset over the course of a day are rarely serious. Most of us suffer from these from time to time. However, the following features would suggest the possibility of an underlying problem and should receive prompt medical attention:

- Sudden, severe onset: "the worst headache I've ever had," "thunderclap headache"
- Any headache associated with altered consciousness or sleepiness
- Any headache associated with nausea and/or vomiting (unless previously, appropriately investigated and clearly attributed to migraine)
- Any headache associated with neck stiffness, fever, visual, or other neurological disturbances
- Any headache following an event or incident while diving, e.g., rapid ascent, omitted decompression stop, etc.
- Morning headaches—unless clearly related to alcohol toxicity

Remedies for Minor Diving-Related Headaches

Suppressing headaches with analgesics does provide subjective relief, but these drugs may interfere with alertness or exacerbate nitrogen narcosis and are not recommended when diving. Most diving physicians would not be particularly concerned with divers taking acetaminophen (or paracetamol) or low-dose ibuprofen, but narcotic or sedating drugs should definitely be avoided.

Better than any treatment, though, is prevention, and there are several quick fix solutions that may be useful in preventing diving-related headaches (and are good diving practices anyway). They include:

- Loosening the mask strap to avoid pressure on the nose, forehead, or cheekbones. If necessary, change to a more comfortable mask. Exhalation through the mask should be easy, and exerting gentle pressure on the mask should not result in pain or discomfort.

- Relaxing the neck during dives. Even though it may spoil your trim momentarily, rotating the body rather than the head to look at objects under water may avoid the strain and the discomfort of hyperextending the neck. Ensure also that the pillar valve is set low enough in the BC and that it does not force hyperextension of the neck to avoid banging the head on it.
- Relaxing during dives
- Taking slow deep breaths. These are relaxing and a more efficient way of removing carbon dioxide. Don't suppress the need to breathe by breathing less. To reduce your air consumption, relax and reduce the amount of carbon dioxide that is produced.
- Staying in shape. Exercise reduces the incidence of headaches.
- Avoiding caffeine and tobacco with diving
- Always following safe diving practices. Spend 3–5 minutes at a safety stop at 3–6 fsw (1–2 msw) below the surface. It is relaxing (weather and conditions permitting) and allows time to reduce the carbon dioxide build up from finning to the surface.
- Wearing adequate thermal protection, especially a hood
- Going for regular dive medical examinations: biennial below age 40, and annually thereafter

Headaches can spoil a diving trip or vacation and detract from the wonderful underwater experience of our unique sport. Many headaches are simple to cure once the cause has been determined. The above mentioned suggestions should allow most divers to steer away from headaches, but remember that unless a headache is easily explained, it is always better to go for a check-up. If they occur frequently, seek medical advice.

INFECTIONS

Infectious diseases remain one of the predominant causes of death and disability in underdeveloped countries. Most pristine diving destinations are in such locations and, as a result, the probability of being exposed to or contracting an infectious disease is relatively high. The type of accommodation, general level of hygiene, and crowding are additional variables. Divers need to know the basic principles for protecting themselves.

Bacteria

Bacteria account for the majority of infectious diseases. Two strategic advantages in prevention and treatment are that bacteria are killed by disinfectants and are treatable with antibiotics. This distinguishes them from viral and fungal infections.

For practical purposes, bacteria fall into four categories: those that primarily infect the skin, those affecting the respiratory passages, sexually transmitted bacterial diseases, and those found in stool or feces.

Skin Bacteria

These include all the bacteria that cause pimples, pustules, or rashes with sharply elevated margins. These bacteria are primarily spread by direct contact and fortunately usually respond well to antibiotic ointments or simple antibiotics. The prevention lies in general cleanliness. It is wise to use anti-bacterial soap when traveling abroad. However, ensure that there is no allergy to these products. Tea tree oil is a remarkably effective antibacterial agent and has the advantage of selectively killing disease-causing bacteria while having minimal impact on normal skin bacteria.

Respiratory Bacteria

These bacteria may cause throat infections or pneumonia. They sometimes follow viral infections and flu to cause sinusitis and middle ear infections. Although inhalation of aerosolized bacteria and droplets may occur when infected individuals cough or sneeze, direct contact with contaminated hands is still the primary method of transfer. Washing hands is one of the simplest and best methods of limiting the chances for getting these infections. If possible and practical, try to avoid being in the proximity of coughing, sneezing, or feverish individuals.

Sexually Transmitted Bacteria

It happens! ABCs: Abstain, Be faithful, and/or use Condoms.

Stool Contaminants

Contamination of water by stool bacteria remains one of the most significant bacterial hazards to man. *Escherichia coli* is an index organism. Reference is usually made to the number of coliforms or *E.coli* in a particular water supply to indicate the amount of contamination with human waste. The ingestion of water or material contaminated by stool bacteria usually results in diarrheal illness. Although these are usually self-limiting, fever, blood in the stool, dehydration, or diarrhea that lasts for more than three days should receive prompt medical attention. Prevention lies in the following principles:

- Be suspicious!
- Drink and use bottled water only—even for brushing teeth. If still water is used, ensure the seal is intact. If this is in question, insist on sparkling water.
- Beware of ice cubes! They are often an unrealized hazard.
- Peel all fresh fruit and wash all fresh produce in potable water—or avoid altogether.
- Boil water or use recommended disinfection remedies (chlorine or iodine).
- Cook all food well and avoid raw food delicacies.

MALARIA

Malaria has become an increasing health problem for travellers to the tropics the world over. Every year, millions of people get infected and a large number of them die. Drug resistance is becoming an increasing problem, whereas the number of safe alternatives continues shrinking. As divers venture deeper into remote tropical regions, they incur an increasing risk of contracting malaria. Lack of medical facilities, transportation, and communication add additional complexity to managing this medical emergency. Understanding malaria prophylaxis and general preventative measures is therefore of the utmost importance. The following section covers the most important considerations in selecting and using malaria prophylactic measures and medications. The treatment of malaria, which is complex and requires close medical supervision, falls outside the scope of this document.

The Three Commandments of malaria prevention and survival are:
- Do not get bitten
- Seek immediate medical attention if you suspect malaria
- Take "The Pill" (anti-malaria tablets/prophylaxis)

Do Not Get Bitten
- Stay indoors from dusk to dawn
- If you have to be outside between dusk and dawn, cover up: long sleeves, trousers, socks, shoes (90% of mosquito bites occur below the knee)
- Apply DEET-containing insect repellent to all exposed areas of skin; repeat every four hours
- Sleep in mosquito-proof accommodation: air-conditioned, and/or proper mosquito gauze
- Buildings/tents, regularly treated with pyrethrum-based insect repellent/insecticide
- Burn mosquito coils/mats
- Sleep under an insecticide impregnated (Permacote®/Peripel®) mosquito net (very effective)

Seek Immediate Medical Attention if You Suspect Malaria
- Any flu-like illness starting seven days or more after entering a malaria endemic area is malaria until proven otherwise.
- The diagnosis is made on a blood smear or with an ICT/rapid malaria finger prick test
- One negative smear/ICT does NOT exclude the diagnosis: Repeat the smear/ICT until the diagnosis is made, another illness is conclusively diagnosed, or spontaneous recovery occurs—e.g., from ordinary influenza.

Take "The Pill"

There are several dangerous myths regarding malaria prophylaxis. Please note that:
- Prophylaxis does not make the diagnosis more difficult
- It does protect against the development of cerebral malaria
- Prophylaxis is not 100% effective—hence the importance of avoiding bites
- Not all anti-malaria medication is safe with diving
- Malaria is often fatal—making prophylaxis justified
- Anti-malaria drugs, like all drugs, have potential side effects, but the majority of side effects decrease with time
- Serious side effects are rare and can be avoided by careful selection of a tablet or combination of tablets to suit your requirements (country, region, and season)

The following drugs are available for the prevention of malaria. Recommendations regarding the preferred prophylactic agents should be obtained from the Center for Disease Control or travel medicine advice organizations prior to departure. What follows is a list of the commonly prescribed drugs and their primary considerations:

(1) **Doxycycline** (Vibramycin® or Cyclidox® or Doryx®, etc.):
- Used extensively in the prevention of chloroquine-resistant malaria. About 99% effective. Not officially recommended for use in excess of eight weeks for malaria prevention, but it has been used for as long as three years with no reported adverse effects. Offers simultaneous protection against tick-bite fever.
- Dosage: 100mg daily after a meal starting 1–2 days before exposure until 4 weeks after exposure
- Doxycycline should be taken with plenty of non-alcoholic liquid
- Side effects: Nausea, vomiting, diarrhea, allergy, photosensitization. May cause vaginal thrush and may reduce the efficacy of oral contraceptives.
- Use in pregnancy: Unsafe (as is scuba diving). Also avoid during breast feeding and in children < 8 years old.

Doxycycline is an agent of choice for divers diving in areas with chloroquine resistance / "resistant malaria."

(2) **Chloroquine** (Nivaquine® or Daramal® or Plasmaquine®):
- Contains only chloroquine. Must be taken in combination with Proguanil (Paludrine®)
- Dosage: two tabs weekly starting one week before exposure until 4 weeks after leaving the malaria endemic area
- Contraindications : known allergy, epilepsy
- Side effects: headache, nausea & vomiting, diarrhea, rashes; may cause photosensitivity (sunburn; prevention—apply sun block)
- Use in pregnancy: Safe. (Note: scuba diving is not considered safe during pregnancy)

(3) **Proguanil** (Paludrine®):
- Must be taken in combination with Chloroquine (Nivaquine® or Daramal® or Plasmaquine®)
- Dosage: 2 tablets every day starting one week prior to exposure until four weeks after
- Contraindications: known allergy to Proguanil. Interactions with Warfarin (an anti-coagulant / blood thinning agent that is incompatible with diving)
- Side-effects: heartburn (tip: take after a meal, with a glass of water & do not lie down shortly after taking Proguanil), mouth ulcers (tip: take folic acid tablets 5 mg/day if this occurs), loose stools (self limiting—no treatment required)
- Use in pregnancy: safe, but must be taken with folic acid supplement: 5mg/day (Note: scuba diving is not considered safe during pregnancy)

The combination of Chloroquine and Proguanil is about 65% effective for resistant *falciparum* malaria. Although not a first choice, its relative safety and limited side-effects may justify its use in certain individuals.

(4) **Atovaquone / Proguanil** (Malarone ®; Malanil ®):
- Registered as a causal prophylactic (kills rather than inhibits the malaria parasite). Safety in diving has not been established. Preliminary data suggests it may be safe for pilots and divers.
- Effective against malaria isolates that are resistant to other drugs
- Controlled studies have shown a 98% overall efficacy of Atovaquone/Proguanil in the prevention of *P. falciparum* malaria
- Dosage: 1 tablet daily for adults, starting 24–48 hours prior to arrival in endemic area, during exposure in endemic areas, and for seven days after leaving the endemic area only
- Dose should be taken at the same time each day with food or a milky drink
- Contraindications: known allergy to Proguanil or Atovaquone or renal impairment (i.e., significant renal disease is likely to be incompatible with diving). Safety in children < 11 kg has not been established.
- Side-effects: heartburn (tip: take after a meal, with a glass of water & do not lie down shortly after taking Proguanil), mouth ulcers. To date Atovaquone has been well tolerated and the most common adverse reaction is headache.
- Use in pregnancy: safety in pregnancy and lactating women has not been established (Note: scuba diving is not considered safe during pregnancy)

(5) **Mefloquine** (Lariam® or Mefliam®):
- About 90% effective
- Dosage: one tablet per week
- Side effects: may cause drowsiness, vertigo, and joint aches and may interfere with fine motor coordination (making it difficult to exclude DCI in some cases)
- Use in pregnancy: probably safe in early pregnancy and may be used with confidence after the first trimester of pregnancy. May be used in breast feeding and babies weighing more than 5 kg.

Mefloquine is considered unsafe for divers and pilots. It is contraindicated in epilepsy but is a good first choice for other travellers.

(6) **Pyrimethamine/Dapsone** (Maloprim® or Deltaprim®/Malazone®):
No longer regarded as effective

(7) **Sulfadoxine & Pyrimethamine** (Fansidar®):
No longer used as prophylactic

(8) **Quinine** (Lennon-Quinine Sulphate®):
Not used for prophylaxis but is the backbone in the treatment of moderate and severe malaria. Serious side effects are not uncommon during treatment

(9) **Artemether** (Cotexin®):
The "Chinese drug." Available in some areas of the world. Not for prophylaxis. Used in combination with other drugs in the treatment of mild to moderate malaria

(10) **Halofantrine** (Halfan®):
Not used for prophylaxis and best avoided for treatment

NOTE:
(1) Prophylaxis significantly reduces the incidence of malaria and slows the onset of serious symptoms of malaria.
(2) All anti-malaria drugs excluding Mefloquine are considered compatible with diving. Safety of Malanil® (Atovaquone/Proguanil) has not been confirmed in diving, but is presumed to be safe for pilots.
(3) Like with all other medication, anti-malaria drugs should be tried and tested on land well in advance of potential exposure.
(4) If unpleasant side effects occur, please consult your doctor.
(5) Whether or not you take prophylaxis, be paranoid about malarial symptoms. Malaria can present in many ways, varying from fever to diarrhea to flu-like symptoms. Always inform your doctor that you have been in a malaria area. Symptoms can start within 7–14 days from first exposure until 30 days (and rarely even months) after leaving a malaria area.

(6) No single medication is 100% effective and barrier mechanisms/personal protection against bites (e.g., mosquito repellents, nets, protective clothing, not going outdoors from dusk to dawn) must be applied.

(7) Any strange symptom occurring during or within six weeks of leaving a malaria area should be regarded with suspicion and requires medical attention.

MOTION SICKNESS AND SEA SICKNESS

Motion sickness is one of the most challenging yet most poorly understood responses to spending time at sea or other unstable platforms. Nearly all divers are affected by it at some time, although sensitivity varies greatly and some appear immune.

One of the reasons why motion sickness is so challenging is that the perception and integration of movement as such is so complex. Various sensory systems collate input that is processed by the brain in an effort to determine position and acceleration of the body. Most activity involving vehicles of propulsion take the human physiology outside its original design specifications and therefore carry the potential of inducing stimuli to which the body would react in other than a normal way.

Teleologically, motion sickness is thought to have its origins as a survival strategy in prehistoric man on experimental diets—that is, eating whatever is found and hoping that it isn't poisonous. Most plant poisons affect the nervous system, but tend to do so differentially. This means that they cause selective or partial disruption of nervous impulses. Over millennia, a survival strategy evolved to empty stomach contents when this occurred to void the noxious substance. The extrapolation to motion sickness is that acceleration and positional instability—particularly where there are conflicting stimuli between the various organs of orientation—may provoke this same survival strategy. However, the knowledge that you would have survived as a Neanderthal eating mushrooms and berries provides little comfort to a diver retching on a boat.

Motion sickness is not limited to nausea and vomiting; it is actually a spectrum of signs and symptoms that evolve over a varying period of time. Awareness of the early stages can sometimes delay or prevent progression to the grand finale:

- Apprehension
- Hypersensitivity to smell
- Pale skin
- Restlessness and withdrawal
- Sweating

- Increased saliva production with swallowing and yawning
- Nausea
- Vomiting (this may be curative or continue to a point of collapse and dehydration)

From a practical perspective there are three key concepts regarding motion sickness:

- Everyone is at risk – but this risk/tendency varies
- Some things make it worse
- Some things make it better

Determining the Risk

By the time an individual reaches a "diving age," they usually know whether or not they have a tendency to get car sick, air sick, or easily become nauseous or dizzy. They also know whether or not they can read a book or follow a map in the car or even if they can risk sitting in the back. The response to driving in a car is useful to determine the likely sensitivity to motion sickness at sea. Although this division is neither exclusive nor particularly scientific, it is useful to determine the need and extent of precautionary measures by classifying divers in four degrees of sensitivity:

- **Grade 1:** Never get sick (at least not yet)—the *back seat reader* types
- **Grade 2:** Get sick on the boat but feel better while diving—*the non-readers*
- **Grade 3:** Also get sick under water—the *obligatory front seat passengers*
- **Grade 4:** Stay sick after diving on return to shore, risk of dehydration— *the must drive myself group*

For the back seat reader (Grade 1) types, no advice is needed other than to request their sympathy and support for the others and to remind them that in prehistoric times they would not have survived to adolescence.

For those who tend to get ill only during a prolonged time on dive boats or when the sea is rough (i.e., the Grade 2, non readers), basic precautions and simple prophylaxis is usually effective. For the others (Grade 3 & 4), prophylaxis is usually required to ensure dive safety, but it comes with additional cautionary advice.

Things That Make It Worse

Sedating chemicals and dietary indiscretions: In general these appear to predispose to motion sickness. Most divers soon discover which food types are more suitable to dive with. In general, non-fatty, complex carbohydrates (e.g., fruit or cereal) are well tolerated. All alcohol should be avoided by all Grade 3 and 4s. However, it is not wise to dive on an empty stomach. Low blood sugar is a risk factor in diving. You should eat something.

Unfavorable sea states: Severe undulation at sea, especially when combined with an inability to see a fixed terrestrial reference point or the horizon, is a significant risk factor for motion sickness. Grade 3 and 4 divers should find the least unstable part of the boat, usually in the middle of live-aboard or larger boats and towards the stern in ski boats during short launches through surf.

Psychological factors: These definitely play a role. Fear of diving may reduce onset time, and fear of becoming seasick is a self-fulfilling prophecy. Offensive odors such as diesel or petrol fumes from the boat engines, raw or decaying food, or even the smell of cooked food may tip some over the edge. Also, the auditory and olfactory assault of fellow divers vomiting over the bows is likely to encourage sympathetic participation by others.

Things That Make It Better

Faith/Traditional remedies: It is said that any remedy, given and taken in good faith, is effective against motion sickness. Although this is not entirely true, it is certainly inappropriate to ridicule or erode the faith of an individual who has discovered a particular precautionary measure that works for him or her. Accordingly, wrist bands, ginger, and other remedies have merit. If it works, it works.

Age: With increasing age, sensitivity to motion sickness appears to decrease. At least not all of aging is bad.

Maintaining orientation: Minimizing the time on the boat (when possible) and reducing the time of not being able to look at the shore or horizon by placing and organizing the dive gear for easy access, assembly, and kit-up, is invaluable. Usually a moving boat is less troublesome than a stationary one—pitching and yawing in the swells. Therefore, use the time on the boat wisely, and plan your activities around this.

Medication: Seasickness medication is controversial due to its sedating or other potentially adverse effects. However, divers will take medication to avoid the unpleasantness of seasickness, and it is pointless ignoring this reality. Accordingly, it is better to provide appropriate advice and precautions on its use. Notably, prevention is better than cure—once motion sickness starts it is more difficult to suppress.

There are four primary considerations when selecting an anti-motion sickness drug:
- Sensitivity to motion sickness (Grades 2–4)
- Duration of the exposure (1–3 days, 3–5 days, >5 days)
- Type of drug and its potential side-effects
- Type of diving planned (risk of nitrogen narcosis or loss of situational awareness)

Anti-motion sickness drugs:

(1) **Scopolamine patches**: These are very effective when applied to clean, thin skin (usually behind the ear) 3 to 6 hours before diving. There are definite contraindications for these drugs, and there are real risks of serious neurological side-effects, including hallucinations, loss of co-ordination, sleepiness, dry mouth, blurred vision, etc. Accordingly, it is only recommended for shallow (< 100 fsw/30 msw) diving over multiple days (>3 days of continuous boat diving) for Grade 3 & 4 individuals who have used it previously without ill effects. Wash the hands immediately after applying the patch, as inadvertent rubbing of the eyes with contaminated fingers will result in full dilation of the pupil and many hours of blurred vision and light sensitivity. Patches are replaced every three days.

(2) **Dimenhydramine**: This is an effective but significantly sedating drug. It may be considered for <3 days of continuous, shallow diving in Grade 3 & 4 individuals who have used it previously without difficulty. The usual dose is 50 mg every 6 hours.

(3) **Cyclizine & Metoclopramide**: Moderately effective for Grade 2 and 3 motion sickness. Again, deep diving is not recommended. Cyclizine dosage is 50 mg every four hours while Metoclopramide is 10 mg every eight hours. Prior use to confirm individual safety is recommended.

(4) **Cinnarizine/Cinnarizine and Domperidone**: Effective for Grade 2 and 3 motion sickness. Minimal side-effects. Dosage of Cinnarizine is 25–75 mg every 6 hours with or without 10 mg of Domperidone. Prior use to confirm individual safety is recommended.

(5) **Phenytoin**: This anti-epileptic drug has been used successfully by astronauts in the prevention of space sickness. It appears to be most effective in Grade 4 motion sickness, and has minimal side effects over 3–5 days of diving. The dosage is 5 mg/kg either as a single dose the night before or in a divided dose mornings and evenings during a dive trip. Its safety is unproven for long term use (>5 days). There are important contraindications to the use of this prescription drug. Prior use to confirm individual safety is recommended.

In closing, motion sickness is common in boat diving. With a little planning it can be limited or even entirely prevented in most people. A few individuals will not be able to dive due to incapacitating motion sickness, but they are unlikely to even attempt diving. For the average person, motion sickness is quite manageable.

TINEA VERSICOLOR (See Dermatology)

PART THREE

COMMON AND IMPORTANT MEDICAL CONDITIONS AND DISORDERS WITH AN IMPACT ON DIVING

COMMON AND IMPORTANT MEDICAL CONDITIONS AND DISORDERS WITH AN IMPACT ON DIVING

BLOOD

ANEMIA AND DIVING

Anemia can be defined as a reduction in hemoglobin, the oxygen carrying protein in the blood, the hematocrit (percentage of cellular content of 100 mL of blood), or total red cell number. In physiologic terms an anemia is any disorder in which the patient suffers from tissue hypoxia due to decreased oxygen carrying capacity of the blood. We usually use the term "anemia" to refer to an absolute anemia, i.e., a reduction in red cell or hemoglobin mass.

In an acute hemorrhage (blood loss anemia), the arterial pressure falls, and the patient rapidly goes into shock simply due to a low blood volume. The sudden, rapid loss of 30% of the total blood volume often results in death unless there is immediate medical care given.

In a slowly developing anemia, e.g., iron deficiency anemia, cardiac output increases, and there is a decrease in hemoglobin oxygen affinity. Anemia is a sign of disease, not the disease itself. The clinical effects include tiredness, lassitude, weakness, pallor, and perhaps fever and low blood pressure. Shortness of breath and chest pain can occur after exercise. Yellow discoloration of the skin may occur in some anemias.

Anemia is dangerous to the diver due to the decreased content of oxygen by the red blood cell mass. Partial pressures are important because they determine the rate of diffusion of a gas, and therefore strongly affect the rate of gas exchange between the blood and alveolar air; however, tissues have to have a certain amount of oxygen per minute in order to live, a need met by oxygen content, not oxygen pressure. The oxygen carrying capacity of one gram of hemoglobin is 1.34 mL. Once oxygen molecules chemically bind to hemoglobin they no longer exert any pressure. The lower the hemoglobin content, the lower the oxygen content, regardless of the arterial oxygen.

The greater the partial pressure of oxygen in the alveolar air of the lung, the more oxygen dissolves in the blood (a restatement of Henry's law). Partial pressures change as a diver descends and ascends in the water column.

Anemia is one of several conditions that NOAA (National Oceanic and Atmospheric Administration) has determined to be relatively disqualifying to diving and requires a case-by-case evaluation.

BLEEDING DISORDERS

Bleeding disorders constitute a wide range of medical problems that lead to poor blood clotting and continuous bleeding.

When someone has a bleeding disorder, they have a tendency to bleed longer than normal due to their inability to form a clot. The disorders can result from defects in the blood vessels or from abnormalities in the blood itself. The abnormalities may be in blood clotting factors or in platelets.

Blood clotting, or coagulation, is the process that controls bleeding. It changes blood from a liquid to a solid. It's a complex process involving as many as 20 different plasma proteins, or blood clotting factors. Normally, a complex chemical cascading process occurs using these clotting factors to form a substance called fibrin that stops bleeding. When certain coagulation factors are deficient or missing, the process doesn't occur normally.

Within seconds of an injury, tiny cells in the blood, called platelets, bunch together around the wound. Normally, quickly, blood proteins, platelets, calcium, and other tissue factors react together and form what's called a clot, which acts like a net over the wound. Over the next several days to weeks, the clot strengthens, and then dissolves or falls off as a scab when the wound is healed.

In people with abnormal bleeding, clotting factors are missing or don't work as they should. This causes them to bleed for a longer time than those whose blood factor levels are normal. Bleeding problems can range from mild to severe. A person with a bleeding abnormality exhibits certain symptoms that include excessive bleeding and bruising, easy bleeding, nose bleeds, and abnormal menses. These people also can have scarring of the joints or joint disease, loss of vision, chronic anemia (low red cell count) from blood loss, neurologic or psychiatric problems, and death, which may occur from large amounts of blood loss or bleeding in critical areas, such as the brain.

Some bleeding disorders are present at birth and are caused by rare inherited disorders. Others are developed during certain illnesses (such as vitamin K deficiency or severe liver disease), or treatments (such as use of anticoagulant drugs or prolonged use of antibiotics). They can include hemophilia and other very rare blood disorders. Other causes of bleeding disorders include:

- Von Willebrand's disease, which is an inherited blood disorder thought to affect between 1% and 2% of the population
- Immune system-related diseases, such as allergic reactions to medications, or reactions to an infection
- Cancer, such as leukemia, which is a blood cancer
- Liver disease
- Bone marrow problems
- Disseminated intravascular coagulation, which is a condition often associated with child bearing, cancer, or infection, in which the body's clotting system functions abnormally
- Pregnancy-associated eclampsia, also known as severe toxicity of pregnancy
- Organ transplant rejection
- Hemophilia A and B, which are inherited blood disorders
- Exposure to snake venom
- Antibodies, a type of immune system protein, that destroy blood clotting factors
- Medicines, such as aspirin, heparin, Warfarin, and drugs used to break up blood clots

Congenital bleeding disorders are very rare, with the exception of hemophilia. Education about them has not been a priority of the medical community. Most have only been recently discovered.

Risks to divers include barotrauma damage to air filled spaces such as the sinuses, ears, or lungs from the bleeding that can occur in these organs, and the decrease in oxygen carrying capacity of the bleeder with anemia. These individuals should be advised not to dive.

BLOOD DONATIONS

This information should apply to any type of diving, since the effect depends on the hemoglobin in the red blood cell mass rather than the partial pressures of gases.

The donor's body replenishes the fluid lost from blood donation in 24 hours. If not anemic, a person can dive in 24 hours after blood donation. It may take up to two months to replace the lost red blood cells. Whole blood can be donated once every eight weeks. The most important part of the blood to the diver is the red blood cell, responsible for the transport of oxygen to the tissues. The fluid part of blood is replenished in about one day. If the diver waits 24 hours and has a normal hematocrit (red blood cell percentage), then diving should be allowed.

Red blood cells are perhaps the most recognizable component of whole blood. Red blood cells contain hemoglobin, a complex iron-containing protein that carries oxygen throughout the body and gives blood its red color. The percentage of blood volume composed of red blood cells is called the "hematocrit." The average hematocrit in an adult male is 47%. There are about one billion red blood cells in two to three drops of blood, and, for every 600 red blood cells, there are about 40 platelets and one white cell. Manufactured in the bone marrow, red blood cells are continuously being produced and broken down. They live for approximately 120 days in the circulatory system and are eventually removed by the spleen.

Apheresis is the process of removing a specific component of the blood, such as platelets, and returning the remaining components, such as red blood cells and plasma, to the donor. This process allows more of one particular part of the blood to be collected than could be separated from a unit of whole blood. Apheresis is also performed to collect plasma (the liquid part of the blood) and granulocytes (white blood cells). There is also a process of "double apheresis" where a doubled quantity of red blood cells (500 mL) are removed, returning all other blood components to the body. This might tend to cause a drop in hemoglobin below normal ranges and require a wait before diving for the red cells to be reproduced, a period of about 120 days.

Approximately 10% of body iron stores are removed with each donation of 250 mL of red blood cells. When appropriate, iron supplements can be prescribed for patients making donations to help increase red blood cell count. Erythropoietin, a hormone, can also be given to stimulate the bone marrow into producing more red blood cells.

LEUKEMIA

Leukemia is a malignancy of the white blood cells. There are two main types: myelogenous leukemia and lymphoblastic leukemia. These can be acute and chronic in their effects on the individual. The most common type of leukemia is chronic lymphocytic (CLL), indicating that the disease of the lymphocytes is slow in its effects on the body.

Acute leukemia is the leading cause of cancer deaths in adults younger than 35 years old. Treatment is usually by anticancer drugs and/or by bone marrow transplantation.

All of the leukemias, whether acute or chronic, are usually serious diseases that result in a limited lifespan. CLL patients often require no treatment and can do relatively well, so they should be assessed on a case-by-case basis. If acute leukemia is in full remission and exercise tolerance is acceptable, scuba diving can be considered—otherwise risks are too high for it to be recommended. The side effects of chemotherapy and radiation treatments and other problems associated with the leukemia make diving unwise.

Complications include anemia, low platelets, and low white blood cell count, depending upon the stage of the disease. A favorable response can be expected in most individuals treated with chemotherapy, radiation, or both. Individuals with leukemia are very sensitive to infections because of changes in their white blood cell count.

Difficulties with diving that might be encountered stem primarily from the effects of the chemotherapy on the immune responses of the body and the possibility of bone marrow depression with anemia and/or low platelet counts. One should not dive while there are any effects of the drugs on the immune system due to the possibility of overwhelming infection from marine organisms. The diver should not be debilitated or weakened from the illness or treatments so as to be unable to perform self and buddy rescue. Blood clotting parameters need to be checked so that hemorrhage from barotrauma will not be a factor.

Anemia will need to be corrected so that there will not be any chance of hypoxia. If there were splenomegaly (enlargement of the spleen), there would be an increased possibility of rupture due to pressure from dive gear and boat reentry (a common problem with boat reentry is rib fracture due to wave action, weight belt, and boat transom trauma). The spleen contracts with simple immersion as part of the dive reflex, causing an increase in the red blood cell mass.

POLYCYTHEMIA VERA (Too many red blood cells)
This is a condition in which the body produces too many red blood cells. There are few references to this condition in any of the major textbooks of diving or hyperbaric medicine. Some symptoms of the condition that might affect diving or mimic diving accidents include headache, dizziness, itchiness, (especially following a warm bath), fullness in the left upper abdomen, red coloration, especially of the face, shortness of breath, breathing difficulty lying down, symptoms of phlebitis, or inflamed veins in the legs.

Other symptoms that may be associated with this disease: vision abnormalities, red skin spots, bluish skin discoloration, and fatigue. Complaints usually can be attributed to the expanded blood volume and hyperviscosity, which may be manifest as weakness, headache, light-headedness, visual disturbances, fatigue, or shortness of breath. Easy bruising and bleeding are common. The face may be flushed, and the retinal veins engorged.

An enlarged liver (hepatomegaly) is frequently seen and over three-fourths of the patients have a hugely enlarged spleen, a situation that would be extremely dangerous to a diver due to possible rupture from pressure from gear and weight belts or trauma from entry and exit with a dive.

Complications of the disease are mainly due to the increased thickness of the blood, increased clotting, and increased blood volume. These include: thrombosis, stroke, heart attack, and heart failure. What changes occur due to increased partial pressures of gases experienced in the diving environment are not known. An increased risk for decompression illness can be theorized due to problems with blood flow.

Problems with clotting frequently occur because of abnormalities of platelet function. Divers with bleeding tendencies have an increased hemorrhage risk associated with barotrauma to the ears, sinuses, and lungs. It is also thought that there is an increased risk of a spinal decompression injury.

Hydrea (hydroxyurea), a medication used to treat polycythemia, can cause some or all of the following side effects: nausea, vomiting, diarrhea, and drowsiness. It may also cause the following symptoms: fever, chills, cough, lower back or side pain, painful or difficult urination, tiredness or weakness, sores in mouth or on lips, unusual bleeding or bruising, black, tarry stools, blood in urine or stools, small red spots on the skin, confusion, dizziness, convulsions, hallucinations, headache, joint pain, and swelling of feet or lower legs.

Another medication, Interferon, has numerous side effects that do not fit with diving. Some of these side effects can alter a diver's level of consciousness and ability to make decisions and participate in buddy responsibilities. It is probable that most diving physicians would be quite reluctant to give their approval for this patient to dive, considering all the possibilities for disaster.

Persons with treated polycythemia with near normal blood counts, a normal sized spleen, and none of the side effects of medication could be allowed to dive on a case by case basis, with the approval of the diver's attending physician.

SICKLE CELL ILLNESS

This is an inherited condition of people of mostly African heritage in which there are abnormal configurations of the red blood cells that have the appearance of "sickles" instead of "lifesavers." They tend to clump in vessels, causing tissue dead areas and anemia, and are triggered by low oxygen conditions. This causes severe pain, tenderness, and loss of mobility and is called a "crisis." The condition can complicate the management of serious decompression illness and can be another cause of aseptic necrosis of bone or bone death.

Sickle cell trait is the name for a condition in which a person carries one sickle hemoglobin producing gene inherited from their parents and one normal hemoglobin gene. Normal hemoglobin is called type A. Sickle hemoglobin is called S. Sickle cell trait is the presence of hemoglobin AS on the hemoglobin electrophoresis. This will NOT cause sickle cell disease, but hypoxia, exercise, and low blood flow will cause sickle cell trait individuals to sickle.

Recommendations to divers and doctors certifying prospective divers concerning sickle cell illness have been under careful study, and these recommendations are changing. Sickle cell traits indicate that an individual has hemoglobin types A and S present in the red blood cell. This situation usually does not cause a problem without very low oxygen tension.

Persons with sickle cell anemia should not dive due to the increased risk of decompression illness and the increased risk of a sickle cell crisis. The person with sickle cell trait should be qualified for diving, since he or she is not at any greater risk from oxygen deficiency in body tissues than the ordinary diver. Should an individual with sickle cell trait become hypoxic while diving (out of air, drowning, equipment failure, etc.) then the cells would sickle. However, it would seem that the risk would be less from the sickling than from other aspects of the situation causing the hypoxia, such as drowning from the unconsciousness caused by the hypoxia.

Hereditary Spherocytosis and Thalassemia

Other anemias caused by red blood cell abnormalities include hereditary spherocytosis or hemolytic anemia and the thalassemias. Hereditary spherocytosis is ordinarily a condition that manifests itself at birth or shortly thereafter. The red blood cells are spherical instead of in the shape of lifesavers. This causes them to be excessively fragile and subject to fragmentation with changes in blood chemistry. There are two other possible dangers that could be averse to diving:

> *Anemia*, with the decreased oxygen carrying potential of a lowered hemoglobin. People with anemia, whatever the type, really have an oxygen-carrying problem. One should not dive if the ability of the blood to transport oxygen and off-load carbon dioxide is compromised in any way. Measurements of anemia include the hematocrit (packed cell volume) and the hemoglobin concentration. Diving is precluded if the hematocrit is 37 or below or the hemoglobin is 12 g·dL^{-1} or below. This is to prevent hypoxia and loss of consciousness while under water—which could lead to drowning.

Splenomegaly, with the possibility of traumatic rupture of the enlarged, fragile organ. The spleen should either be small or surgically removed before a diver can be certified as "fit to dive." If one has had the spleen removed, the diver should have full immunizations against the *pneumococcus* and should be aware of greater susceptibility to marine infections.

Thalassemia or Cooley's anemia is due to abnormal genes in the hemoglobin molecule and has many variants. Most of these have no clinical significance and do not relate to diving. However, one must infer danger if there is anemia below Hb of 12 g/dL (oxygen transport) or if there is an enlarged spleen. Enlarged spleens can rupture from very minor trauma.

As with most blood diseases, the level of illness, response to treatment, and many other factors have to be considered before allowing a person to dive. Many with these conditions can dive without risk, if not severely anemic, or if there are no other intercurrent complications related to the breakdown of hemoglobin with resultant iron storage problems.

Understandably, one should not dive with a low hemoglobin level or if weakened or debilitated from the illness or the treatment of the illness. This can sometimes be quite severe.

CARDIOVASCULAR

AORTIC ANEURISM
The aorta is the largest artery in the body. It takes blood from the heart to the rest of the body and runs through the chest and abdomen. For various reasons this vessel may develop a weakness and become dilated. This makes it more prone to rupture, with catastrophic bleeding causing death if not surgically repaired at once.

Any physical exercise likely to cause a sudden rise in blood pressure may precipitate such a rupture. It is therefore advisable to have an aneurism evaluated and surgically repaired before undertaking a vigorous recreational sport such as scuba diving.

BLOOD PRESSURE
For many years a "normal" blood pressure was accepted to be below a systolic pressure of 140 mm Hg (during contraction of the heart) and a diastolic pressure of 90 mm Hg (during the period of relaxation of the heart). Today there is a move to get closer to 120 over 80 mm Hg. Extreme or chronic elevations in blood pressure may cause stroke due to rupture of blood vessels in the brain. Long term effects can cause heart, kidney, and eye problems as well as an increased risk of coronary artery disease or so-called heart attack.

Conversely, blood pressure that is too low (also called hypotension) may cause reduced blood flow to the brain with dizziness, nausea, and even lapse of consciousness, especially due to changes in posture. Individuals prone to hypotension are usually aware of feelings of impending black-out upon standing up rapidly. Medications such as Effortil are sometimes prescribed but are not considered safe with diving.

There is a tendency for blood pressure to increase with age, a sedentary lifestyle, and obesity. High blood pressure has been associated with sudden death due to coronary artery disease, especially in older divers during the increased exercise of diving. Another phenomenon that has been associated with elevated blood pressure is acute pulmonary edema of immersion (i.e., congestion of the lungs with fluid in divers). Divers affected by this condition may suddenly become very short of breath under water, and upon evaluation, have fluid in their lungs.

In order to prevent problems due to chronic high blood pressure, various medications are commonly prescribed to artificially lower it. These may have adverse effects, in particular, the ability of the cardiovascular system to respond to stress and exercise. Divers or student divers with blood pressure problems require assessment by a health care professional familiar with diving medicine.

Control of blood pressure by loss of body weight, restriction of salt in the diet, and regular moderate exercise is safe and appropriate, as well as through use of selected medications. It is unwise to dive with uncontrolled high blood pressure. Borderline hypertensives or individuals taking medication to control their blood pressure should take a maximal stress exercise electrocardiogram test to assess how the diver and their cardiovascular system respond to the exertion of recreational diving and to detect early coronary artery disease and dangerous disturbances in heart rhythm.

CHOLESTEROL

Cholesterol is a kind of fat used in the body for such things as making new cells. However, under certain inherited conditions and lifestyles, such as a high intake of fatty foods, the levels may increase and cause hardening of the arteries, leading to coronary artery diseases, heart attack, or stroke. Cholesterol levels are measured by means of a blood sample. Desirable cholesterol is < 160 mg/dL. Normal cholesterol is < 200 mg/dL. Borderline cholesterol is 200 mg/dL to 239 mg/dL. High cholesterol is 240 mg/dL or higher. Total cholesterol can be measured with a simple needle prick test, but this is only a screening test. Blood cholesterol is expressed in three forms; these contribute to the total cholesterol, but have different implications for health. They are usually determined by means of a fasting blood test called a lipogram:

Low Density Lipoprotein Cholesterol (LDL) is the "bad" form responsible for blocking blood vessels and causing heart attack or stroke.

Ideally the LDL level should be < 100 mg/dL with a borderline level of 130 to 139 mg/dL and a high level of 160 to 189 mg/dL.

High Density Lipoprotein Cholesterol (HDL) is the "good" form, as it helps to prevent the LDL from blocking the blood vessels and appears to protect against heart attack or stroke.

Ideally the HDL should be 60 mg/dL or higher with 40 to 60 mg/dL acceptable, and below 40 mg/dL low. The ratio of HDL to LDL is usually considered and should be more than 20%.

The third form, triglycerides, is found in only small amounts in the blood, but a high triglyceride with a high LDL may increase the risk of heart attack.

Borderline high triglyceride is 150 to 199 mg/dL. High triglyceride is 200 mg/dL or higher.

Causes of high cholesterol include genetic disorders, overweight, smoking, lack of exercise, and eating a diet heavy in saturated fats.

Cholesterol problems are usually asymptomatic and go undetected unless specifically tested. It is generally recommended that all people over the age of 35 be tested. People with relatives who have suffered or died from heart attacks—especially at a young age—should definitely be tested for elevated cholesterol. Although a healthy diet containing low fat will lower the cholesterol levels in most people—and is strongly recommended for all—people with hereditary cholesterol problems will require medication. Such medication is usually safe with diving as long as there are no complications of the high cholesterol or side effects from the medication that would make diving unsafe. If unaddressed, cholesterol problems will lead to early and frequently sudden death that may be precipitated by the exercise of diving. Accordingly, it is important to lead a healthy lifestyle and to control cholesterol so as to reduce the risk of cardiovascular disease.

CLOTTING—DEEP VEIN THROMBOSIS (DVT)

Although this condition is not specifically associated with diving, it is increasingly associated with flying. As many divers fly to distant pristine dive spots, the possibility is there. This is also a common complication of major surgery and injuries to the lower limbs. Some caution is therefore advisable if this applies.

This condition, although well known in medical fields, came to prominence in 1977 when the term 'economy class syndrome' erroneously first appeared, suggesting a life threatening condition from especially long, cramped air travel, but in fact, it can affect all people who are sedentary or recumbent for extended periods of time.

Deep vein thrombosis (DVT) is a condition where blood clots form in the deep veins, usually in the legs or lower abdomen and pelvis. A far less serious condition of blood clots in the superficial veins is called phlebitis and is usually only of cosmetic importance, although if ulcerations form, diving is contraindicated until they have healed.

The problem with clotted deep veins is that pieces of these large clots may become dislodged and move up the circulation to the lungs where they can cause severe breathing difficulties or even death due to lack of oxygen. This risk is greatest when veins above the knee are involved. Rarely they may contribute to other serious medical conditions such as stroke and heart attack. While phlebitis is commonly accompanied by signs of redness or tenderness, DVT may have no signs or symptoms at all, or only some mild pain and swelling or local tenderness deep in the legs followed maybe several days later by sudden death.

There is much controversy as to the numbers affected, but it has been estimated that 1 in 100 patients with DVTs above the knee will die of complications. As many as 300 people per year die from DVT as a result of flying. Prevention is therefore important.

Prolonged immobilization is one of the key causative factors. Thus, long air or even long distance car, bus, and train travel in cramped seats, or bed rest after surgery, for example, can possibly precipitate DVT.

At greater risk of DVT also are pregnant women, women taking oral contraceptives, individuals over the age of 40 or with a history of cardiovascular disease or stroke, high blood pressure, or high cholesterol. Other factors which increase the risk are a history of a previous DVT incident, a history of inflammatory bowel disease, or a history of recent surgery. The greater the distance traveled, the higher the risk also.

A number of suggestions have been made to help prevent DVT. These include walking about the flight cabin as permitted, drinking plenty of fluids other than alcohol to prevent dehydration adding to the likelihood of clot formation, wear loose and comfortable clothing, exercise of your legs by flexing and extending the ankles while in your seat, wear compression stockings if at extra risk of DVT, avoid crossing the legs, stop smoking, lose weight, elevate your legs where you can.

Aspirin is not recommended as a blood thinner. Divers who have made a very long flight to a destination may be advised to wait 24 hours before diving and until they are rehydrated and rested and the possibility of DVT is lessened. Since diving tends also to increase dehydration, it may potentiate any latent DVT effect from a long flight.

Treatment for DVT will involve the use of anticoagulants to dissolve the clots such as Coumadin (Warfarin or Dicoumarol) and Heparin. If these are being taken, they can affect bleeding from diving hazards such as blunt trauma or injuries from barotrauma of the ears, sinuses, or decompression sickness, and the increased hemorrhage may potentiate injury. Although divers apparently have no difficulty while taking Coumadin, most diving medicine experts would advise not to dive while taking this medication.

The constrictive actions of diving equipment such as belts and wetsuits may also add to DVT.

CORONARY ARTERY DISEASE (CAD)

Coronary artery disease (CAD) is well known today as it affects nearly 3 million, and over 700,000 die every year in the United States. It is commonly called "hardening of the arteries" and is due to deposition of cholesterol in the coronary arteries supplying blood to the heart muscle. This causes a partial or complete block, causing lack of blood and therefore oxygen to the muscle. If such lack of oxygen is prolonged, the heart muscle will die (called heart attack or myocardial infarction) or can lead to irregular heart beats (dysrhythmias) resulting in sudden death.

A number of factors potentiate the likelihood of CAD, including smoking, high fat and cholesterol diet, increasing age, increased blood pressure, diabetes, a family predisposition, and obesity.

Although symptoms are commonly thought to be pain in the chest (angina), quite often following heavy exertion or sudden excitement, many individuals have no symptoms before a sudden fatal heart attack.

With an aging population and therefore an aging population among divers too, there is a real increased risk of such cardiovascular deaths in scuba divers over the age of 40. Indeed 20%–30% of fatalities in sports divers may be due to CAD.

If symptoms are present, some medications such as beta blockers or nitroglycerin may help, but eventually in most cases coronary bypass surgery will be required. It has been suggested that sports divers over age 40, or even those under 40 who are obese and out of condition, see a cardiologist and take an exercise electrocardiogram as described in the section on coronary bypass surgery. Such an exercise tolerance test should successfully reach 13 METs (1 MET is equivalent to normal resting oxygen consumption). Swimming against a 1 knot current will require 8 METs, so 13 METs is the potential for an emergency reserve. (See also Fitness to Dive, page 49).

If CAD is present and coronary bypass recommended, then after surgery and with sufficient time for healing, an increasing exercise regime, and further stress electrocardiograms, it may be possible to return to diving.

CORONARY BYPASS SURGERY

Coronary artery bypass surgery is a quite common procedure today, especially in the older population. It involves transplant of a vessel from the leg to re-establish blood supply of a blocked coronary blood vessel supplying blood to the heart muscle.

Many years ago it was considered that divers who had had coronary bypass surgery should not dive. Today divers may be fit to dive provided their post operative cardiac function permits this, and there is no significant cardiac damage or tendency to have rhythm abnormalities.

A period of 6 to 12 months is usually recommended post surgery to permit healing and recovery. After this, a potential diver should be evaluated by a cardiologist, be free of pain, and have a normal stress electrocardiogram and an exercise tolerance test (See Fitness to Dive).

A recommended regimen for a diver who has had bypass surgery of the heart is rehabilitation for three to four months followed by regular swimming or other conditioning. At six months a stress electrocardiogram should be done to show that adequate blood flow is sustained to the heart muscle during exercise. If this is done with normal blood pressure and no serious changes in heart rhythms result, a return to diving may be contemplated.

Commonly today, "stents" (small tubes to keep the coronary blood vessels open) are often implanted. However, these have a high rate of blocking again after a few months. Again, the individual should enter the regime above to ensure the heart can function adequately in the diving environment.

CRAMPS (CLAUDICATION)

Painful spasms of the muscles, commonly of the calf of the legs or soles of the feet, are known as cramps. Other muscles, such as those of the thighs, upper limbs, and even the abdomen may be involved. The pain is often very strong, but temporary and usually resolves after a short time with some residual soreness.

To assist relaxation of the muscles affected, passive extension is advised plus massage. Divers seem to be especially prone, perhaps because it seems to affect muscles not used to the heavy exercise involved. Swimmers, too, are often affected. Clearly severe pain, while in or under water, creates the danger of drowning. To mitigate the occurrence of cramps, divers or swimmers are advised to keep physically fit by exercising regularly, keep well hydrated with electrolyte balanced products like Gatorade, have well-fitted, not over-tight equipment such as fins, keep warm but not overheated or too cold, and eat a nutritious diet.

HEART ATTACK (MYOCARDIAL INFARCTION)

A heart attack occurs from coronary artery disease (CAD), leading to blockage of the arteries to the heart by cholesterol and the resulting lack of oxygen delivered by the blood to the heart muscles. Small blockages may cause minimal damage and have little or no effect until a large blockage may damage large sections of the heart muscle and cause a sudden heart attack. At this time, the heart ceases to function and results in sudden death, often without warning.

Some 20%–30% of scuba diving deaths are the consequence of cardiovascular problems, and this is more common in those over 40 years of age. The cause is coronary artery disease (CAD), which is discussed elsewhere in this section. (See also Irregular Heartbeat, Cholesterol, and Bypass Operation.)

The first indication of a potential heart attack may be a crushing-like pain in the chest and numbness or pain in the left arm, or without warning, a heart attack may be sudden, with failure of the heart, resulting in hospitalization or death. The exercise required in diving for a diver with a heart suffering from coronary artery blockage may result in sudden death due to the inability to get the extra amount of oxygen required for the heart to function. Should the diver recover, then a cardiologist experienced with diving medicine needs to decide if the diver can return to diving after suitable medical evaluations, including a stress electrocardiogram.

It may be necessary, in a severe case, to have coronary bypass surgery or the insertion of "stents" (small tubes to keep the coronary blood vessels open). Again after the surgery, with a sufficient time of 3–4 months for healing followed by swimming, conditioning, and a stress electrocardiogram at 6 to 12 months, it may be possible for the diver to return to diving. It should, however, be realized that it is likely that there may have been some residual damage done to one or more parts of the heart muscle at the time of the heart attack, which may make for a greater risk for further heart attacks in the future.

HEART VALVE PROBLEMS

The problem of mitral valve prolapse is discussed elsewhere, but other forms of heart valve problems may be a contraindication to diving. Such factors as regurgitation or backflow from a valve between chambers of the heart or valve obstruction to transfer of the blood will affect the efficiency of the heart especially if required to work hard, as when swimming under water. As such the presence of valvular heart disease usually results in a recommendation not to dive.

Divers who have artificial valves inserted are also not recommended to dive. Aside from potential failure of the valves under the heavy exercise is the use of anticoagulants commonly used with such valve implants. This is likely to cause excessive bleeding, which could add to the dangers to the ears from barotrauma and to decompression sickness in sites such as the spinal cord. These divers should be advised to have a stress electrocardiogram with an exercise tolerance test (see Coronary Bypass Surgery and Fitness to Dive).

IRREGULAR HEART BEAT (DYSRHYTHMIAS)

Most divers with normal hearts will not have serious dysrhythmias, although minor irregularities may occur sometimes without a problem. Normal hearts beat between 60 to 100 times per minute. In healthy athletes, such as runners, it is not unusual for their hearts to beat as slow as only 40–50 per minute. With such an athlete, increased exercise will cause the beat to increase in rate. Should it not do so, then it may be a more serious indication of heart defects requiring medical intervention. Other common causes of slowing of the heart or bradycardia are medications in common use today to control increased blood pressure such as beta blockers.

Normal individuals also often may have extra beats or skip a beat. These may be precipitated by drugs such as caffeine, alcohol, stress, dietary supplements, decongestants, analgesics, anti-allergy medicines, or fatigue. These extra heartbeats can occur in the atrial or upper chambers of the heart when the condition is called supraventricular or atrial dysrhythmia. If they occur in the lower heart chambers it is called ventricular tachycardia. Should the irregularities be frequent, then careful medical evaluation by a cardiologist experienced with diving medicine is required.

Those with such serious, frequent irregularities may be well advised not to dive because of the potential for sudden loss of consciousness and therefore drowning or dying of heart failure. This may be triggered by the diver simply putting the face down in cold water. Such cases have occurred not only under water, but on the surface swimming back to the boat.

If the irregular heartbeats are of a minor nature and can be sufficiently controlled without additional problems, then the individual may be fit to dive. However, very often the therapy and medications are associated with other factors that are not compatible with fitness to dive.

It is probably wise for a potential diver with any irregularities of the beating of the heart to have a complete medical evaluation by a cardiologist prior to diving.

MITRAL VALVE PROLAPSE (FLOPPY VALVE SYNDROME)

This is a quite common condition of the heart, especially in women, and is present in some 1.4% to 17% depending on age of the population. Sometimes called a "click-murmur syndrome," it was first noticed in the 1960s. The changes in heart sounds are caused by the extension into the main pumping compartment of the heart, the left ventricle, of components of the mitral valve as a result of excess and loose tissue. No symptoms may result or in a few cases there may be unusual chest pain, palpitations, a feeling of air hunger (dyspnea), and fatigue. Interestingly, mitral valve prolapse also is often associated with panic disorders.

Usually a diver who has had no symptoms and has been prescribed no medications such as beta blockers should be able to dive without concern, and reassurance should be all that is necessary.

If there is chest pain, palpitations, or abnormal heart beats which might produce palpitations, these should be controlled by appropriate medications such as a beta blocker. Although this medication may affect the degree of exercise level achievable, it may not be a problem unless in an emergency situation.

It has been suggested also that a 12 hour recording be made of those individual's heart activity who do have mitral valve prolapse and wish to dive before passing them as fit to dive.

PACEMAKERS AND IMPLANTED HEART DEFIBRILLATORS

Commercial and military divers are not permitted to dive with such heart stimulators. However, for sport diving, the decision is based on individual evaluation.

Pacemakers and defibrillators are usually required due to a malfunction of the neuroelectrical impulses controlling the beat of the heart. This can result in fainting or, if the cause is a previous heart attack, the diver may be limited in his or her ability to handle the extra exercise requirement of diving.

Pacemakers are usually installed over the heart in between the rib-cage and the skin and muscle. Today they can be quite small and will control unusual electrical conduction in the heart that might otherwise lead to malfunction. The heart defibrillator is not really a pacemaker. This device gives a shock to the heart when life threatening effects of heart contraction occur. This could likely be fibrillation, in which the heart cells depolarize and contract rapidly but without the normal coordinated pumping action. Quick action is needed to intervene to prevent death. Today Automatic External Defibrillators (AEDs) are increasingly common on aircraft and in public places for the general public to be able to shock somebody with fibrillation back to normal rhythm.

Pacemakers, when implanted, need to safely work to pressures equivalent to at least 130 ft (40 msw) for recreational scuba diving and be capable of rapid increases or decreases in pressure and changes in temperature.

Before being accepted for diving, the cardiologist should expose the diver to a stress electrocardiogram with exercise test (see Coronary Artery Bypass Surgery and Fitness to Dive) workload.

Since a number of recreational diving fatalities every year are due to cardiovascular problems, any diver with a history of cardiovascular disease with compromised exercise tolerance should be discouraged from scuba diving and requires a thorough evaluation by an experienced cardiologist. Those with defibrillators are usually advised not to dive because of the risk of sudden death while under water.

PATENT FORAMEN OVALE (PFO)

Commonly called the "hole in the heart," patent foramen ovale (PFO) is an opening between the upper right and left chambers of the heart, which collect the blood to be pumped by the ventricles or lower heart chambers. When babies are still in the uterus of the mother, blood bypasses the lungs and goes directly around the baby's body. Once born, the upper right and left chambers are required to pass the blood through the lungs, and the foramen (window) closes in most cases. However, this hole, or PFO, is still found after birth in 25–30% of the adult population.

Thus, bubbles formed in decompression on the venous side of the body may transverse to the arterial side through this patent hole. It is not necessarily easy, because the blood pressure on the left side (arterial) is higher than the right side (venous). However, a strong Valsalva effect on trying to clear the ears or heavy leg exercise, such as pumping up and down, can trigger the bubbles to transverse through the hole. Such Valsalva-induced right-to-left shunts was shown in 18.5% of non-diving volunteers.

The hole may vary in size. In general, 60% of PFOs are small and not a real problem, but 40% are large and could allow bubbles to enter the arteries and cause arterial gas embolism or cause severe decompression sickness (DCS). Although the actual role of PFO in the incidence of DCS remains unclear and there is little conclusive evidence of the increased risk of a PFO, the presence of a skin rash soon after surfacing or severe symptoms such as paraplegia may implicate its presence.

Nevertheless, the risk of DCS in divers with a PFO is small and current research does not support the view that a PFO contributes significantly to the risk of DCS. Nor is a PFO in a diver with severe neurological DCS necessarily a contraindication to continued diving. As a consequence, it is not recommended that there should be wide screen testing for all divers for the present of a PFO.

DCS occurring in a low risk dive, or repeated DCS with no indication of the reason, or the occurrence of severe neurological decompression occurring from dives well within the decompression table limits may merit investigations for the presence of a PFO.

It has also been suggested that divers may wish to stop strenuous arm, leg, or abdominal exercises after diving, as this could precipitate shunting of blood through a PFO.

If a PFO is found it may be closed by a transcatheter occlusion and the diver may return to diving without this potential extra risk. There is, of course, risk to this invasive procedure that may encourage divers with PFO to choose more conservative alternatives. The simplest is to restrict dive profiles to those less likely to produce bubbles. There is no increased risk from a PFO if there are no bubbles present in the heart. This strategy will also reduce the risk of bubbles crossing into the arterial circulation via any of the other avenues that are not affected by closure of the PFO.

VARICOSE VEINS

A varicose vein is a permanently distended vein commonly seen in the legs due to weakening of the blood vessel walls. They can be treated by injection including collapse of the vessel or various surgical interventions. Diving has no specific action on varicose veins. Indeed the water pressure may be supportive. However, there is an increased risk of injury and hemorrhage due to contact with underwater rock or coral or trauma when getting on or off a boat, etc. A wet suit or support bandages are recommended.

DERMATOLOGICAL

ATHLETE'S FOOT

Due to the nature of diving, wet skin is part of scuba diving, but it can aggravate many skin disorders. Athlete's foot is a fungal infection due to *Tinea pedis*.

The condition results in an itchy skin with burning, peeling, cracking, and a red discoloration. It is especially prevalent between the toes and the bottom of the feet. Some individuals are more susceptible than others, and recurrences may occur after treatment. From a diver's viewpoint, it can be transmitted and should be treated and preferably eradicated before diving.

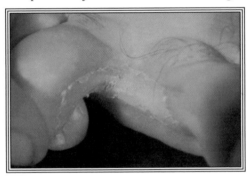

Figure 7 Athlete's Foot

Treatment at first can be with over-the-counter antifungal creams. The feet need to be kept dry after diving or swimming, especially between the toes. The use of talcum powder and cotton socks may be helpful. It may be a good idea to help prevent many dermatological diseases to wear sandals in public showers and pools. Diving booties should not be shared and should be kept as dry as possible.

If the condition does not heal after two weeks, if blisters form, or if the infection is spreading and there are signs of a bacterial infection with pain, pus, and fever, then you should consult a physician as antifungal medication may be required.

Scuba divers are not prevented from diving because of athlete's foot but should take additional care due to the wet environment.

RASHES

There are many kinds of rashes but only those likely to be caused or affected by diving are considered here. Due to exposure to moisture from salt or fresh water, any acute or chronic dermatitis may be exacerbated, as may be bacterial skin infections like acne. Allergic reactions also may be induced from wetsuit glue or detergents.

Atopic dermatitis or eczema presents with intense itching and a red raised rash and sometimes fluid filled blisters, particularly on the hands, neck, face, and legs.

Common in babies and children and sometimes called eczema, it can go on in some individuals into adulthood. The condition often occurs in families and may have a genetic link and can be triggered by contact with irritants such as dyes in face masks and wetsuits, stress, dry skin, and heat. The condition need not prevent diving, but the diver may wish to ensure the skin is well moisturized and kept in a cool, non-humid environment when not diving.

Psoriasis is a chronic rash that affects 2% of the population and is caused by too rapid growth of the cells of the skin, commonly occurring on the elbows and knees, scalp, feet, and lower back. The rapid growth causes patchy red skin with whitish scales. These may itch and be tender to touch. Treatment by a dermatologist is recommended.

For divers the condition may be embarrassing and cause some discomfort putting on wetsuits, etc., and could cause aggravation, but it is not a contraindication to diving.

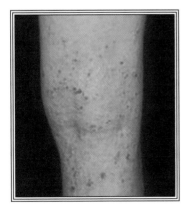 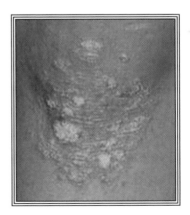

Figure 8 Atopic dermatitis, or eczema (left), and psoriasis (right)

SKIN CANCERS

Over 1 million people living in North America contract skin cancer every year most often due to over exposure to the sun. This is especially likely in divers who may travel to resorts in very sunny climates and be exposed between dives on the dive boats, snorkeling, or just tanning on the beach. There are three types—basal, squamous, and melanoma.

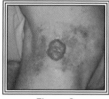

Figure 9

Basal cell carcinoma is a relatively benign cancer not life threatening and relatively the most common. It usually is seen on the head, face, and torso. It may show as a new smooth skin bump which may be shiny like a mole with a pearl-like appearance or just as a red irritated area or a small sore that bleeds and will not heal. Treatment requires a visit to the dermatologist for surgical removal and biopsy.

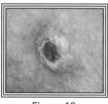

Figure 10

Squamous cell carcinoma is also relatively benign. It shows as a persistent small red lump much like a wart that does not heal. Treatment involves surgical removal of the lump. Both basal cell and squamous cell cancers are more likely in freckled, light skinned people who may be of Celtic origin with red or blonde hair and who have experienced severe sunburns at an early age.

Many such cancers could be prevented by protection from the sun with suitable clothing to cover the arms and legs and a wide brim hat. Sunglasses with ultraviolet protection are also advised. Any exposed skin should be protected with frequent application of sunscreens with an SPF (Sunscreen Protection Factor) of 30 or more. Tanning booths should be avoided.

Figure 11

Melanoma is a very serious form of skin cancer affecting the pigment producing cells which grow aggressively and may spread to other parts of the body, causing death. It is most important to catch melanoma early, as it may be surgically cured at the initial stages. Signs of melanoma are particularly related to any sudden change in growth or color of a mole which may be a dark color and irregular in shape. They can be quite small and may bleed. Treatment requires surgical removal and biopsy as soon as possible. Prevention, as with basal and squamous cell carcinoma, is to avoid the sun and tanning salons. Divers may be at increased risk due to frequency of exposure to the sun. Those taking certain photosensitive medications should be extra careful not to develop severe sunburns while in the sun on dive boats, etc.

SUNBURN AND HEATSTROKE (See Also Skin Cancers)

Sunburn is caused by the ultraviolet (UV) component of sunshine. While some individuals, due to a high melanin content of their skin, exhibit a fine tan, others, with freckled, fair skin, blue eyes, etc., may develop a red, sore, and painful skin. If it is severe this may also develop into more generalized symptoms such as fever, nausea, and vomiting. Vision problems and cataracts are other possible problems from too much exposure to the sun. Above all is the increased risk of skin cancers (See Skin Cancers).

Divers should be extra careful on open dive boats with no shade or in resort areas with hot sunny conditions. The worst time of the day is when the sun is highest, between 10 a.m. and 2 p.m.

The reflection of the sun from water surfaces, white sand, white boat decks, etc. can add to the sunburn risk. The closer to the equator, the higher the sunburn risk, too.

The remedy is to frequently apply sunscreen or sun blocking lotions with an SPF of 30 or more. Adequate protective actions include wearing a hat with a wide brim, sunglasses with UV protection, and light, loose fitting clothes covering the arms and legs. Many medications such as antibiotics like tetracycline or creams for the treatment of acne amplify the action of the sun on the skin and serious sunburns can occur from even short exposures.

Heatstroke or Sunstroke

In conjunction with sunburn, over-exposure to the sun can be associated with heatstroke, a serious and potentially fatal condition. This may have signs or symptoms such as loss of consciousness, convulsions, a core temperature over 104°F (40°C), confusion, anxiety, restlessness, rapid heartbeat, vomiting, and a hot, dry, flushed skin with no sweating. This is a life threatening condition which requires emergency medical intervention as soon as possible and first aid to cool the patient. While waiting for professional medical care, this may be activated by putting the individual in a cool or cold room, removing clothing, and bathing the skin with cold or ice cold water. Do not place the victim in an ice water bath. Instead place ice bags around the neck, armpits, and groin. Ideally, monitor the rectal temperature and try to reduce it to 102°F (39°C) or lower. Temperature recordings taken from the ear or mouth are not recommended. If the individual is conscious and coherent they may be given cool fluids to drink, such as Gatorade, but caution is advised, as many heatstroke victims are not sufficiently stable to drink or swallow safely. Unless medically trained, do not give over-the-counter medications to try to reduce the temperature.

Clearly a diver affected by sunstroke is not fit to dive for several days. When fully recovered, however, the diver could return to diving.

GASTROINTESTINAL

ABDOMINAL SURGERY

In the past, surgical interventions in the abdomen utilized large incisions (laparotomy) to permit the surgeons to examine the abdominal contents directly. This imposed all the risks for infection, scarring, and non-healing of the abdominal wounds. Recovery was usually long and many days were required in the hospital. Today, however, endoscopic (i.e., while looking inside) surgery permits same-day surgery in many cases. This technology permits access to the abdomen through several small incisions—often less than an inch or two in length. Through these incisions the surgeon can both see and carry out appropriate surgical procedures by means of an endoscope. Endoscopy has significantly reduced the risk of infection, shortened hospitalization, and improved the time for recovery.

This is important to the diver. Although there are few or no direct effects of diving on abdominal surgery, clearly a laparotomy is likely to be more debilitating during recovery than endoscopy. Diving may be in water with various degrees of contamination, so to prevent infection, the smaller the surgical wound, the better. In either case, diving should not occur until after the surgical incision is well healed, which may take as much as six weeks. This will give sufficient time for the supporting abdominal muscles to heal. It will also permit time to deal with a small number of abdominal surgeries that end up trapping parts of the bowel, leading to what is called incisional hernias.

The attending surgeon can usually best advise when to return to swimming or diving and when the fatigue and reduced fitness resulting from major surgery are likely to be over. Until then, divers should not be lifting dive tanks or other heavy diving equipment. A gradually increased program of physical therapy could be of help.

BOWEL OBSTRUCTION

An obstruction of the bowel can be caused in a number of ways. These include twisting or entrapment of the intestines, possibly within a hernia (see Hernias), adhesions or scarring due to infection, and diseases of the gut or unusual abdominal compression. The symptoms include acute abdominal pain often accompanied by nausea and vomiting.

It is unlikely that anybody with an acute bowel obstruction would be in the mood for diving. The condition is painful and in need of immediate hospitalization and urgent evaluation and treatment by a physician. Over-distension of the obstructed or entrapped bowel may result in bursting with life-threatening infection of the abdominal cavity (peritonitis).

Once treated and recovered, the individual may return to diving.

COLOSTOMIES

Various diseases and disorders require the contents of the large bowel (i.e., the colon) to be rerouted through the abdominal wall rather than to the anus, i.e., a colostomy. Colostomies may be the result of the surgical treatment of cancer of the large bowel, Crohn's disease (a chronic inflammatory disease of the intestines), traumatic injury, etc. If the opening involves the small (i.e., the ileum) rather than large bowel (colon), it is called an ileostomy. These then require fitting of a removable drainage bag to collect bowel contents.

Unless the underlying disorder or its treatment provides problems for the diver, the management of a colostomy is relatively straight forward. In general it presents little problem to divers accustomed to them, although it may unnerve unfamiliar buddy divers. Concerns that colostomy bags may expand and burst on ascent appear unfounded. The wetsuit usually supports the bag and the bowels can accommodate the modest build-up of intestinal gas and contents during the dive. Obviously, the bag may become dislodged due to unusual movements of the diving equipment, and the contents of the bag may be spilled, but this is more of a nuisance than a danger.

Unlike colostomies, an ileostomy functions slightly differently. The contents of the ileum are more liquid than those of the colon, so it is common to create a type of reservoir to allow for some accumulation before intermittent drainage is required. This is achieved by creating a loop of the small bowel under the skin called a "continent," "moderate" ileostomy, or Koch Pouch. To then relieve the contents, a small nipple valve is included that can be emptied regularly by means of small rubber catheter. This creates the possibility for obstruction if there is a rapid accumulation of gas—such as if a diver swallows a lot of compressed air while diving. However, the authors are unaware of any serious consequences resulting from diving with "ostomies." However, the diver would be wise to evaluate his or her particular situation both with the surgeon or physician involved and, whenever available, a physician experienced in diving medicine.

ABDOMINAL CRAMPS

Painful spasms of the muscles, commonly of the calf of the legs or soles of the feet, are known as cramps. However, other muscles, such as those of the thighs, upper limbs, and even the abdomen may be involved. The pain is often very strong, but temporary, and usually resolves after a short time with some residual soreness.

To assist relaxation of the muscles affected, passive extension is advised plus massage. Divers seem to be especially prone, perhaps because it seems to affect muscles not used to the heavy exercise involved. Swimmers, too, are often affected. Clearly, severe pain, while in or under water, creates the danger of drowning. To mitigate the occurrence of cramps, divers or swimmers are advised to keep physically fit by exercising regularly, keep well hydrated with electrolyte balanced products like Gatorade, have well-fitted, not over-tight equipment such as fins, keep warm but not overheated or too cold, and to eat a nutritious diet.

GALLSTONES

The gallbladder is an organ associated with the liver. Its primary use is to collect and concentrate bile, which is then introduced into the upper intestine to assist with digestion. Because the gall bladder concentrates various salts and other compounds, it is possible that sediment or even crystals may form. These are called gallstones and may be made up of cholesterol or bile salts and range in size from very small flakes to more than 2 inches in diameter. They are associated with a number of intestinal problems but are often symptomless by themselves.

When symptoms do occur, these are usually related to acute, intense pain in the upper right side of the body, under the rib cage, and may be accompanied by nausea and vomiting. Once any acute inflammation has settled, gallstones are usually removed together with the gallbladder.

Some 600,000 individuals receive gallbladder surgery each year and about 10% of people over 40 have gallstones. In the past, surgical intervention involved laparotomy through a large abdominal incision. Today endoscopy access through only two or three small holes causes less pain and a makes for a quicker recovery and a faster return to diving!

For divers the primary concern would be developing a gallbladder attack while in a remote location or on a live-aboard. Travel insurance is an important consideration to allow the diver to get to a modern, experienced medical facility for treatment including surgery. Individuals who experience intermittent cramping or pain under the right side of the ribcage may wish to have gallstones or other gallbladder disease excluded before taking on a long trip to remote locations.

GASTROENTERITIS

Infection or irritation of the intestines is a common, every day malady. It goes by various synonyms including, traveler's diarrhea, food poisoning, stomach flu, and other less flattering colloquial names. Travelers—including divers—are particularly at risk and the nausea, vomiting, and diarrhea that develop may be mild to completely debilitating. It also causes dehydration, which is a risk factor for decompression illness.

There are three kinds of gastroenteritis: bacterial, viral, and parasitic.

Bacterial:
Bacteria commonly contaminate food supplies, particularly ground meat, poultry, eggs, fresh fruits, vegetables, and salads. *Eschericia coli (E.coli)* and *Salmonella* are common culprits. These infections are usually short-lived, with diarrheal illness and limited associated malaise.

Viral:
There are many viral illnesses with a gastroenteritis component. These are particularly prevalent in epidemics as may occur on cruise ships, nursing homes, college campuses, etc., where people are in close quarters. The Norwalk virus has been implicated in many of these outbreaks. Symptoms include vomiting and watery diarrhea, flu-like manifestations with fever and headache, and abdominal cramping. These may continue for several days and the condition is highly contagious. In severe cases hospitalization may be required.

Parasitic:
Parasitic infections are common in developing countries and include amebic dysentery and giardia infections. Dysentery implies the presence of blood in the stool—always an ominous sign which should prompt immediate medical attention. Giardia infections may last for many days and are associated with copious diarrhea, intestinal gas, and cramping. Antibiotics such as metronidazole (Flagyl ™) are required.

Prevention of all forms of gastroenteritis start with good basic hygiene and frequent washing of the hands as well as decontamination of surrounding surfaces with antibacterial agents or halogen (chlorine or iodine) bleaches.

Contaminated clothing should be cleaned in bleach or boiling water. All food liable to spoilage should be refrigerated. Care should be taken eating shell fish and raw fish especially—when in doubt...don't.

With the condition being as common as it is, particularly in third world countries where divers travel, it is a near certainty that you will develop a diarrheal illness at one stage or another. Fortunately, with the exception of parasitic and bacterial dysenteries, the infection itself is not really a problem. The major concern is dehydration. Far more important than food is active rehydration using safe water sources and isotonic solutions containing some glucose (e.g., Gatorade). For diarrheal illnesses other than those presenting with flu-like symptoms (i.e., viral infections) and specifically if there is blood in the stool or the disease lasts more than 72 hours, antibiotics are usually prescribed. Cipro® is popular for bacterial infections and Flagyl® for giardia and amebic dysentery.

As a rule it is not recommended to suppress the diarrhea with Lomotil® or Immodium® as this traps the infective agent in the body and may prolong the illness. Over-the-counter drugs to help prevent the diarrhea, such as Pepto-Bismol, may be helpful in mild cases.

Since dehydration is believed to increase the risk for decompression sickness, divers may need to wait for a few days until they have recovered and rehydration is complete.

HEARTBURN

Heartburn is the non-medical name for gastroesophageal reflux disease (GERD). It is caused by an abnormal reflux or backflow of the stomach acid and contents into the esophagus. Symptoms include a burning sensation or pain behind the breastbone and may be accompanied by a sour taste or even regurgitation of food or a sense of bloating and nausea. Commonly it occurs after eating especially spicy foods or general overeating. It may last for several hours. Lying down or bending over will make it worse.

The condition occurs in 20% of adults at least once per month, especially in those over the age of 45. Severe heartburn may occur in 5%–15% of individuals and it is present in 80% of pregnant women. Drinking alcohol and smoking will exacerbate heartburn. Obesity and hiatus hernia are additional risk factors for heartburn (see Hernia).

There are several situations during diving that may exacerbate heartburn. In particular the constriction by the wetsuit, weight belt, and buoyancy compensator combined with needing to bend over to don fins, etc., are likely to provoke an attack of heartburn in individuals who suffer from it regularly.

It is wise to avoid foods such as acidic fruit juice, bread, savory mince and even bananas shortly before diving. Most people quickly develop their own lists of "no-no" foods. During ascent, due to expansion of compressed air swallowed during the dive with equalization, reflux may also cause regurgitation of stomach contents. Severe reflux may be dangerous under water as it may impair breathing or even result in aspiration (i.e., breathing in) of stomach contents. People who are woken up at night with coughing due to reflux are particularly at risk. Although mild and infrequent heartburn can usually be managed effectively with over the counter antacids, regular or severe episodes—especially in lean individuals—may justify formal medical and eventually surgical treatment.

Simple tips to reduce heartburn include the following:

- Do not combine food and liquids (i.e., if possible eat and drink two hours apart)
- Avoid eating or drinking within two hours of retiring to bed
- Avoid food that is known to cause heartburn
- Avoid aspirin and anti-inflammatory drugs—known to aggravate heartburn
- Avoid or cut back on smoking, alcohol, caffeine, and spicy food
- Lose weight—a reduction in intra-abdominal pressure can reduce reflux by 30%.

HERNIAS

A hernia is a protrusion of body tissue into the space of another. It can be applied to the spine, i.e., herniated disk; stomach, i.e., hiatus hernia; or intestines.

Usually the non-specific word "hernia" refers to a weakness of the abdominal wall which allows soft tissues—and sometimes the intestines—to protrude from the abdominal cavity towards the skin. There are several locations where they occur: Inguinal hernias are the most common and occur in the groin region. Femoral hernias may be confused with inguinal but are due to bulges from the lower abdomen into the upper thigh. Incisional hernias can occur after abdominal surgery. Umbilical hernias develop around the navel, and epigastric hernias develop in the middle of the abdomen. Hiatus hernias occur when part of the stomach bulges out of the abdomen into the chest cavity.

The symptoms associated with inguinal hernias include tenderness or severe pain in the groin or heaviness, swelling, and tugging or burning sensation in the groin, scrotum, or inner thigh. This may be relieved only when lying down. It is possible that a bulge may be caused without any pain.

Hiatal hernias may involve heartburn (see Heartburn) and esophageal reflux, or they may be asymptomatic.

Treatment commonly involves surgical repair of the hernia. There are some 750,000 carried out each year in the United States. If not, then there is danger of trapping a piece of the bowel in the hernia. Such an obstruction, "incarceration," or strangulation can result in severe infection as the loss of blood supply to that loop of intestine results in tissue death (infarction) and infection. Surgery usually cures more than 90% of hernias. Trusses are not generally advised as they do not prevent trapping.

Although rare, the risk to the diver is that the trapped loop of bowel containing air will expand during ascent and may rupture. For these reasons, it is best to have a hernia surgically repaired before diving. Prevention of a hernia or its recurrence can be assisted by taking plenty of exercise and avoiding obesity or sudden weight loss. Chronic heavy coughing or straining at bowel and urine relief should be avoided, and lifting heavy weights improperly.

Interestingly, surgical repair of a hiatus hernia can result in "gas-bloat" syndrome in divers when the inability to belch after successful surgery causes distension of the stomach with gas. In extreme cases, this may result in a rupture of the stomach on ascent.

INFLAMMATORY BOWEL DISEASE (IBD)

Inflammatory bowel disease (IBD) is a chronic condition that causes inflammation and sometimes ulceration of the bowel and affects some 600,000 people in the United States. The two most well known forms are ulcerative colitis and Crohn's disease, but it can also affect the joints, eyes, and skin. Symptoms include bloody diarrhea or constipation, nausea, vomiting, acute abdominal pain, fever, and loss of weight. Although usually not life-threatening, these diseases can be very debilitating and may involve accompanying depression. There also is an increased risk of colon cancer with ulcerative colitis.

The disease may start with intermittent attacks followed by more prolonged attacks accompanied by anemia, electrolyte disturbances, dehydration, poor absorption of fluids, liver disease, and a generalized fatigue.

Mild cases, with only occasional symptoms, may be treated with medication such as corticosteroids and aspirin-like agents, but severe cases may involve surgical removal of sections of bowel.

Divers often travel to isolated dive sites or on live-aboards where an acute attack may be difficult to treat. Divers with active symptoms of IBD should not dive. However, some divers with good control of the inflammation or in remission may be fit to dive.

PANCREATITIS

Pancreatitis is an inflammation of a specialized gland in the abdomen called the pancreas. The pancreas is a surprisingly complex organ that produces two sets of products: (1) those released in the blood stream that affect the absorption, breakdown, and utilization of glucose as well as the function of the digestive organs, and (2) those released directly into the intestinal canal and involved with the digestive process.

Pancreatitis may be acute or chronic. Acute pancreatitis is serious and may be life threatening. It is associated with severe pain and distension in the middle of the abdomen, which may spread directly to the back. It may occur after a heavy meal or drinking alcohol. Other signs or symptoms may include nausea or vomiting, fever, and rapid pulse. Chronic pancreatitis is a more insidious problem. It presents with ongoing mild abdominal pain and distension, loss of weight, bad smelling and large amounts of feces, and ultimately even the development of diabetes when the organ is shriveled, scarred, and calcified.

Treatment for acute pancreatitis is aimed at pain control, keeping the bowels unobstructed, and trying to prevent the extreme fluid loss that may occur. If the pancreas actually ruptures, it forms a collection of fluid in the abdomen (called a false or pseudocyst); surgery may be required. Chronic pancreatitis may be a result of alcoholism or a variety of inflammatory conditions. Chronic pancreatitis is treated by avoiding fatty foods and alcohol and taking medication to compensate for the loss of products previously produced by the pancreas.

Although there are far more common causes for an acute abdominal crisis—such as appendicitis—acute pancreatitis may affect divers also, particularly in situations of binge drinking. The take-home message is to avoid dietary and alcoholic indiscretion but also not to ignore acute abdominal pain until it becomes a life threatening crisis. Those with mild chronic pancreatitis who are not under medication for pain, not ill or fatigued, and are able to eat normally will probably be able to dive safely.

PEPTIC ULCERS

It is estimated that 5% to 10% of the general population develop peptic ulcers at some stage during their lives. These ulcers are due to damage to the lining of the stomach often causing a crater-like sore in the lining of the stomach or duodenum (first part of the small intestine). Those in the stomach are less common and are called stomach ulcers; those in the upper small intestine are common, associated with stress, and called duodenal ulcers. The collective term is peptic ulcers.

The most common causes are irritation of the stomach lining due to higher acidity or destruction of the protective lining by aspirin, non-steroidal anti-inflammatory (NSAID) drugs, or infection with *H. pylori* bacteria. Treatment is by antacids and antibiotics for infections.

Symptoms may include upper left abdominal pain often relieved by antacids; loss of appetite, weight loss, and general fatigue; bleeding and possible perforation; bloating and nausea after eating; vomiting after meals; and black tar-like stools due to the bleeding into the intestines.

Left untreated, some ulcers may heal but at least half such cases will recur. However, modern medications are very effective and surgery is rarely necessary.

It is inadvisable to dive with an active peptic ulcer, particularly in remote locations. The symptoms of such an ulcer can come on rapidly and can be severe and disabling. Once the ulcer is healed and there are no further symptoms, then diving should be possible.

VOMITING

Vomiting is associated with a number of normal and abnormal conditions, including pregnancy, motion sickness, overheating, gastroenteritis, etc. Often it is due to inflammation or irritation of the stomach lining from chemicals or infective agents. In countries with poor sanitation and health control, it is a common feature of gastroenteritis syndromes (see Gastroenteritis). The symptoms of vomiting—abdominal cramps, diarrhea, fever, headache, etc.—may last for one to several days. Anti-emetics are not always effective, and as many are taken orally, may not be absorbed before being expelled. However, the most important part of treatment for vomiting is to replace the acute loss of fluids and dehydration which—in divers—may also increase susceptibility to decompression sickness.

Vomiting may also be a feature of sea sickness (see Motion Sickness). This affects some divers more than others, and not everyone who gets sea sick ends up vomiting. Fortunately, sea sickness can usually be managed fairly well with medication or non-chemical means (see Sea Sickness). Medication often causes drowsiness and other side effects and needs to be tested by the diver at least 24 hours before diving to ensure these will not present problems.

For divers, vomiting from any cause may be a problem under water. Vomiting through a regulator presents certain practical problems—such as the caliber of the exhaust port—and food may block the one-way valve on the exhaust port and cause leaking or obstruction. Some recommend removing the regulator, but this is reputed to be equally dangerous as the large inhalation after vomiting may come before the regulator is restored and result in aspiration and drowning. In practice, however, this has not been as much of a problem as suggested.

Prolonged and uncontrolled vomiting may require hospitalization to ensure adequate rehydration.

Prevention is the best treatment by ensuring food is adequately refrigerated and hygienically prepared (see Gastroenteritis). Wash hands frequently and cook all meat and chicken to a temperature likely to kill bacteria.

GENITO-URINARY

ABORTION AND MISCARRIAGE

The terms abortion and miscarriage both imply the termination of pregnancy. Miscarriage is reserved for spontaneous and unplanned loss of gestation prior to 20 weeks, and it affects 10%–15% of pregnancies. Abortion covers the entire spectrum of premature terminations of pregnancy. The cause or circumstances are often qualified by means of several descriptive modifiers such as: spontaneous, medical, legal, illegal, septic, threatened, partial, inevitable, etc. Spontaneous loss of pregnancy prior to 12 weeks may be due to genetic abnormalities, poor adherence to the uterine wall, or hormonal imbalances. If all the products of conception are expelled, it is called a complete miscarriage and no further medical treatment is required. Some miscarriages may seem to be little more than a slightly heavy menstruation and can even go unnoticed and they require no special precautions. In the absence of pain, fever, or prolonged bleeding, there is no reason to avoid diving within seven days of an early, complete, spontaneous miscarriage. In abortions after eight weeks gestation, surgical clearance of the womb is usually required. Abortions by choice, for whatever reason, also require both medical and surgical interventions and require a longer period of healing. The larger the fetus, the bigger and more hazardous the procedure. A recovery period of at least six weeks is usually recommended where hospitalization and surgical interventions are required. This allows the body to return to its normal physiological state and reduces the chances for infection.

BREAST SURGERY—IMPLANTS

The modern world with its ever increasing search for perfection has had a proportional impact on cosmetic surgery. As such, there is a surprisingly large number of women who sport breast implants. In spite of all the fears about silicone leakage and its consequences, the frequency of breast implant surgery has diminished very little. Women with such implants may end up scuba diving and have concerns about their safety. To these we can offer the reassurance that breast implants appear to be impervious to the pressures of diving.

There are certainly anecdotal cases of implants being dived outside their prospective recipients and subsequently being seen to develop bubbles during decompression. But the direct exposure to inert gas at high pressure in these experiments by far exceeds that which these prostheses would be exposed to inside their human carriers. Therefore, six weeks after placement and in the absence of any complications, diving can be undertaken with complete safety. The same is true for calf and other silicone prostheses.

HYSTERECTOMY

Removal of the uterus is a very common gynecological procedure. It is usually performed as a treatment for excessive menstrual bleeding, abnormal menstruation, deep coital pain, following complications of pregnancy, or following the development of benign or malignant tumors of the womb, cervix, or vagina. In women before menopause, hysterectomies are usually performed without removing the ovaries. This allows normal hormone production to continue, prevents osteoporosis, and actually maintains the normal menstrual cycle, but without the actual menses (i.e., vaginal bleeding). In post menopausal women the ovaries are often removed as a precaution. As long as the underlying reason for the hysterectomy is not disqualifying, most women should be able to resume diving after clearance by their surgeon—usually after six weeks. The vaginal and/or abdominal wounds are then strong enough to withstand the rigors of exercise and exposure to water.

KIDNEY STONES

Our kidneys are designed to concentrate impurities and water-soluble waste products to allow us to discharge them from the body with a minimal loss of water. Certain of these waste products have a tendency to form crystals and—if these form in the kidney or in the tube between the kidney and the bladder (the ureter)—they are called kidney stones. Some people have a genetic predisposition to form kidney stones, but most kidney stones develop due to chronic hypohydration when the urine becomes hyperconcentrated to conserve water. Kidney stones are said to be one of the most painful of human afflictions. The pain is excruciating and usually migrates between the small of the back and the groin. Depending on the size of the stone—some of which can actually be visualized on x-rays—they may either be passed spontaneously or require surgical intervention. The latter may include lithotripsy—a process of passing ultrasonic shock waves through the body to break up the crystals—or kidney surgery. Any surgery immediately introduces the usual six week prohibition to dive in the absence of any complications. In terms of preventing kidney stones, there are two primary strategies. For those with a natural tendency to form kidney stones, medication and the avoidance of certain foods and chemicals may be necessary. For those who only develop them when they take in too little fluid, the remedy is obvious—avoid dehydration and take copious fluids, up to three liters per day. As a rule it is healthy to keep urine clear (i.e., almost colorless) without the artificial diuretic effects of alcohol or caffeine. Kidney stones do not have any direct affect on diving. Of greater concern is the possibility of sudden incapacitation due to acute pain, but this is unlikely during the short underwater excursions of recreational diving.

MENSTRUATION

Menstruation (cyclical vaginal bleeding) is a normal event in women of childbearing age, usually between 12 and 46 years. It is the result of an interaction between two hormones—estrogen and progesterone—on the lining of the uterus or womb. After 21 to 28 days there is an abrupt decrease in hormones, resulting in shedding of this lining with bleeding. Most cycles are 21–35 days in duration with menses (i.e., bleeding) lasting for 3 to 10 days with a total blood loss of 30–40 milliliters. Menstruation may be associated with discomfort or pain in the back, lower abdomen, and thighs. There are various possible menstrual abnormalities ranging from too frequent to absent, and extremely painful to painless. Oral and other contraceptives affect menstruation and this introduces further variables. As far as diving is concerned the issue is relatively simple: (1) There is no specific reason not to dive during menstruation. There is conflicting evidence whether women are more susceptible to decompression illness during menstruation, but the risk—if any—remains small and it is wise to dive conservatively at all times anyway. (2) Menstrual fluid and blood have not been shown to attract sharks and the risk of getting attacked as a result is miniscule. (3) Tampons are safe with diving and will not cause "womb squeeze" or any other dangers. (4) Women who are very uncomfortable during menses (bleeding) or take anti-inflammatory medication to control pain and bleeding should consider not diving at that time.

PREGNANCY

Little is actually known about the effects of compressed gas diving on the unborn human fetus. However there are several potential concerns:

- The fetus has an independent circulatory system which interfaces with that of the mother for the exchange of oxygen and nutrients. Accordingly, it also relies on the mother's circulatory system for inert gas exchange. This piggy-back system introduces a whole new set of variables for which regular dive tables make no provision.

- Diving not only raises the partial pressure of nitrogen, it also increases oxygen partial pressure. This may or may not be harmful for the unborn— we simply do not know.

• If decompression illness or gas embolism were to occur, this would have potentially devastating consequences for the fetus. In addition, the effect of subsequent recompression therapy may have adverse effects, although some research in Russia on carbon monoxide poisoning has suggested that a single hyperbaric treatment is safe.

Several studies have tried to define the risk of diving while pregnant. Experiments with animals—usually sheep, goats, or dogs—have suggested an increased risk of deformities in early pregnancy and still birth when DCI occurred closer to full-term. However, these experiments have typically involved diving profiles far more extreme than humans would ever do willingly. For ethical reasons, actual human research has been limited to questionnaires and surveys of women who voluntarily or unknowingly continued to dive while pregnant. Such questionnaires tend to prompt a response from those who experienced problems. This causes false high results due to so-called self-selection bias and the evidence is therefore not particularly convincing. Nevertheless, the rate of birth defects in these women has still been reassuringly low and we know that even uncomplicated, full-term pregnancies have a 1%–4% incidence of fetal abnormalities. So while there is certainly potential for harm, at least the risk appears to be relatively low and is certainly not an indication for a medical abortion. So why all the concern? Well, if one were to dive and a birth defect were to result—from whatever cause—and this affects the child for the rest of its life, the burden of guilt would be great. For those parents who avoid smoking and drinking and maintain a healthy lifestyle for the sake of the unborn child, it makes no sense to then go diving. It is only nine months, after all. Snorkeling is safe during pregnancy and can be enjoyed in most places where casual scuba diving is done. If, for whatever reason, diving is undertaken during pregnancy, it is appropriate to realize that the most vulnerable stage is the first 12 weeks. This is when the limbs and organs are almost fully formed. After this they still grow and differentiate, but are near perfect miniatures. This is also the period of morning sickness, so the incentive to dive is often suppressed together with other appetites.

HEAD, EYES, EARS, NOSE, AND THROAT

APHTHOUS ULCERS (ULCERS OF THE MOUTH)

Recurrent aphthous ulcers of the mouth and tongue are a common medical complaint. They typically start in childhood or adolescence as recurrent small, round, or oval-shaped ulcers with defined edges, red borders, and yellow or grey floors. The cause is unknown, but it does not appear to be infectious, contagious, or sexually transmitted. Immune mechanisms appear to play a role and some people have a genetic predisposition to develop them. It may also be associated with other so-called auto-immune conditions where the body directs its immune defenses against itself. Aphthous ulcers may be brought on by a variety of conditions: vitamin and iron deficiency, intestinal inflammatory disorders, smoking cessation, stress, trauma, pre-menstrual hormonal changes, pregnancy, food allergies, sensitivity to a frothing agent in healthcare products such as sodium lauryl sulphate (SLS), immune deficiencies, and medication, especially anti-inflammatory drugs.

Approximately two-thirds of the population are affected by aphthous ulcers at some time. Treatment is symptomatic and Orabase® with cortisone ointments are commonly prescribed. Although these ulcers may impair the ability to comfortably keep a regulator in place, they present no other major problems in diving. Because the ulcers are non-infective there are also no specific risks associated with sharing regulator mouthpieces with someone with aphthous ulcers.

BLINDNESS

Blindness is not a disease as such. It is the complication of a variety of eye diseases, trauma, birth defects, and infections. It is defined as the inability to see at 20 feet (6 meters) what the normal eye should be able to see at 200 feet (60 meters). This is expressed as a fraction—thus 6/6 (20/20) for perfect vision and 6/60 (20/200) or less for blindness if vision cannot be improved by wearing corrective lenses or glasses. Vision is made up of a number of sub-systems and sub-processes. Each of these can be disrupted, with the ultimate result being an inability to see clearly, interpret what is seen, or to see anything at all.

To begin with, light of sufficient brightness and within the range of color (i.e., wavelength) visible to the human eye needs to pass through the transparent, skin-like layer in front of the eye called the cornea. The cornea is unique and very vulnerable. It cannot recover from more than trivial injuries. It is also one of the few parts of the body that may be transplanted. The reasons for needing to do so is that there are a number of illnesses that may make the cornea opaque or weak, even allowing it to burst.

The cornea is not only a transparent membrane, it also acts as a second lens in that it bends light so as to allow it to pass through the pupil. This effect is important enough to potentially disrupt vision if its shape is irregular (i.e., astigmatism). Fortunately this also allows vision to be surgically corrected by manipulating its curvature via refractive surgery by blade or laser.

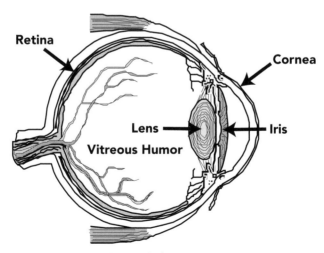

Figure 12 The Eye

Behind the cornea is the iris (disk-like muscle) with a hole in the middle—the pupil. The iris determines eye color and light passes through it towards the lens. The iris controls the amount of light to enter the eye—much like the f-stops in a camera lens. Certain disorders may paralyze or narrow the iris, preventing it from adapting appropriately to light intensity.

Immediately behind the iris is the lens. This transparent, flattened sphere or disk allows light to bend and converge on the retina so as to form sharp images. The lens has an ability to adapt its shape so that objects can be observed in focus at a variety of distances. Mismatching of the cornea, lens, and retina axis are responsible for a need for an additional lens—glasses—to restore visual acuity. Opacity of the lens (e.g., cataracts) or the inability to change shape (i.e., loss of accommodation) will also affect the ability to see clearly.

Next, light passes through a gel in the substance of the eye called the vitreous humor. This jelly-like substance is also transparent but it may become contaminated with particles such as blood clots. When looking at a white surface and rapidly glancing to one side it may be possible to see shadows passing "in front" of the eye. These are called "floaters" and are particles trapped within the vitreous. They are insignificant in small quantities, but if they interfere with vision it may require a synthetic replacement of the vitreous.

The retina is a complicated lattice of specialized nerve and support cells able to react to light and color that generate electrical impulses that are transported to the brain and interpreted as images. The retina contains a particularly sensitive area—called the macula—where the sharpest images are formed. Macular degeneration—an eye disorder affecting the area of sharp vision—eventually destroys this area, leaving the individual with only "corner of the eye" vision. The retina requires derivatives of vitamin A to see in the dark, and a deficiency may result in night blindness. The circulation to the retina runs next to the optic nerve, which is attached at the rear end of the eye and links it to the brain. Once the artery enters the eye it divides like a spider's web over the retina to ensure an even delivery of oxygen and nutrients. Complete interruption in blood supply results in immediate total blindness in that eye. Some conditions, like glaucoma, are more gradual (see Glaucoma). The optics from both eyes' nerves converge to form a junction called the optic chiasm. Here nerve fibers pair up to split the visual fields from both eyes into distinct left and right sides, or half spheres. The nerve fibers transporting images from the left side of someone looking straight ahead spread over the right side of the brain like a light beam. Damage to the brain in this area—as in a stroke—may result in loss of vision in the opposite side of both eyes. Eventually the nerve fibers again converge at the very back end of the brain in what is called the occipital lobe. This is why a severe injury to the back of the brain may result in blindness. In the setting of diving, vision is required for safety and enjoyment of the experience. It is a minimum requirement for divers to be able to read their gauges and handle their dive gear. There are blind people who dive, but they are entirely dependent on their buddies for their safety and, as a result, at least two seeing divers should support one blind diver. Diving does not appear to have any significant effect on diseases affecting the eye. The only exception is disorders that weaken the cornea. If the tensile strength of the cornea is compromised, mask squeeze (or suction on the eye) may cause it to rupture. This is why diving should be avoided for a period of time after penetrating eye surgery (see Eye Surgery and Refractive Surgery).

COLOR BLINDNESS

This is a genetic condition, usually transferred by females to their male offspring. It results in a deficiency in the ability to appreciate distinctions in color, especially the red/green combination. The impact is usually minor other than problems with selecting matching apparel, and possible problems in distinguishing color-coded signals and signs. High-risk occupations such as bomb disposal and aviation that depend heavily on correct color interpretation may disqualify individuals with abnormal color vision. One benefit of having problems with color vision is that the illusion created by camouflage is less effective. For this reason, color-blind individuals were used as spotters in the Vietnam War to detect hidden strongholds and airfields. Similarly, such individuals may also be able to distinguish better the presence of animals and fish who blend into their environment under water. Divers with color blindness could not rely on color to differentiate gas cylinders or regulators while diving.

CONTACT LENSES

Contact lenses are one of three ways in which inherited or age-related deterioration in visual acuity may be corrected; the others are corrective glasses and refractive eye surgery. Contacts are not appropriate for everybody and certain eye conditions preclude their use. Nevertheless, they are amazing pieces of plastic. As the name suggests, they are in contact with the cornea of the eye and correct its refractive index (light bending or focusing properties). This restores the ability of the eye to form a sharp image on the retina. Contact lenses have gone through a series of evolutionary developments over the past three decades. As the cornea has no circulation of its own, it must obtain its oxygen directly from the environment. Accordingly, gas permeable contact lenses were eventually developed to allow this process to continue even with the contact lens in place. The older hard (PMMA) lenses were non-gas-permeable and caused numerous problems. Divers who wore them sometimes suffered from visual blurring and corneal irritation as the lenses did not allow nitrogen to escape—resulting in bubbles between the eye and the lens. Fortunately they are almost obsolete nowadays. Today's contact lenses are all gas permeable and present no problems to divers. They come in two primary types: soft and rigid gas permeable (RGP) lenses. Each has specific characteristics and wear and care regimens. In addition to lens composition, there are now also disposable and durable varieties of lenses. Disposable lenses are discarded daily. The advantage is that if they are lost while diving, the impact is trivial. More durable soft lenses with a one-week to one-year lifespan may pose greater inconvenience and cost if lost. The same is true for RGP lenses that may last for years with regular care. There are two major pitfalls in the use of contact lenses:

- Prolonged wear, especially overnight and beyond the manufacturer's recommendations. This can lead to corneal ulceration and even blindness.

- Use of inappropriate cleaning agents that may damage the lens or the eye. New contact lenses wearers may be confused by the large number of cleaning solutions available today. Always follow manufacturer's recommendations or get professional advice. Experienced users may become complacent over time and resort to cleaning lenses with saliva or even tap water. This is courting disaster by inviting infection and corneal abrasions. Contamination with acanthamoeba for instance may actually result in complete loss of vision.

Any redness of the eye or hypersensitivity to light associated with the wear of contact lenses should prompt discontinuation of their use and urgent medical attention. As far as diving is concerned, there are only two additional considerations:

- Contact lenses may be lost if the face mask is accidentally dislodged or removed during diving. Keeping the eyes closed when the mask floods does help minimize the chances.

- It is also unwise to depend entirely on contact lenses when traveling, especially if losing them may affect diving safety. Consider the alternative of having corrective lenses built into the face mask. Also, always carry spare contact lenses and cleaning liquid and have a set of conventional glasses as a back-up.

DEAFNESS

The inability to hear or to hear normally may be an inherited or acquired disability. It spans a spectrum of impairment ranging from slight hearing loss to complete deafness. Loudness of sound is expressed in decibels (dB). The decibel scale is logarithmic (non-linear or exponential): a 10 dB increase indicates a one-hundred fold increase in loudness. Below (Table 3) is an outline of common noise levels and their decibel equivalents.

Table 3. Common Noise Levels and Decibel Equivalents

Loudness (dB)	Noise Description
0	Threshold of hearing (human with good ears)
10	Human breathing at 3 m (20 ft) away
20	Rustling of leaves
40	Residential area at night
50	Quiet restaurant
70	Busy traffic
80	Vacuum cleaner
90	Loud factory
100	Pneumatic hammer at 2 m (6 ft)
110	Accelerating motorcycle at 5 m (15 ft)
120	Rock concert
130	Threshold of pain
150	Jet engine at 30 m (100 ft)
180	Rocket engine at 30 m (100 ft)

Hearing loss is classified as mild (26–40 dB), moderate (41–55 dB), moderately severe (56–70 dB), severe (71–90 dB), and profound (90 dB). A hearing loss of more than 70 dB is considered deafness, although significant difficulties with communication can already be experienced at lower levels of hearing loss.

The process of hearing depends on a number of synchronized mechanisms and transfer systems as well as interpretation within the brain. Each step may affect hearing if abnormal. The normal process is that sound waves are directed by the pinna (outer ear shell) to the external ear opening and into the external ear canal. They travel down the one-inch tube towards the ear drum (tympanic membrane [TM]). The TM looks a little like a modern audio speaker; it is conical in shape, but instead of having a magnet at its base, it has an attachment to a lever made of bone, called the *malleus* or hammer. This lever has two joints connecting it to two adjacent bones, the *incus* (anvil) and *stapes* (stirrup) that amplify sound waves fourteen times. The stapes rocks on top of an oval membrane called the oval window.

Behind the membrane is a miniature spiral tube, incarcerated in bone, called the cochlea. It is made up of three fluid compartments, with the middle one lined with trigger hairs that react to different wavelengths of sound. High pitched sounds with short wavelengths cause a reverberation of the trigger hairs closest to the oval window. Lower sounds reverberate higher along the spiral. Activation of the trigger hairs causes them to transmit electrical impulses, which are transferred to the brain. Exposure to very loud noise tends to damage the trigger hairs closest to the oval window. This explains the loss of high pitched hearing in individuals exposed to such noise. Malfunction of the trigger hairs may generate spontaneous discharges without a sound stimulus. This "ringing in the ears," or *tinnitus*, is common to many conditions in which hearing is damaged. Any disturbance in sound conduction from the external ear up to the trigger hairs is called conductive hearing loss. The fault is usually mechanical. Damage or dysfunction of the trigger hairs, auditory nerve, and brain is called nerve (or sensori-neuronal) hearing loss. It is an electrical problem. For obvious reasons, deafness may pose a problem to diving safety, both on shore and in the water. However, if this aspect can be overcome, there is no need to disqualify someone from diving on the basis of the hearing deficiency alone. There are three exceptions:

- Conditions that may be exacerbated by diving, such as a perforated TM
- Previous barotrauma of the inner ear with deafness, which disqualifies someone from diving on the basis of risk for further injury
- Conditions where deafness and vertigo may coexist—such as Meniere's disease—on the basis of the vertigo and the risk of disorientation under water

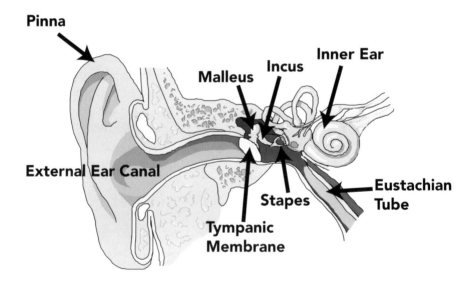

Figure 13 The Ear

Temporary hearing loss as a result of diving is most commonly related to middle ear squeeze, with or without a perforation. Rarely, inner ear damage may result from forceful attempts at equalizing. Lastly, a less common cause of deafness is inner ear decompression sickness. This is rarely seen in < 80 fsw (24 msw) air diving. Deafness after diving should always prompt medical attention.

DENTAL

Tooth problems fall into three categories as far as diving is concerned: (1) bad teeth, (2) missing teeth, and (3) no teeth.

Bad Teeth

These include cavities and corrupted fillings that contain a gas cavity. Diving may result in implosive or explosive barotrauma as the gas space contracts and expands according to Boyle's law. In most cases, and everyday recreational diving, dental barotrauma is both rare and managed relatively simply by terminating the dive. This may be more complicated when people travel abroad or dive deep with compulsory in-water stops. Commercial divers and diving instructors working in remote locations would do well to have their teeth checked meticulously. Tooth ache and dental mishaps are one of the most common claims on travel insurance! It is wise to have your teeth checked prior to anything but the briefest of trips.

Missing Teeth

The absence of some teeth is not particularly troublesome unless they impair the ability of the individual to hold the regulator securely in place. Dental plates, bridges, and implants are usually not a problem but it is wise to check the security of the devices before undertaking diving or the individual may lose more than their smile.

No Teeth

Fortunately, the tendency to remove teeth at the first sign of decay has all but disappeared. Nevertheless, there are divers who are edentulous (toothless) and wear dentures. Most dentures are loose, i.e., they are affixed with a type of temporary glue to keep them from becoming dislodged during daily activities. This may not stand up to the rigors of holding a regulator in the mouth, and the ability to do so should be confirmed. Dental implants by means of titanium screws are becoming more popular. These devices are quite secure and unlikely to cause problems.

DEVIATED NASAL SEPTUM

The nasal septum is a part-bony and part-cartilaginous partition that divides the nasal passage into two distinct channels with an associated nostril. It has a very rich blood supply and the most common origin of nose bleeds is from its foremost area. The exact cause of septal "skewness," or deviation, is unknown and it usually of little consequence unless it impairs air flow through the nose or drainage of mucus from the sinus cavities.

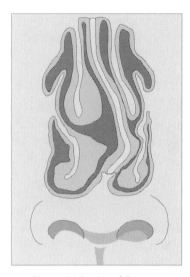

Figure 14 Deviated Septum

In patients over the age of 14 years, approximately 70% of nasal septa are deviated (skewed) to some extent. The deviation can be classified into three grades according to severity:

- Grade I: any deviation that does not contact the lateral nasal wall structures
- Grade II: contact with lateral nasal wall structures which reverses with decongestion
- Grade III: contact with lateral nasal wall structures which persists after decongestion

Only grades II/III correlate with nasal and sinus problems by obstructing the openings for sinus drainage. When the finding of a deviated septum corresponds with a difficulty to equalize on the same side, it is attractive to associate the two. This assumption is not firmly grounded in science, but the presumed mechanism whereby surgical correction of a deviated septum corrects equalizing problems is due to a correction in air flow. Turbulent air flow may cause mucosal irritation and engorgement and it is thought that by alleviating the turbulent flow, the congestion can be reduced. Surgery involves a 60–90 minute procedure with relatively few complications. Anecdotally, many divers report an improvement in their ability to equalize as well as relief in chronic sinusitis, bad breath, and even snoring.

EAR SQUEEZE (MIDDLE EAR BAROTRAUMA)

Approximately 65% of all divers will suffer from middle ear squeeze at some stage during their years of diving. Diving to a depth of as little as 4–6 fsw (1.2–1.8 msw) without equalizing will already cause some degree of barotrauma. If equalizing is still unsuccessful by the time the pressure on the ear drum reaches the equivalent of 6–33 fsw (1.8–10 msw) of sea water pressure, the eardrum may rupture. Divers who have experienced ear drum rupture often describe momentary relief of pain as the tension on the ear drum is relieved. They then suffer a brief spell of extreme dizziness as cold water rushes into the middle ear and comes in contact with the inner ear. As the water warms to body temperature, the dizziness settles, and the diver may believe that their equalizing problems are over and the now fluid-filled middle ear has no need for equalization. However, there is usually significant deafness upon return to the surface, followed by severe pain some 2–5 hours later due to an inflammatory response to the water. Between minor irritation and perforation of the ear drum is a spectrum of gradual tearing and bleeding within and behind the ear drum. Middle ear barotrauma should be treated by a medical professional. Nasal and systemic decongestants are invariably prescribed in an effort to normalize Eustachian tube function—the key to a healthy middle ear. Return to diving should be delayed until pain has disappeared, signs of damage have resolved, perforations have closed, and the ability to equalize with ease has returned. (Also see Diving Nuisances—Ear Problems and Deafness)

EYE SURGERY AND REFRACTIVE SURGERY

It is important for individuals who have undergone eye surgery to allow an appropriate period for wound healing before resuming diving. The underwater and hyperbaric environment introduces a number of unique risk factors that should be considered:

- Marine organisms:
  These may cause infections when they contaminate denuded skin and membranes of the cornea, sclera, conjunctiva, or lid tissues. These pathogens may enter the eye through unhealed corneal or scleral wounds and result in vision-threatening inner eye infections (endophthalmitis). The risk of infection due to contact of the eye with water is much greater when diving in potentially contaminated ocean, river, or lake water than when showering or bathing in chlorinated city water

- Gas in the front or back of the eye (anterior chamber or vitreous cavity):
  This may be affected by changes in pressure and result in vision-threatening barotrauma within the eye.

- Negative pressure in the air space of a face mask caused by a mask squeeze: This may result in bleeding of the eye surface (subconjunctival hemorrhage), and lid bruising and swelling (raccoon eyes), and could theoretically cause the rupture of incompletely healed corneal or scleral wounds.

- Recompression, hyperbaric oxygen, and other in-chamber (dry) dives: Only gas in the eye remains a consideration

There are no controlled studies specifically addressing the requisite length of convalescence before a return to diving after eye surgery. The recommendations below are based on the application of wound healing observations in other studies and on clinical experience.

Refractive Surgery and Diving:

LASIK (laser-in-situ keratomileusis):
Laser refractive surgery is a safe and effective means of correcting refractive errors in divers. Photorefractive keratectomy has been allowed for U.S. Navy divers since 1996. Laser-in-situ keratomileusis (LASIK) is presently a more commonly done procedure. Although this procedure presents the potential for both inflammation and trauma under the corneal flap as well as traumatic dislocation of the flap, these conditions have not to date been reported as complications of diving. Visual acuity appears to be maintained in the hyperbaric environment. Acute hyperbaric stress does not appear to significantly alter refractive power after corneal surgery.

Summary on LASIK and diving:
- There are no case reports that document diving-related complications after LASIK
- There are at least three potential complications that might occur in post-op LASIK patients as a result of diving:
   (1) Globe rupture from face mask barotrauma (unlikely)
   (2) Interface keratitis (infection of the flap interface)
   (3) Flap displacement from interface bubbles
- Complications that might impact the safety of divers include:
   (1) Halo
   (2) Glare
   (3) Night diving complaints
   These decrease from 25+% early to about 4% in one year.
- It is recommended waiting a *minimum of one month* before resuming diving after LASIK. This should always be discussed with the personal ophthalmologist, so that he or she will be able to add any special knowledge about your specific situation that would be relevant.

Radial Keratotomy:

There are often inquiries about radial keratotomy [RK], a surgical procedure with long-term implications for diving. RK is currently a widely performed corneal sculpturing (keratorefractive) procedure. Individuals whose nearsightedness (myopia) has been corrected with this procedure are prohibited from entering diving programs in the Navy. Applicants who have had this procedure may not even be allowed to serve in less visually demanding Navy positions. Two recent reviews of RK in the military have recommended that the procedure continue to be disqualifying for Navy divers and for Army aviators. Edmonds, Lowery, and Pennefather recommend that no one who has had RK be allowed to dive unless they have face masks designed to equalize the pressure within the mask to that of the ambient pressure. The Davis and Bove text states that until further data are available, a person who has had RK should be permanently disqualified from diving.

Summary on RK and Diving:

Divers may suffer from:

- Halos and glare
- Variation in visual acuity during the day
- Progressive farsightedness
- Regular astigmatism
- Decrease in best corrected visual acuity
- Recurrent corneal erosions and ulcers
- Increased susceptibility to traumatic corneal rupture; possible barotrauma induced rupture of RK incisions in the hyperbaric environment, although there are no reports of this occurring.[13] Sport divers who have had radial and astigmatic keratotomy that does not entail full thickness corneal incisions or prolonged topical steroid therapy *may be allowed to dive after three months.*

Photorefractive keratectomy (PRK):

PRK is a new refractive surgical procedure. Unlike radial keratotomy, it entails no corneal incisions, which may decrease the ability of the cornea to withstand blunt trauma. Published studies of the outcomes of PRK have shown this procedure to be relatively free of post-operative complications when compared to RK.

Summary on PRK and Diving:

- Few post-operative complications
- In the absence of post-operative complications, pain, and light sensitivity, diving may be resumed *two weeks after surgery*

---

13. Dr. (CAPT) Frank Butler, a very experienced U.S. Navy eye surgeon, has seen only one clinically significant case of facemask squeeze in many years of association with Navy and sport diving activities. Most of the reports of corneal rupture following RK have been the result of direct blunt trauma to the eye. Also worthy of note are the reports of blunt trauma severe enough to cause swelling and hemorrhage and facial fractures in which radial keratotomy scars remained intact.

Corneal Surgery:
In corneal surgery with full thickness incisions, very little healing is noted in the first week, followed by a rapid rise to about 30% of normal strength at one month. Wound strength then gradually increases to approximately 50% of normal by three to six months. Penetrating surgery in which full thickness incisions are made in the cornea should be followed by a six month convalescent period.

Cataract Surgery:
For cataract surgery, the post operative waiting period varies with the type of incision used. There should be a three month's wait if a non-corneal valve incision is used. If a corneal valve incision is used, the clear corneal type requires a two month wait and the "scleral tunnel" needs only a one month waiting period.

Glaucoma Filtering Surgery:
This is a relative contraindication to diving but, if approved, requires about a two month wait before diving.

Pterygium (Conjunctival Thickening) Excision and Conjunctival Surgery:
These require two weeks of convalescence and there should be a one week wait after corneal suture removal.

Argon Laser Trabeculoplasty or Iridectomy and Yag Laser Capsulotomy:
No wait required.

Vitreoretinal Surgery (e.g., Vitrectomy, Retinal Detachment Repair, and Pneumatic Retinopexy):
There must be a two month waiting period before diving, with assurances that all air or gas has been absorbed. A two week wait would be sufficient for retinal cryopexy or laser photocoagulation for breaks.

Oculoplastic Surgery, Skin Grafts, and Strabismus Surgery:
A two week wait is recommended, with the caveat that there must be complete coverage (epitheliazation) of skin grafts and that there is no air-filled prosthesis.

GLAUCOMA

Glaucoma refers to a collection of eye diseases affecting the optic nerve and consequently vision. It is usually related to increased pressure within the eye. This pressure eventually causes deformity of the optic disk (i.e., where the optic nerve enters the eye), and a disruption in the circulation to the retina. The distant areas are affected first with loss of "corner of the eye" vision. If untreated, the condition may ultimately result in tunnel vision and finally blindness.

The condition is usually painless and 50% of people only realize they have glaucoma when they have already suffered a serious loss of vision. Pressure within the eye is a function of fluid production and drainage. Overproduction or limited drainage will have the same net effect. Drainage occurs through channels closely associated with the iris (i.e., the colored disk) of the eye. In angle-closure glaucoma, the channels may be blocked if the pupil is dilated and the iris is bunched up (much like the biceps bunches up when it is contracted). Certain medications—particularly anti-motion sickness medication—cause the iris to contract (pupil to dilate) and may precipitate an acute bout of glaucoma. This disease has a rapid onset, with redness of the eye and sudden loss of vision. Open-angle glaucoma is caused by a mismatch in fluid maintenance without obvious abnormalities in the drainage system. This is painless and invisible and causes visual deterioration over months to years. There are other, more rare types of glaucoma, including normal pressure, childhood, congenital (i.e., inherited), and secondary glaucoma. The latter is due to complications from eye infections, trauma, etc. The implications of glaucoma on diving are significant even though the pressure of diving has no net effect on the pressure within the eye. Ironically, the concern is therefore not so much the undiagnosed cases of chronic glaucoma (although these run the risk of blindness long-term), but rather those taking medication for it. The treatment of glaucoma includes medication that affects the diameter of the pupil or increases drainage of fluid from the eye. However, these agents also affect blood pressure and heart rate and it is important for individuals on anti-glaucoma medication to be assessed for exercise tolerance (see the section on Diving Fitness, page 49). Particular care should also be taken with anti-motion sickness medication.

Glaucoma is an important consideration, but not necessarily a contraindication to diving. Expert dive medical advice is recommended.

GROMMETS / PE TUBES

Grommets, tympanostomy, or PE (polyethylene or pressure equalization) tubes are miniature cylinders inserted through the ear drum as a temporary surgical solution to certain acute middle ear infections as well as chronic dysfunction of the Eustachian tube. The middle ear is in a constant process of forming a vacuum as oxygen is absorbed. Accordingly, the Eustachian tube is needed to allow replenishment of oxygen and to equalize pressure with the outside world. This also allows the eardrum to move freely in response to sound waves. Persistent failure of the Eustachian tube results in a retraction (stiffness) of the ear drum; deafness, with a build up of fluid in the middle ear; infection; and sometimes rupture, as pus accumulates and forces its way through the ear drum. If the problem cannot be overcome by treating the Eustachian tube dysfunction, or if pus, blood, or thick fluid accumulates behind the ear drum, surgical intervention is required. This involves cutting a hole in the ear drum (i.e., myringotomy) and ensuring ventilation and drainage by means of PE tubes that artificially aerate the middle ear for a period of time. During this time the middle ear remains vulnerable to infection and contamination by water through the external ear. Accordingly, it is advised to avoid submerging the ear or swimming for the 4–12 months it takes for the tubes to fall out, which they usually do spontaneously.

 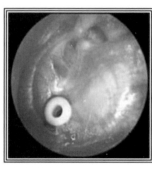

Figure 15
Grommet (left)

Figure 16
Tympanic membrane with grommet inserted (right)

Diving with PE tubes is obviously contraindicated for the same reasons. Once the PE tubes are out and if the individual is able to clear the ears, diving is possible again. Some divers use special ear protective cups (ProEar® masks) to prevent the entry of water through the PE tubes, but this is strongly discouraged. These devices are not foolproof and entry of water into the middle ear may cause severe dizziness and disorientation under water as well as the risk of infection.

HAY FEVER

Hay fever or allergic rhinitis is an inflammatory condition of the nasal passages and membranes with characteristic symptoms of sneezing, nasal congestion, nasal itching, and a runny nose. It may also affect the eyes, ears, sinuses, and throat. The reaction is due to a complex immune response to foreign airborne particles, usually from plants (e.g., pollen) or animals (e.g., hair or skin scales). Amazingly, it affects nearly 20% of the population, which is why pollen counts are broadcasted nationally. Although hay fever is certainly not life-threatening, it can affect quality of life and cause a number of health and, of course, diving-related problems. There is also an important association with asthma. Individuals with hay fever are most likely to present with equalizing problems or chronic episodes of sinusitis. Treatment involves suppressing the allergic response by counteracting its effects (e.g., antihistamines), reducing the body's sensitivity to allergens (e.g., desensitization therapy), or providing immunosuppression in the nose (e.g., cortisone aerosols). The latter has the benefit of actually reducing the long term tendency to hay fever, and it may break the vicious cycle between hay fever and chronic sinus infections.

Although hay fever as such is not a contraindication to diving, it is important to confirm the ability to equalize as well as exclude concurrent asthma or chronic sinusitis in those who suffer from it.

LOSS OF HEARING (SEE DEAFNESS)

NOSE BLEEDS (EPISTAXIS)

Epistaxis is defined as sudden-onset bleeding from the nostril or nasal cavity. It is a common reason for visits to emergency departments and carries significant social and psychological impact. More than 90% of cases require very little intervention and can be managed with simple first aid measures.

The source of bleeding may be in any part of the nose, but the front is most common. Here a converging network of arteries in the nasal septum provides a relatively vulnerable area that may bleed in response to even relatively trivial trauma. Many remedies have been recommended, but the most appropriate appears to be bending the head forward and pinching the nose just below the bony part and above the nostrils—almost as if equalizing the ears.

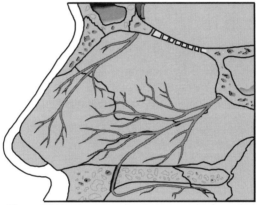

Figure 17 Nasal system showing network of arteries

Firm pressure should be applied and maintained for at least ten minutes. Epistaxis affects one in seven people; it peaks bimodally: in the 2–10-year age group (due to foreign bodies and nose picking) and in 50–80-year-olds (due to fragile blood vessels or hypertension). The incidence is also increased in dry climates and during winter months. Regular nose bleeding requires further investigation into bleeding tendencies, medication, recreational drug use, tumors, etc., but isolated events are almost always benign. Diving has implications on nose bleeding for at least two reasons:

- The cause of the nose bleed may be related to barotrauma of the sinuses, ears, or even lungs, and this should be considered and treated as necessary.

- The act of pinching the nose to equalize may provide sufficient trauma to the front of the nose to precipitate nose bleeding. It may also dislodge partially formed clots and change a simple isolated nose bleed into a repetitive affair. If this appears to be the case it may be helpful to equalize by occluding the nostrils rather than pinching the nose. The area of bleeding can also be treated with silver nitrate to reduce bleeding episodes.

Ear and sinus barotrauma usually have a definite association with pain during descent, and this should be determined.

PERFORATED EARDRUM
(Also see Grommets/PE Tubes & Ear Squeeze)
The ear drum (or tympanic membrane) is a paper thin piece of skin that is attached to a series of three bones that transfer sound waves from the external to the inner ear.

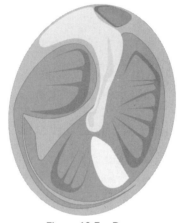

Figure 18 Ear Drum

The ear drum partially seals off the middle ear from the environment and pressure equalization occurs through a tube between the back of the throat and the middle ear—the Eustachian tube. The ear drum may rupture or tear as a result of two fundamental problems:

- High pressure differentials between the external ear and the middle ear, such as during diving, flying, or trauma (e.g., explosive shocks or a blow to the ear)
- Infections with a buildup of pus ultimately resulting in rupture. Pressure-related ear drum perforations usually heal without difficulty within 2–6 weeks.

Once the eardrum is healed, diving may be resumed as long as the ability to equalize is unaffected. However, if the perforation is very large, if the Eustachian tube function is abnormal, or if there is underlying infection, it may result in a chronic perforation. If the eardrum fails to heal after six weeks, it may need to be patched using skin from the external ear. This is called a tympanoplasty.

Once this has healed the eardrum is typically stronger than before and diving is permitted as long as the diver can equalize. Diving with a perforated eardrum is strongly discouraged due to the risks of infection and dizziness under water.

RINGING IN THE EARS (TINNITUS)

Tinnitus is the subjective perception of sound—usually ringing—in the head or the ears, in the absence of an external source. The term tinnitus derives from the Latin word *tinnire*, meaning "to ring." It is estimated that between 10% and 15% of the population are affected, and it is commonly associated with other ear diseases and disorders. It is not uncommon for people to report tinnitus after exposure to explosions or very loud noises. Although annoying, this type of tinnitus is usually very short in duration. Lasting forms of tinnitus are associated with underlying ear problems and structural damage. Surprisingly little is known about the origins of tinnitus although many theories abound. One plausible theory is that damage to the hair cells in the inner ear, from a variety of causes, results in spontaneous electrical discharges. In other words, the hair cells provide signals without being stimulated by sound. In a sense this is like "epilepsy" of the inner ear.

Tinnitus associated with diving is an important concern. The two most important causes are barotrauma (i.e., pressure-related damage) to the inner ear and decompression illness. If a diver has problems equalizing and shows signs of middle ear injury, it is more likely to be barotrauma. This form of ear injury seems to be quite common amongst breath-hold divers and spear fishermen who make multiple descents and often neglect their ears in favor of conserving air. Unless tinnitus subsides within a few hours, it should be medically evaluated. However, if associated with deep or mixed gas diving, tinnitus—with or without deafness—may be due to decompression illness. This requires immediate medical attention and prompt recompression.

Tinnitus is not a contraindication to diving unless it is associated with balance disorders (e.g., Meniere's disease) or is the result of previous inner ear barotrauma with rupture of the oval or round windows.

SINUSITIS

Sinusitis, or sinus infection, is an inflammatory condition of the sinuses and nasal passages. It commonly follows simple head colds or other conditions resulting in blockage of the holes and tunnels connecting the sinus cavities to the nasal cavity. The function of the sinuses or paranasal sinuses, as they are sometimes called, is not completely understood. Theories include improving humidification of air, providing better resonation and speech projection, and reducing the weight of the human skull. There are four pairs of sinuses. They are arranged around the nasal cavity as follows: above, frontal sinus; in the middle, ethmoid sinus; behind, sphenoid sinus; and below, maxillary or cheekbone sinus. The sinuses are lined with specialized mucous membranes with hair-like projections—*cilia*. These miniature hairs sweep mucus towards the ostia (openings to the nasal cavity) from where it is transported towards the back of the throat and swallowed. If the mucus cannot be removed, the sinuses become, in a sense, constipated. It then does not take much time for an infection to occur. The combination of blockage, pressure, and inflammation then cause the classic symptoms of pain around the nose and eyes that is exacerbated by leaning forwards. Acute sinus infections can last up to eight weeks and may occur one to three times per year, often in association with head colds. Chronic sinusitis lasts longer than eight weeks and may even continue throughout the year.

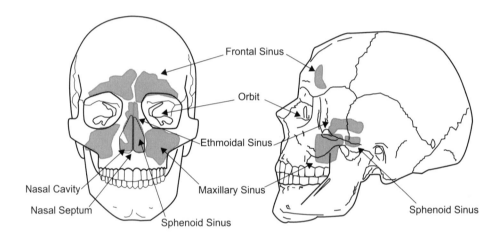

Figure 19 Paranasal sinuses

The implications on diving are primarily related to the gas-filled nature of the sinuses and the need for them to be equalized during changes in ambient pressure. Usually diving does not affect the sinuses and divers are not even aware of the process of equalizing. The openings between the sinus and nasal cavities allow simple, passive equalization throughout. If the passages are blocked, however, pain results very quickly, as the sinus cavities are completely incompressible. Unlike the ear, they do not have a compliant wall, such as the ear drum, that is able to bulge in to accommodate slight volume changes. With the sinuses there is an immediate tug on the mucous lining of the sinus, and swelling and bleeding can occur even at shallow depths. The frontal sinus is most commonly affected, because it has a thin, winding tunnel connecting it to the nasal passage that easily becomes blocked. Next is the maxillary sinus, and this may present as toothache because of the proximity to the upper teeth.

It is unwise to force your sinuses. The maxillary sinus lies just under the eye, and the extreme pressures of diving may even cause an implosive injury with a fracture of the bony plate dividing the sinus and the eye. Barotrauma may also complicate the underlying sinusitis and cause severe infection and even meningitis. Never dive with acute sinusitis. Chronic sinusitis, on the other hand, has a variable effect on diving. About 50% of divers who dive with chronic sinusitis actually experience an improvement of their problems. This may be because every dive is essentially like a sinus rinse, with mucus being expelled as gas expands in the sinus during ascent. However, the other 50% of divers continue to battle with their sinuses and need consultation with an ENT surgeon experienced in diving medicine.

SWIMMER'S EAR (OTITIS EXTERNA)
—See Diving Nuisances page 74

VERTIGO AND MENIERE'S DISEASE

Vertigo is a false sensation of spinning, or your surroundings spinning around you. It is not a disease as such, but the result of some disturbance in the inner ear and nerve pathways responsible for detecting motion and preserving balance. Dizziness, on the other hand, is a non-specific description of faintness or lightheadedness. It is not synonymous with vertigo, which is a very specific condition.

The most common cause of vertigo is called Benign Paroxysmal (acute onset) Positional Vertigo or BPPV. The cause is not completely understood. A popular theory is that following head trauma, with aging, or spontaneously, some of the crystals from the "gyroscopes" in the inner ear that detect movement or acceleration become separated and interfere with the detection of angular acceleration or spinning. The result is that when the head is held in a certain position, it provokes a sensation of spinning, i.e., vertigo. The classic presentation is that of a person turning in bed and within seconds experiencing an episode of vertigo that subsides over less than a minute. It usually requires no treatment and tends to improve with time. Unless the spinning episodes are significant and occur during diving, it is not a contraindication.

Meniere's disease is a more serious condition. Again, the exact cause is obscure, but it is thought to be due to a build-up of pressure inside some of the compartments in the inner ear, leading to both deafness and vertigo. The association with hearing loss is important, as is the tendency of vertigo to build up over hours rather than starting abruptly and subsiding as in BPPV. Meniere's disease is a contraindication to diving, as it destroys the ability to assess orientation accurately under water.

There are many causes of dizziness other than inner ear barotrauma and ear drum perforation associated with diving. It is useful to know the most likely causes according to when they occur during the dive. This not only assists in knowing when dizziness is likely to be serious, but also to know how to remedy the problem.

During Descent

During descent, dizziness may be associated with a benign condition called alternobaric vertigo (i.e., vertigo due to pressure differences in the middle ear). It occurs in certain susceptible individuals in whom the ears equalize at different rates and the brain interprets the difference in pressure as a rotation. Inner ear barotrauma and the stimulation of cold water are other possible causes of vertigo, even with the eardrum intact, but especially following rupture. Individuals who suffer from BPPV may experience significant episodes when descending head first on a dive. If they do dive at all, the positions that provoke vertigo should be intentionally avoided.

At the Bottom

Dizziness that starts upon reaching the bottom is uncommon in shallow recreational diving. Possible causes depend on the type of diving, diving apparatus, depth, and gas mixtures the diver breathes. In recreational diving with open water scuba, these causes include nitrogen narcosis, carbon dioxide retention, motion sickness, poor diving visibility, medication, and alcohol, as well as middle ear barotrauma and alternobaric vertigo. In commercial or technical diving, other causes must be considered, including gas-switch decompression sickness (also called counterdiffusion). Extreme pressure may cause vertigo independently due to the high pressure nervous syndrome (HPNS). This is particularly possible with dives > 400 fsw (122 msw) in depth. The possibility of gas contamination and low oxygen levels must also be considered as potential causes of dizziness and vertigo.

During Ascent

Here the possibilities of alternobaric vertigo and inner ear decompression sickness need to be considered. Some divers have persistent dizziness following shallow dives in which they did not report any problems equalizing. The possibility of inner ear irritation has been suggested. Finally, there are a myriad of other causes of vertigo, including multiple sclerosis, stroke, inner ear infections, migraine, irregular heart beat, low blood pressure, etc. Usually the underlying cause is known to the diver, and this becomes the primary consideration rather than the vertigo associated with it. Diving is usually contraindicated for the same reasons listed above.

IMMUNOLOGICAL

HIV, AIDS, AND OTHER BLOOD BORNE ILLNESSES

HIV & AIDS

Human immune-deficiency virus (HIV) infections and the resulting Acquired Immune Deficiency Syndrome (AIDS) have become a world-wide epidemic. It has now spread to every country in the world and by 2003 it had infected an estimated 40 million people worldwide. The incidence ranges from 1:100,000 to 24% of the population, depending on the socioeconomic status of the country. Over 1.1 million people in the United States are infected with HIV, but the truly devastating impact is in Sub-Saharan Africa. Originally limited to same-gender promiscuity and intravenous drug users, HIV/AIDS has now become an indiscriminate illness affecting both genders, all ages, and all levels of society. The primary method of transmission is sexual exchange of body fluids. Intravenous drug abuse, exposure to infected blood, and blood transfusions are secondary means of acquiring the infection. There is no evidence that the infection may result from exposure to saliva or tears, although these can contain the virus. Unless there are ulcerations in the mouth, transmission via the exchange of a regulator mouthpiece, for example, is extremely small. However, contact with blood is very hazardous and barriers (i.e., gloves and one-way resuscitation devices) are recommended. Fortunately, the virus is quite fragile and unable to remain infective outside the body for all but the briefest of times—dry equals dead.

The evolution from HIV infection to AIDS is variable in duration. It starts as a flu-like illness with swelling of the lymph nodes, followed by increasing episodes of infections and cancers, ultimately leading to death. AIDS-related death is not a direct consequence of the HIV infection *per se*, but is due to various other infections or cancers that eventually escape the control of a weakening immune system. Accordingly, in impoverished countries, death may occur within one to two years due to a constant bombardment with infective agents. In developed countries, the improved hygiene, with suppression of the infection by modern antiretroviral medication, may result in life expectancies exceeding 10 years.

155

The relatively long latency of the disease (i.e., the period from becoming infected until actually showing manifestations of the disease) is both a blessing and a curse. It provides individuals with at least a reasonable period of good health after contracting the illness, but at the same time it affords a long period in which the disease can be transmitted to others. There is also a period of six weeks to six months following infection in which the usual blood tests—based on the body's response to the virus rather than the virus itself—are still negative. This has previously been the cause of transmission via transfusion with "uninfected blood."

The effects on diving are varied:

- HIV infection may directly affect the nervous system and cause memory loss, an inability to concentrate, or nerve-related pain. Obviously, this would render diving unsafe.
- HIV causes periods of diarrhea, at which time there is significant risk of dehydration
- Transmission of the virus during dive training or an exchange of regulators is extremely small. Casual sex—especially if unprotected—is by far the greatest risk for contracting the disease. As a general rule, individuals with symptomatic HIV infections should not dive.

Hepatitis B & C
Hepatitis B and C are liver viruses transmitted by an exchange of body fluids. Risks and precautions are similar to HIV, but these viruses are more infective. Fortunately, hepatitis B can be prevented by active immunization. There is no prophylaxis or treatment for hepatitis C. Both diseases have an asymptomatic carrier status in which the individual does not appear ill, but may transmit the disease. There is some concern that hepatitis C may potentially be transmitted via an exchange of regulators. Cleaning of mouthpieces with household bleach or other standard disinfectants will eliminate this possibility. Symptomatic individuals are unfit to dive.

RAYNAUD'S DISEASE AND SYNDROME AND AUTOIMMUNE DISEASES
Reynaud's disease and syndrome are phenomenons of arterial spasm in the extremities, resulting in acutely painful pallor (e.g., whiteness due to lack of circulation) of the hands and/or feet, followed by a bluish discoloration, and finally redness as the circulation is restored and compensates for the interruption by a widening of the blood vessels.

Reynaud's disease is usually diagnosed before age 40 years and occurs five times more frequently in women than men. The difference between the "disease" and the "syndrome" is that the disease has no associated underlying cause.

The syndrome is associated with certain autoimmune disorders (i.e., illnesses due to the body's immune system attacking itself). The phenomenon may be precipitated by exposure to cold or vibration. Accordingly, diving may be a trigger for the syndrome. Unless the underlying illness presents a safety hazard due to skin ulcerations or joint, lung, or kidney problems, Reynaud's is not a contraindication to diving as long as it can be avoided by adequate thermal protection of the hands and feet.

Figure19 Reynaud's Disease

Autoimmune Diseases

This catch-all name includes a whole myriad of illnesses in which the body launches an attack on itself. Sometimes it is provoked by exposure to an infective agent that has chemical similarities to parts of the body, like rheumatic heart fever. In this case a relatively trivial throat infection causes an immune response that may permanently damage the heart valves. Other examples include insulin-requiring diabetes mellitus, rheumatoid arthritis, scleroderma, possibly multiple sclerosis, systemic lupus erythematosis, etc. It may also include problems related to the rejection of a transplanted organ. Treatment for these diseases usually focuses on suppressing the immune system and treating or compensating for the damage to the body. As far as diving is concerned, there are three primary concerns:

- The immunosuppression may make individuals prone to infection
- Many immunosuppressants and anti-inflammatory agents affect the ability of blood to clot, with a resulting bleeding tendency. Any injury or decompression illness would be complicated as a result
- The deterioration of various organs due to the immune disorder may also be prohibitive: cardiac failure, kidney failure, lung fibrosis, and joint immobility may all disqualify an individual from diving.

MUSCULOSKELETAL CONDITIONS

AMPUTATIONS

Amputees dive regularly, and with care, training, and assistance perform well as divers. Several things need to be discussed in so far as the risks involved are concerned.

First, there needs to be an investigation into the reason(s) why the amputation(s) occurred and whether there are associated diseases or risks. Usually there are four reasons for amputations: (1) trauma, (2) infection, (3) cancer, and (4) poor circulation. Each of these has different safety-related considerations in addition to the loss of the limb itself.

Although traumatic amputations usually don't imply other underlying disease, there may have been associated trauma to vital organs and brain injury, with a risk of post-traumatic epilepsy.

Rapidly propagating infections like gas gangrene and "flesh-eating-bug" infections are rare, but may result in amputation. Once healed, the individual is usually otherwise fit. More chronic infections are usually associated with poor circulation.

Many young people develop bone and cartilage cancers that eventually require an amputation to effect cure. If the cancer has been eradicated, and there is no aftermath of complications due to chemotherapy or radiation, diving may be undertaken as mobility allows it.

Finally, more than 50% of non-traumatic amputations are related to diabetes and vascular disease. These may have bearing on a diver's general medical fitness, ability to exercise, and risks for stroke and heart attack. There is a practical dilemma of exercise testing in amputees, as most tests require the use of our legs. However, sit-ups and arm exercises are sometimes used to assess cardiovascular fitness.

Some amputees develop phantom pains for a period of time after the amputation. These pains can be severe and need medication. Other times it may feel as though the limb is still there and they may even have bizarre sensations such as itching in a foot that is no longer attached to them. Although the pain is unlikely to be confused with decompression illness, the medication used to treat phantom pains may be unsafe with diving and it may deny them the use of an artificial limb required for mobility and safe diving.

Younger amputees tend to adapt very quickly and effectively to the loss of their limbs. They are usually able to take care of themselves and may resent being assisted unless this is requested. As an instructor or dive leader, it is usually wise to let them know that they can ask you for help if needed, but not to impose it otherwise. Usually they will have a specific buddy they dive with, but if not, try to team them up with experienced and relaxed divers who will be able to take the challenge in their stride with minimal fuss.

Artificial limbs or prostheses usually do not pose a problem for diving as long as they are waterproof, do not upset the diver's buoyancy, permit improved mobility above and below water, and are a help rather than a hindrance. The weightlessness of water offers many divers with disabilities a wonderful opportunity to escape the ravages of gravity. It is most gratifying to teach and take these people diving.

ANKYLOSING SPONDYLITIS ("BAMBOO BACK")
Ankylosing spondylitis is a chronic, persistent disease that primarily affects the spine of young men in particular and may eventually lead to stiffness of the back. The joints and ligaments that normally permit flexibility of the back become inflamed and eventually may cause the bones (vertebrae) to grow together (fuse), resembling notches in a bamboo on x-ray. The cause is unknown but genetics seem to play a role. The condition is diagnosed by a history of persisting non-traumatic back pain, followed by x-rays of the back and certain blood tests that show the inflammatory nature and genetic association of the disease. Treatments may include: exercise, non-aspirin anti-inflammatory medicines, sulfasalazine (aspirin analogue), non-surgical self-help systems, and surgery. This is one of the few inflammatory conditions where exercise is recommended, and diving may fall into this category.

While individuals are unlikely to pursue diving during flare-ups and acute episodes of pain, diving can be undertaken in periods of remission, as long as flexibility is adequate for diving safety. Depth and pressure would have little effect on the condition, and treatment poses little specific risk to the diver, with the exception of high doses of sulfasalazine that may cause stomach ulcers and a bleeding tendency. Altered posture might present a problem with gearing up, water entry, and exit but is probably manageable with proper planning and assistance.

BACKACHE

Most back ailments are located in the region of the lower back and are related to muscle, bone, nerve, and ligamentous problems. The pain is usually the result of muscle spasm, nerve impingement, inflammation of the joints and membrane (periosteum) covering the bony vertebrae, or combinations of these factors. Low back pain from any mechanical cause usually also features spasm of the large, supportive muscles alongside the spine (*erector spinae* muscles). The spasms and stiffness generally add to the pain from the original, underlying cause.

Some of the more common back problems are:

- Small shearing fractures (i.e., spondylolyses) or compression fractures of the spine from abuse or osteoporosis (thinning out of bone)
- Rupture or herniation of intervertebral disks
- Degeneration and narrowing of the disks
- Poor alignment or shifting of the vertebrae (i.e., spondylolisthesis)
- Spinal stenosis (narrowing of the spinal canal)
- Strain or tears to the muscles or ligaments supporting the back
- Spine curvature abnormalities (like scoliosis or kyphosis) which may be inherited and seen in children or teens
- Other medical conditions like fibromyalgia and spondylitis

Back pain unrelated to the vertebral column can be caused by a number of diseases of the abdomen and pelvis. These include bladder or kidney infection, pancreatitis, kidney stones, diseases of the uterus or ovaria, and intestinal obstructions, infections, and perforations.

Diving obviously should be limited in situations where there is acute back pain with decreased ability to function.

Pain medications and muscle relaxing drugs may add to the problem of reduced alertness and exacerbation of nitrogen narcosis. Divers with chronic back pain controlled by exercises, pain medications, and muscle relaxants may run the risk of re-injury from the excess weight of carrying heavy gear, boat rides through surf, injury from water entry and exit, and worsening due to the hyperextended head-up position required during diving. On the positive side, divers often report relief of back pain under water due to the weightlessness of the dive. Divers experiencing transient lower back discomfort while wearing a weight belt under water may find relief by grabbing his or her knees and holding a flexed stretch for 10–15 seconds.

BODY WEIGHT

Questions are often asked about diving while overweight, or with a high body mass index and percent of body fat. There is no question that the medical and diving-related risks are increased in obese divers (possibly indicated by a BMI > 30 kg/m²).[14] There are several reasons why obesity is important in considering whether or not a person is "fit to dive."

Obesity and Decompression Illness

As yet there is no conclusive evidence that an increased percentage of body fat increases the risk for decompression sickness. Higher DCS rates have been associated with increasing age, with a gradual increase in skinfold thickness (i.e., percent body fat) being one feature of the passage of time.[15]

Theory has it that nitrogen preferentially dissolves in tissues of the body with a high gas solubility and blood flow. Nitrogen is very soluble in adipose (fat) tissue and, accordingly, the hypothesis is that fat becomes a reservoir for nitrogen. Upon decompression, nitrogen may rapidly leave the adipose tissue and gas bubbles would encroach on the venous system where they would be carried to the heart and lungs. If the gas bubble loads to these organs were high, the lung capillaries may become blocked or bubbles may pass through the lung vasculature or a PFO (i.e., a patent foramen ovale in the heart) and embolize the brain. This might lead to a vein-to-artery "stroke" and neurological DCS.

Cardiovascular Disease Risk Increase

BMI

In some areas of the world where medical fitness is more stringently regulated than the USA, a high BMI (body mass index) would disqualify an individual from diving.

---

14. The body mass index is an imperfect but very useful way to relate height to weight and derive a value that can be compared across a large range of age and body variables. It is determined by dividing the individual's weight in kilograms by the square of their height in meters. So an individual who weighs 70 kg and is 1.7 meters tall will have a BMI of 70 ÷ (1.7 x 1.7) = 24.2 kg/m². The normal range is 18.5–24.9; underweight is < 18.5; overweight is 25 to 29.9, and obese is > 30 kg/m². BMI does not consider body composition. Body builders, for example, would have high values due to the extra muscle mass.
15. A higher incidence of decompression sickness was reported in US Navy divers with a greater skinfold thickness in 1984 by Dembert et al. Similarly, McCallum reported a higher incidence of decompression illness in obese commercial divers, whereas Chryssanthrou noted the incidence of osteonecrosis (bone death) to be higher in those who had a higher degree of obesity. However, whether this was due to the amount of fat or merely the additional weight of the diver has not been adequately resolved.

Obesity and lack of exercise are risk factors for diabetes mellitus, blood lipid disorders, hypertension, and ultimately coronary artery disease. The BMI, being a marker for obesity, is often used to evaluate these risks indirectly. Many diving physicians feel that a BMI greater than 30 suggests a critical reduction in exercise tolerance and an increased risk for coronary artery disease and heart attack that are incompatible with diving. (Note: it is possible for truly muscular and fit people to have high BMIs, so scores should be applied intelligently).

Appetite Suppressants
Medications given for appetite suppression introduce several risks to diving. Most drugs are stimulants that cause changes in mood and blood pressure, both of which may prove dangerous with diving. The additional effect of nitrogen narcosis on these medications is unknown.

Diabetes (See section on diabetes and diving, page 209)
The overweight person is also at increased risk for diabetes. Unknown and untreated diabetics are at risk for wide swings in blood sugar levels, often brought on by stressful situations such as diving and cold water. Low blood sugar (hypoglycemia) is a risk factor for insulin-requiring diabetics and may be a cause of drowning. The potential influence of hyperglycemia on diving safety requires further investigation.

Decreased Pulmonary Function (Hypoxia, CO_2 Retention)
Due to an increase in intra-abdominal pressure and a reduction in movement of the diaphragm, obese divers are at risk for carbon dioxide build-up and black-out under water. This may be evaluated with a Pulmonary Function Test (PFT). Low vital capacity (i.e., the maximum volume that can be exhaled after a maximal inhalation) and a reduced FEV_1 (i.e., the Forced Expiratory Volume in 1 second, the volume of air that can be exhaled in the first second with maximal effort following maximal inhalation) may indicate an increased risk. Reduced ability to exercise may contribute towards:

- Increased risk for DCS
- Decreased ability for self rescue
- Decreased ability for buddy rescue
- Increased risk of panic in stressful situations due to limited exercise tolerance and CO_2 build-up

CARPAL TUNNEL SYNDROME
Carpal tunnel syndrome occurs when tendons or ligaments in the wrist become enlarged through inflammation or swelling, causing a pinching of the nerve that supplies the muscles at the base of the thumb and sensation in the thumb, index, and middle fingers. Causes include work-related cumulative trauma to

the wrist (e.g., typing and computer-based work), pregnancy, fluid retention, diabetes, and obesity. Symptoms may include a burning, tingling numbness in the thumb, index, and middle fingers as well as an inability to grip or make a fist. Treatment includes immobilizing the wrist in a splint, anti-inflammatory drugs, injections of cortisone in the wrist to reduce the swelling, or surgery.

Problems in diving relate to a loss of manual dexterity. This may include difficulty donning gear and inability to perform self or buddy rescue. In theory, the symptoms could be confused with DCS, but the prior history of tingling may eliminate this possibility.

If surgery is performed, one should be able to return to diving after complete healing of all incisions and satisfactory rehabilitation as determined by the operating surgeon. A reasonable period of time would be 4–6 weeks—barring complications or wound infections.

Healed nerve and tendon release operations are thought not to impose any restrictions on diving.

COMPRESSION FRACTURES OF THE VERTEBRAE

Compression fractures of the vertebrae occur when the vertebral body is squashed flat by impact or trauma along the length of the spinal column (e.g., falling from a height). This condition may also occur spontaneously due to osteoporosis (the most common cause) or tumors. When the fracture occurs as a result of osteoporosis, the vertebrae in the chest and lower spine are usually affected, and symptoms may be worse with walking. With multiple fractures angulation may occur, either forward or to the side, that may put pressure on the spinal cord, producing symptoms of numbness, tingling, or weakness. Symptoms depend upon the area of the back that is affected; however, most fractures are stable and do not produce neurological symptoms.

People with compression fractures with nerve root or spinal cord deficit symptoms, even if episodic, should not dive until the problem is surgically repaired. Symptoms of numbness and pain may be mimicked by decompression sickness and present problems in differentiation after a dive (also see section on Back Pain). Weight bearing and donning gear on the surface can be real problems to the affected diver, even though once in the water they are more comfortable with the absence of gravity effects.

Diving should be postponed until the back is surgically stabilized. With significant symptoms, it wouldn't take much to become paraplegic. Ironically, if the diver were paraplegic and stable, then we could make some arrangement for him to dive, but that's certainly not what we want!

A diver has to carry his equipment on land (boat) and be able to perform hard physical work on occasions. Weight-bearing, with grade 3 spondylolisthesis as described above, can certainly lead to nerve root compression, resulting in severe pain, paralysis, and loss of function. In addition to causing its own difficulties, this can mask neurological symptoms caused by decompression illness. Until surgically repaired, significant spondylolisthesis would be disqualifying; a three month post operative period should be allowed and no diving at all if there are significant residual symptoms.

DISK HERNIATION AND SPINAL SURGERY

An intervertebral disc is a fibrofatty cushion of tissue between each vertebral body of the spinal column. This can become weakened and protrude into the spaces between and behind the vertebral bodies, pressing on nerves and spinal cord tissue. This causes pain and neurological symptoms, such as numbness and loss of motor function of the extremities.

Confusion with the symptoms of DCS leads some authorities to consider an unoperated herniated disc disease to be a contraindication to scuba diving. In addition, many aspects of diving may aggravate the condition, such as donning or carrying heavy gear. Someone with neck and lower back disc problems causing nerve root irritation (also called radicular neuropathy, damaged nerves with pain,numbness, and muscle weakness) should not dive until this has been surgically repaired. It is recommended that divers discuss this with their surgeon in terms of weight-bearing, climbing, and the hyperextended neck position that is required with scuba diving.

Those with lumbar herniated discs without protrusion can and do dive; however, there is a definite risk of acute herniation with the lifting activity and the strain of getting back into the boat. Acute herniation can mimic a decompression accident.

It is wise to be familiar with any neurological abnormalities related to a chronic back problem so as not to confuse these with new symptoms of decompression illness. If possible, carry a physician's note providing an accurate medical description of any problems.

Most diving physicians feel that post-surgical and healed vertebral fusions are not restrictive to further diving. These are theoretical although unproven concerns about an increased risk of bubble formation in regions of the spine where there has been some disruption of blood supply. In the absence of evidence, conservative diving is recommended.

Return to Diving Post-surgery

There are no set guidelines that govern the return to diving after disc surgery. This will depend to a great extent on the type of surgery, presence or absence of complications, whether or not a fusion has been done, and if there have been any complicating factors, such as a wound infection or residual symptoms.

Generally, a person may return to diving in three months with the approval of the operating surgeon.

There is an absolute contraindication to diving after disc surgery that has failed and results in chronic moderate to severe pain requiring regular analgesics, or persistent weakness or neurological abnormalities, or spinal instability, or spinal narrowing (stenosis).

DYSBARIC OSTEONECROSIS

Dysbaric osteonecrosis is the death of a portion of bone due to inadequate decompression. It is thought to primarily affect the upper arm (humerus), thigh (femur), and shin (tibia) in relation to the shoulder, hip, and knee joints, respectively. Although the definitive pathologic process is poorly understood, there are several hypotheses:

- Build-up of nitrogen bubbles in or around blood vessels in bone
- Gas-related, osmotic gas or drawing in of blood and fluid causing pressure-related disruption to the circulation
- Bubble-related breakdown of fat cells in bone with subsequent blockage of blood vessels by oil and fat (i.e., fat embolization)
- Thickening of blood causing sludging and blood vessel blockage

The injury in the bone is often symptom-free to begin with and may only be discovered by a random x-ray. Eventually, as the shoulder or hip joints start to deform and collapse, there may be significant pain and disability, often requiring artificial replacement of the joints. The diagnosis and classification of severity is made by x-ray/magnetic resonance imaging (MRI) showing area of dead bone, cysts, and attempts at bone healing.

Fortunately, this illness appears to be uncommon in recreational divers but it is of greater concern to saturation divers and caisson workers.

The issue of further diving is largely moot to recreational divers. If it does occur, then the extreme diving, likely to have been the cause, should be discontinued. If there is pain and disability, these would be disqualifying until treated. Once the joints are replaced, diving may be resumed after a suitable recovery period. Deep diving should probably be avoided in future for the sake of the remaining limbs.

For commercial divers, this is a bigger problem. Usually the recommendation is that diving should be discontinued in the case of bone death affecting the surface of the hip or shoulder joints, but other asymptomatic problems are probably irrelevant to further diving safety other than prompting closer observation.

As with all joint problems, weight-bearing, self and buddy rescue, and entry/exit problems should also be addressed by the divemaster/instructor/employer.

FIBROMYALGIA

Fibromyalgia (FM) is an increasingly recognized chronic pain illness. It is characterized by the presence of multiple tender points and a constellation of symptoms. Typically there are widespread musculoskeletal aches, pain and stiffness, soft tissue tenderness, general fatigue, and sleep disturbances.

The cause is unknown; the diagnosis is one of exclusion and the treatment is symptomatic.

It is entirely possible that a person with this condition will seek to become certified in scuba diving because of the perceived benefits of weightlessness. The instructor should be aware of the psychological aspects of the condition and the medications that some of the patients require for relief. Antidepressants and pain relievers are often required that can blunt the senses and cause decreased ability to think clearly and exercise good judgment. The additive effect of nitrogen narcosis clearly increases the risk for deeper diving.

FRACTURES

Acute bone injury, fracture, sprain, and other inflammatory processes should all put a temporary dampener on diving activities. Collectively, these may result in:

- Loss of mobility and dexterity (donning and doffing gear, entry and exits from water)
- Adverse affect on self- or buddy rescue abilities
- An obvious inability to dive with non-waterproof, plaster of paris cast or splint
- Possible alteration in the uptake of inert gas at the site of injury
- Possible wound infection by marine organisms
- Possible reinjury or delayed healing.

Accordingly, divers with acute bone or joint injury or inflammations should not return to diving until:

- The injury has healed and there is a full range of motion and strength
- Residual pain is minimal and will not interfere with diving or diving safety

- There is no longer a pattern of pain or injury that may be confused with DCI
- Until the treating physician has given the go-ahead

Consideration should be given to the positioning of diving gear, straps, and equipment and what effect this will have on weight-bearing and the possibility of further injury to underlying structures.

Diving After a Fracture

Healed fractures generally are thought not to impose any restrictions on diving. Generally, a fracture should be properly healed in 4–6 weeks, barring complications. However, there is the theoretical, unproven caveat that there is an increased risk of bubble formation in regions of bone where there has been some disruption of blood supply, leaving an increased or decreased vascularity.

There are a couple of other factors that one might consider:

- Even though healed, there is a period during which the fracture will still be vulnerable to further injury. During this time the limb or area should be protected and consideration should be given to the pressure applied to the affected arms or legs when exiting the water or climbing back into boats, and the effects of heavy scuba gear together with the positioning of the gear. Divemasters and buddies should be involved and asked for assistance as needed.
- There is significant loss of muscle strength and sometimes actual muscle wasting (atrophy) with a fracture and disuse while repairing. This recovers with use, but may cause temporary weakness and tendency to cramp while finning.

Diving With a Cast

Although diving with a fracture is discouraged in general, modern casts—unlike plaster of paris—do make provision for getting wet.

Waterproof cast construction uses a waterproof cast liner made of Gore-Tex to replace the traditional stockinette and cast padding. The Gore-Tex liner repels water and permits evaporation, allowing bathing, swimming, sweating, and hydrotherapy without any special drying of the cast or skin. Fiberglass casting tape is then wrapped around the waterproof liner.

If the fracture or sprain is not significant, and if it does not affect mobility, or if the individual can actually don dive gear and function adequately with the splint or cast, or if the individual is no longer on pain medication, and if common sense suggests diving might be performed safely, then diving may be considered with approval of the treating physician.

JOINT SURGERY AND METALLIC IMPLANTS

Once fully recovered, there need be no diving limitations or restrictions on diving with a knee or hip replacement, nor any other metallic inserts or implants. The effects of pressure are irrelevant to artificial implants and the laws of Boyle, Dalton, and Henry—gas compression and inert gas absorption—do not apply. Theoretically, there may be an increased chance of gas bubble formation in scar tissue or areas of deranged blood supply, but this has no firm basis in human or animal studies.

Mobility and strength are more pertinent concerns, i.e., ability to walk around with heavy gear prior to entry and climb ladders (or shore) for exits. All wounds should be completely healed and the diver should have been released by the surgeon for full weight-bearing activities. Physical rehabilitation should have been accomplished.

One should be able to dive the usual limits of sport diving without any restrictions. Divers usually notice a change in their buoyancy characteristics and may need to adjust their weighing due to their newly acquired internal weights—the artificial joints.

Diving After Knee or Hip Reconstruction

Much depends on the original cause of the disease or disability. Generally, the guidelines for the new diver are much more stringent than for an experienced diver who is returning from an injury. The sport diver should have no problem as long as there is good range of motion and the diver is able to bear weight.

The candidate must have appropriate mobility and dexterity and must be able to withstand the rigors of physical fitness required for their personal safety and that of others.

RHEUMATOID ARTHRITIS AND OSTEOARTHRITIS

Risk Factors for Arthritis

The inevitability of aging brings with it an increased prevalence of bone and joint problems, one of the most common being osteoarthritis. Given the amount of use and abuse to which we put our bodies, it is surprising that the musculoskeletal system does not "wear out"; paradoxically it actually thrives on this and adapts to usage. If cared for, it can "last a lifetime."

Rheumatoid arthritis, on the other hand, is irreverent to age and may affect divers of all ages. Women appear to be more susceptible to rheumatoid arthritis and systemic lupus erythematosis (SLE), whereas men suffer more readily and severely from ankylosing spondilitis. However, like gender, age very strongly affects the incidence, expression, and impact of musculoskeletal diseases. Some conditions only occur in childhood; others, like SLE and ankylosing spondylitis, usually start in young adults. Polymyalgia rheumatica and giant cell arthritis rarely begin in those less than 55 years of age. Rheumatoid arthritis (RA), SLE, gout, and other major inflammatory rheumatic diseases are expressed differently if they begin in older patients. The reasons for all these variables are unclear, but the common features to all are disability, medication, and pain.

Diagnosis of arthritis still depends more on careful interrogation of symptoms and examination. The assessment of pain, disability, and handicap is often more difficult, involving investigation of functional abilities, as well as hopes, fears, needs, and aspirations. This assessment requires careful documentation in prospective divers for comparison in the case of a possible bout with decompression sickness. Most musculoskeletal disorders cause chronic pain and disability without having a great effect on life expectancy. The prevalence is therefore highest in older people.

In the absence of disabling pain or medication incompatible with diving, and with appropriate assistance by buddies and divemasters, selected individuals with joint disease may dive. However, as with any disability or disorder preventing self- or buddy rescue, one should combine two able-bodied individuals to one disabled diver. With minimal assistance with entrances and exits, the arthritic diver can usually manage a moderately difficult dive with ease. The underwater "weightlessness" of scuba diving not only relieves the relentless onslaught of gravity on our bodies, but even permits those with bone and joint problems a glimpse of freedom. Some arthritic divers have described significant relief from pain at depth.

Treatment

A few types of arthritis are treatable with specific therapy (e.g., gout can be completely controlled with drugs and Lyme disease with antibiotics), but there are no "magic bullets" for most chronic rheumatic disorders. Most arthritic divers will want to know about the effect of diving on the drugs they are taking, such as aspirin, NSAIDs, steroids, and the numerous other medications in use for secondary (fallback) treatment of certain arthritic illnesses (gold, Cyclosporin, Immuran, etc).

Scuba diving can be an important part of the physical therapists armamentarium. Physical therapy is useful for prevention of more rapid deterioration as well as for treatment of symptoms. In early disease, the maintenance of muscle strength and a full range of joint motion will help prevent subsequent disability. Physiotherapy often plays a central role in rehabilitation and pain management.

None of the drugs used to treat most forms of arthritis alter consciousness and therefore are not dangerous to the diver from that perspective. However, anti-inflammatory agents do alter bleeding tendencies and these should be considered (see section on bleeding disorders, page 98). Other drugs blunt the immune system, and divers need to be aware of the increased possibility of infection in polluted water.

In late destructive disease of any type, joint replacement, and, less commonly, deliberate surgical joint stiffening (arthrodesis) can be performed. Joint prostheses from metal or silicone pose no problem to the diver in that they are not air containing and thus are not affected by changes in pressure.

Conditions easily misinterpreted as arthritis by the layperson include phlebitis, arteriosclerosis obliterans, cellulitis, edema, neuropathy, vascular compression syndromes, the stiffness of Parkinson's disease, periarticular stress fractures, myositis, and fibromyositis. Accordingly, a diver presenting with a history of arthritis should be carefully interviewed to verify if it is indeed joint-related and—if in doubt—referred for dive medical assessment. Add to this the joint pains associated with "bends" or decompression illness, and you have the possibility of confusion in diagnosis.

The foot and ankle deserve additional attention: the prospective diver should test his weight bearing ability with full equipment and weight belt. Inability to handle the weight need not preclude one from diving, but should prompt the buddy to be aware of the risks of such disability. Since finning is such a vital part of safe diving, disorders of the foot and ankle may have great impact on the enjoyment and safety of diving.

SCOLIOSIS
The spine has natural curves when viewed from the side. The lower back bends slightly inward and the upper part of the spine bows a little outward. Viewed from behind, however, the spine appears straight with little side-to-side curvature—except in people who have scoliosis. With scoliosis, the spine curves to the side.

Of every 1,000 children, three to five develop scoliosis severe enough to need treatment. Scoliosis occurs rarely in adults. Sometimes, it's a worsening of a condition that began in childhood but wasn't diagnosed or treated. In other cases, adult scoliosis may result from a degenerative joint condition in the spine.

Usually scoliosis is painless. Most cases are mild, requiring only follow-up and observation. In more severe cases, the spine can rotate as well, resulting in prominent ribs on one side of the body and narrowed spaces between ribs on the other. Severe scoliosis can cause ongoing back pain and difficulty breathing. Surgery may then be necessary.

Probably the main concern with diving with scoliosis is the possibility of decreased lung function. Some cases are so severe that the chest cavity is distorted and the affected person may have difficulty breathing and a reduced lung capacity. This would need to be assessed carefully to be sure that the diver will not suffer from carbon dioxide build-up due to inadequate breathing at depth or run the risk of airway obstruction with barotrauma or a "burst lung."

Another concern would be the vulnerability of the unstable spine to injury, such as from lifting heavy weights and tanks. Proper fitted gear and a good degree of physical capacity and cardiac reserve (the ability of the heart to handle stressful situations) might also play an important part in the decision to dive.

There will likely be more difficulty with gearing up, entries, and exits, but, once submerged, this difficulty disappears in the relatively gravity-free environment of diving. If in doubt, the opinion of the treating physician and a diving physician should be sought.

TENDONITIS / BURSITIS

Tendons are the thick fibrous cords that attach muscles to bone. They transmit the power generated by a muscle contraction to move a bone. Tendonitis is inflammation or irritation of a tendon.

A bursa is a space surrounding a joint that is covered by fibrous tissue. It is similar to the "housing" around moving parts of a machine; it is both protective and lubricating. Bursitis is inflammation or irritation of a bursa.

Since both tendons and bursae are located in or near joints, inflammation in these soft tissues will often be perceived as joint pain and may be mistaken for arthritis. Movement aggravates the pain, and stiffness and pain are prominent at night. There is a concomitant decrease in function as the pain and stiffness increases.

Injury or overuse during work or play is the most common cause of tendonitis and bursitis. Rarely, infections and medications can cause the inflammation (cholesterol medication; ciprofloxacin, etc.). Tendonitis or bursitis may be associated with diseases such as rheumatoid arthritis, gout, psoriasis, thyroid disease, and diabetes.

Diagnosis is mainly by medical history and physical examination since tendons and bursae are generally not visible on x-rays. MRI and ultrasound may be useful in the detection of bursitis and tendonitis in some cases. Aspiration (fluid drainage) and evaluation of liquid drained from a swollen bursa may help to exclude infection or gout. Blood tests may be ordered to confirm underlying conditions, but are generally not necessary to diagnose tendonitis or bursitis.

Treatment of these two conditions is based on the underlying cause. In overuse or injury, reduction or avoidance of the precipitating activity is useful. The use of various therapeutic modalities, especially ice, may help to reduce inflammation and pain. An adequate warm-up before and correct posture during exercise are useful. Braces, splints, using a cane or support, anti-inflammatory medications, steroid injections, and physical therapy are all helpful in the treatment of these conditions.

A potentially serious complication of tendonitis is rupture of a tendon, with the most common being a tear of the Achilles tendon. This usually requires surgical intervention to repair it. Otherwise, surgical intervention for other forms of tendonitis or bursitis is uncommon.

In addition to possibly worsening the condition, diving would not be wise during the acute phase of the illness due to the functional limitations of the diver. Depending on the part of the body involved, there might be difficulty donning and doffing gear, water entry and exit, in water locomotion, and self- and buddy rescue, any of which might lead to a cascade of events leading to a diving accident.

Medications required for pain relief could blunt the ability of the diver to multitask as necessary in the underwater environment. Diving should only be undertaken once the acute inflammatory process has subsided and the person is able to function normally.

NEUROLOGICAL, PSYCHOLOGICAL, AND PSYCHIATRIC

ANXIETY DISORDERS

Anxiety is a complex feeling of apprehension without an identifiable cause. In its extreme form it is called *panic*. Fear is similar to anxiety in many respects, except that it is directed towards something specific—usually understandably so (e.g., large predatory sharks). A phobia, on the other hand, is also a fear of something specific, but it is exaggerated to an irrational extent and may be incapacitating. The individual suffering from it realizes that the fear is illogical, but is unable to control it. Examples of phobias include acrophobia (fear of heights), claustrophobia (fear of confined spaces), agoraphobia (fear of open spaces), and arachnophobia (fear of spiders).

Anxiety is a very common condition. Symptoms may range from mild to severe. They may include breathlessness, a bouncing, racing heart rate, and other physical sensations. One particularly dangerous form of anxiety is panic. During an episode of panic an individual perceives their survival to be threatened and becomes irrational. They manifest instinctive behavior—even if this endangers themselves and others. In the setting of diving this may include removal of dive gear, breath holding, and rapid ascent. Panic may be the final stage in a series of escalating trivial stressors encountered during a dive. Alternatively, as in the case of individuals suffering from baseline or so-called *trait anxiety*, it may follow a single mishap, such as the loss of a mask. Another type of anxiety-related illness is *panic disorder* or panic-attacks. Individuals suffering from this condition may suddenly and inexplicably get the feeling that they are about to die. In the US, panic disorder has a lifetime prevalence of 1.5%–3.5%. One-third to one-half of these individuals also have a fear of open spaces, or agoraphobia, whereas 50% to 65% have associated major depressive illness.

Phobias
Phobic disorders have a lifetime prevalence as high as 10%–13%. They encompass several subcategories of anxiety conditions, some of which may be relevant to diving, such as claustrophobia (fear of enclosed spaces) and acrophobia (fear of heights—which may appear when diving in clear, deep water).

Post Traumatic Stress Disorder
Surprisingly, some divers experience sufficient psychological trauma during dive training to ultimately manifest a post-traumatic stress disorder (PTSD). This syndrome—associated with flash-backs, nightmares, and problems adapting to normal life after the event—is a real entity. Others may have repressed fears related to episodes of near drowning in their youth that suddenly reappear when they are reintroduced to the aquatic environment. Most anxious divers ultimately drop out of the sport, hopefully unharmed. Occasionally, however, there are some who try to overcome their fear and these may be "time bombs" vulnerable to panic.

The implications of anxiety disorders in diving are quite obvious. Erratic or irrational behavior, prompted by these disorders while in a non-breathable environment, may easily lead to injury or death. Therefore, in the evaluation of students and divers, it is important to emphasize the need to declare phobias and anxiety disorders in advance. One should pay attention to an individual's motives for diving or learning to dive (e.g., love of water vs. a partner coercing them to dive against their will). If necessary, one should provide such "dragooned divers" with a medical excuse to escape without losing face. Inability to equalize the ears, being invisible to others, may provide anxious individuals with a means of leaving the sport with their egos intact.

One should observe how divers behave in anticipation of the dive. For example, are they calm or erratic in their preparations? One should be prepared to intervene when the first manifestations of anxiety appear, whether above or under water. Simple reassurances provided for simple stressors may prevent fatal complications later on. When in doubt about an individual's psychological ability to cope under water, try to delay their encounter and, if necessary, obtain medical advice.

ATTENTION DEFICIT DISORDER (ADD)

Attention deficit disorder (ADD) has become a household term.[16] The name is actually misleading. Rather than an inability to concentrate, individuals suffering from it are unable to regulate their attention. They may either become distracted by non-relevant stimuli, or become fixated on one specific stimulus to the exclusion of all else. Essentially, these individuals are trying to absorb everything at once and accordingly are unable to focus on one thing at a time. ADD or ADHD may exist in a pure *attentional* form, a *hyperactive* form, or *a combination* of the two. Persons suffering from ADD may have problems with the following mental processes: (1) adapting to a changing environment, (2) organizing their thoughts, (3) planning and setting goals, (4) separating emotion from reason, (5) retrieving from short term memory, and (6) controlling verbal and motor impulses. The exact cause for ADD is not fully understood, but appears to involve chemicals and interconnections in the frontal part of the brain. The prevalence is around 3%–7% in US children. It affects boys two to four times as often as girls, and approximately 50% of children are still symptomatic as adults. Many patients are ultimately able to compensate sufficiently to lead successful and productive lives.

With ADD, the implications on diving are fourfold. Firstly, an inability to reliably focus on safety factors such as depth, time, and cylinder contents puts a diver at obvious risk. Secondly, an inability to concentrate may affect the process of learning and deny the student the benefit of the safety information they receive. Thirdly, impulsivity and involuntary activity may endanger them in water. Lastly, the medication used to treat ADD may increase the risk of seizures and have unpredictable interactions with nitrogen narcosis. It is therefore recommended that persons with the diagnosis of ADD be evaluated by a psychiatrist or an experienced diving physician before enrolling them for dive training. Children with the condition will probably be unsuitable for diving instruction. However, adults who have been able to pass high school or college exams, are able to drive a car safely, and no longer need medication may be able to dive safely.

---

16. There are many synonyms for this condition: attention deficit disorder with and without hyperactivity, attention deficit hyperactivity disorder, hyperkinetic impulse disorder, hyperactive syndrome, hyperkinetic reaction of childhood, minimal brain damage, minimal brain dysfunction, undifferentiated attention deficit disorder. It is abbreviated as AD/HD, ADD, ADD/ADHD, ADHD.

BELL'S PALSY

Bell's palsy is a one-sided paralysis of the muscles of facial expression due to damage of the associated nerve. The cause is unknown, although there are several theories. The condition affects 1 in 65 individuals. The peak incidence is in the third and eighth decades of life. Up to 85% of individuals make a rapid and full recovery; 10% have minor difficulties, and 5% have severe, permanent deformity. The best outcome is observed in those individuals where function already starts to recover within two to three weeks of the onset.

Diving-related concerns are largely limited to the diagnostic confusion the condition may create. It is particularly important to distinguish Bell's Palsy from *facial baroparesis* (pressure-related paralysis of the face). This unusual condition—which may seem identical to Bell's palsy—is the result of pressure in the middle ear compressing a portion of the facial nerve and causing paralysis. It presents abruptly, virtually immediately after diving, and may also be confused with gas embolism or stroke. The outcome is good, with no need of treatment, but further diving is discouraged to avoid permanent injury.

Divers with acute Bell's palsy may experience some difficulty in blinking or closing the eyes during mask clearing. The facial nerve also supplies a muscle in the ear that dampens loud sounds. Accordingly, such divers may experience significant discomfort related to, for example, the noise of exhaled bubbles passing their ears under water. Wearing a hood may offer some relief.

BRAIN SURGERY

Trauma and brain tumors are the most common indications for brain surgery. They tend to primarily affect younger individuals and these may subsequently present themselves for dive training—even for the purpose of physical rehabilitation. The concerns related to any brain surgery are largely threefold: (1) the chances of loss of consciousness or epilepsy, (2) the impact of the underlying condition and its effect of dive safety, and (3) the extent to which the injury, tumor, or surgery has affected the individual's mental and physical abilities.

In general, individuals who have had any open skull surgery will not be able to dive safely. Even with the appropriate suppressive medication, epilepsy may still occur, and the consequences of losing consciousness under water are unacceptable. If confronted by a highly motivated diver with a history of brain surgery, it is strongly recommended that a certificate of diving fitness be obtained from an experienced diving physician with the consensus of a neuro-surgeon. If the element of epilepsy has been excluded, then the intellectual and physical capabilities of the individual need to be considered. In addition to their ability to care for themselves, the responsibility towards their dive buddies also deserves some thought. Where these are in doubt, two able-bodied and preferably experienced divers should be partnered with the disabled diver.

BULIMIA AND ANOREXIA

Eating disorders are complex psychological conditions frequently associated with other mental and physical ailments. It is unlikely that the diagnosis will be volunteered by a prospective diver, but on occasion family members or partners may request advice about diving safety.

Bulimia

Bulimia is a particular type of eating disorder in which the person binge-eats, followed by voluntary vomiting and/or the use of laxatives, diuretics, and excessive exercise to prevent weight gain. It affects 1%–3% of women and 0.1% of men during their lifetime. As far as diving is concerned, there are three key concerns:

1) **Underlying psychological stability of the individual.** Persons with bulimia often have other psychological or psychiatric disorders, making them susceptible to panic or even suicide. Professional assessment is therefore advised.

2) **Physical complications related to the efforts at weight loss.** Repetitive vomiting may result in erosive damage to the teeth, tearing of the esophagus, and inhalation of stomach contents, with lung damage. Tooth decay may affect the ability to keep a regulator in place or cause tooth squeeze. Damage to the lungs—sometimes indistinguishable from asthma—may predispose to lung barotrauma.

3) **Biochemical effects related to the efforts at achieving weight loss.** Vomiting, excessive use of diuretics, or laxative abuse may cause life-threatening changes in the body's salt and electrolyte balances, with heart beat abnormalities, seizures, cramps, and general muscular weakness. Again, this justifies professional assessment.

Anorexia Nervosa

Anorexia differs from bulimia in that it is not associated with binge-eating. Individuals intentionally starve themselves below minimum weight levels due to disturbed perceptions in body image. It is largely limited to the female gender and affects 1–2 per 200 women in the US. The starvation makes the individuals extremely vulnerable to cold, low blood sugar, and low blood pressure. In addition, there may be physical weakness and psychiatric disturbances. Diving is not recommended and a professional medical opinion should be sought.

CONCUSSION

Concussion is loosely defined as a minor, closed injury to the brain following impact to the head. It is associated with no, or only a very brief, loss of consciousness or memory. Although not a life-threatening injury, it can present with long-term problems. Any loss of consciousness suggests a more serious

177

injury, with an associated risk of post-traumatic epilepsy. Post concussion syndrome, as this is called, may consist of prolonged symptoms, including:

- Recurrent headaches
- Dizziness
- Memory impairment
- Incoordination
- Hypersensitivity to light and noise
- Concentration and attention problems
- Depression
- Anxiety

Unfortunately, the severity of the concussion, or even the number of concussions, is not proportional to the risk for developing these complaints, making it hard to predict problems. Fortunately, most patients with concussion recover fully within three days and are headache free within 2–4 weeks of the injury. Return to diving may be considered within six weeks of the injury if no long term problems have developed. Any loss of consciousness, or a lapse in memory either before or after the event for a period longer than 30 minutes, suggests a significant injury to the brain and approximately a 5% chance for post-traumatic epilepsy within the next two years (see Convulsions, Seizures, and Epilepsy). Accordingly, such individuals, and those with persisting problems, need formal assessment by a neurologist and diving physician before diving may be considered.

CONVULSIONS, SEIZURES, AND EPILEPSY

Convulsions or seizures actually describe the external appearance of someone experiencing spontaneous, uncoordinated electrical discharges within the brain, resulting in spasmodic muscular contractions.

Seizures have a multitude of causes, but for practical purposes these may be divided into those that are predictable and those that are unpredictable. Predictable seizures include single episodes of convulsions related to low blood pressure, severe dehydration, reactions to recreational and medical drugs, low blood sugar, etc. Some diving medicine experts include sleep or nocturnal epilepsy within this category. What distinguishes these types of seizures from epilepsy is that they have a known and predictable cause or onset. Therefore, in the absence of the precipitating cause, further seizures can be avoided reliably.

Epilepsy means having recurring, unpredictable seizures, usually of an unknown cause. By definition, at least two seizures are required before the diagnosis of epilepsy is made.

The primary concern with all these conditions is that a loss of consciousness under water is likely to result in death by drowning unless, by a turn of good fortune, the individual:

- Does not lose the demand valve (regulator)
- Is discovered before drowning
- Does not breath-hold during ascent with a rescue attempt as a result of laryngospasm or an inability to exhale
- Receives effective resuscitation immediately at the surface
- Never has cardiac arrest

Unfortunately, this is a long wish list to be met and the death rate with unconsciousness under water is between 30% and 70%. In the case of a seizure under water, it may be even higher.

Diving induces many of the stimuli known to independently precipitate an epileptic seizure: flickering lights, hyper- or hypoventilation, and sensory deprivation. So, if there is even a marginal risk for seizures, this may be increased even further by diving.

Finally, even though an individual has not had epilepsy for a number of years or after a certain age, statistics still indicate that the probability of another convulsion is greater than in the rest of the "normal" diving population (believed to be less than one percent).

Certain training associations, such as the British Sub-Aqua Club, do accept medical clearance for individuals who have been seizure-free—on no medication—for five years, or after three years if the last seizure occurred during sleep only. This position, made by their medical advisory panel, is based on evidence that the chances of developing another seizure decreases exponentially over time and approaches near normal levels after five years. There are no data, however, that evaluate the risk specifically for the stresses of diving. Ultimately, it is up to the diver to decide. Most diving physicians are very reticent to encourage an individual with a known risk factor to face an elevated or unquantified risk, for which the adverse outcome is likely to be fatal.

Two elements must be considered in summarizing the current recommendations concerning epilepsy and diving.

First, most diving physicians are of the opinion that they would not feel confident about advising a person with a confirmed diagnosis of epilepsy that it would be safe to dive, unless seizures or unconsciousness were due to:

- Fainting with ultimate seizure activity due to remaining upright in the presence of low blood flow to the brain
- Other causes of acute low blood pressure, low blood sugar, medication, or recreational drugs
- Fever, but not after the age of five

Secondly, there is scientific evidence that suggests that individuals who have been free of seizures, without medication, are unlikely to have further seizures after a period of five years. This encourages continued efforts to further our understanding of the relationship between epilepsy and diving.

Expert opinion is advised in all these cases.

DECOMPRESSION ILLNESS
Decompression illness (DCI) encompasses the gas bubble disorders of arterial gas embolism and decompression sickness.

The objective of this section is not to explore its causes, but to explain how a previous episode of DCI may affect future diving fitness. Accordingly, previous DCI may be considered according to five parameters:

- Predictability
- Severity
- Response to treatment
- Risk of recurrence
- General diving medical fitness

Predictability
Predictable DCI occurs when divers have violated known depth-time parameters, ascent rates, have omitted decompression, or have held their breath during ascent. The disorders that result from this are explicable and therefore, in a sense, predictable. Unpredictable DCI suggests that individuals have some as yet undefined risk factor that has led them to sustain DCI following a "safe" dive profile. DCI that is impossible to predict is consequently impossible to prevent with any measure of certainty.

Severity
Decompression illness affecting the brain, spinal cord, inner ear, lungs, or heart is considered severe. Individuals experiencing these forms of DCI are more likely to be seriously ill and may sustain permanent damage and suffer ongoing disability as a result.

Response to Treatment

Response to treatment provides a measure of the extent of the DCI injury. Divers who make a full recovery with a single recompression treatment are likely to have suffered less damage than those in need of multiple, extended, or complicated treatments.

Risk of Recurrence

This determination is made not only in terms of how likely the DCI is to recur, but also how devastating it might be if it does. For instance, an individual who has already lost a large part of the spinal cord or one of his or her vestibular organs will become completely debilitated with a subsequent injury. In contrast, a person who suffers from elbow pain after a long technical dive, which subsides quickly with a single recompression, need not be precluded from future diving.

General Diving Fitness & Diving Activity

The overall fitness of a diver who has suffered DCI must also be considered. If the diver has recovered fully from a predicted episode of DCI without permanent scarring, psychological or neurological impairments, or other long-term sequelae, they are more likely to return to diving than someone with underlying diseases or risk factors.

Guidelines on resuming diving after DCI vary, but common recommendations are shown in Table 4:

Table 4. Guidelines for resuming diving after DCI

DCI	Predictable?	Resolved with decompression?	Danger of reccurence?	Otherwise Fit?	Resume Diving
Pain-Only	Yes	Completely	None	Yes	7 days
Pain-Only	Yes	Partially	Little	Yes	4–6 weeks
Serious	Yes	Completely	None	Yes	6 weeks
Serious	Yes	After 6 weeks	Low	Yes	6 months
Any	No	—	—	—	Unfit
Any	—	No	—	—	Unfit
Any	—	—	Yes	—	Unfit
Any	—	—	—	No/Poor	Unfit

DEPRESSION

Depression, or Major Depressive Disorder (MDD), is one of the more common psychiatric disorders. It is generally underdiagnosed and accordingly under-treated. The cause has not been determined clearly, but there are many theories surrounding brain chemical imbalances. The lifetime incidence of MDD is 20% in women and 12% in men. MDD as a disorder contributes to suicides, medical illness, disruption of interpersonal relationships, drug and substance abuse, and absenteeism.

Suicide is a leading cause of death in the US, with approximately 200,000 attempts every year; half of these are associated with MDD. In 1998, there were some 30,000 completed suicides.

To meet the definition of MDD, at least five characteristics should be present within the same two-week period. These should represent a change from previous functioning and include either a depressed mood or a diminished sense of interest or pleasure, as well as:

- Significant weight loss or gain
- Lack of or excessive sleep
- Agitation or slowing of activity
- Fatigue or loss of energy
- Feelings of worthlessness
- Diminished ability to think or concentrate or indecisiveness
- Recurrent thoughts of death, ideas of suicide, suicide attempts, or a specific plan to commit suicide

The implications of MDD on diving are threefold:

- Diving provides a relatively convenient method for suicide and this should be evaluated with the same suspicion as the presence of a firearm in the house.
- Anti-depressant medication may have an unpredictable and variable interaction with diving. Most importantly, it may reduce self-appraisal and awareness of errors of judgment.
- Inability to concentrate and indecisiveness may affect a diver's safety under water. One should, however, be careful in considering those individuals with external causes for their depression for whom diving provides an important escape. It may not only be cruel and unnecessary to deny such individuals the pleasures of diving, but it may even be dangerous by removing one of life's few consolations from them.

Divers with MDD, whether or not they are on medication, should be carefully evaluated by an experienced diving physician. Diving in excess of 80 fsw (24 msw) is discouraged due to possible interactions between drugs and nitrogen narcosis.

HEADACHE (Also see Diving Nuisances: Headaches)

Headaches are common. They not only represent one of the most frequent symptoms in medical practice but also are extremely common in diving. The mechanism for headache is relatively obscure, as the brain itself does not experience pain. However, the membranes surrounding the brain and the blood vessels contained within them can generate painful impulses when stretched or irritated. Accordingly, inflammation of the membranes surrounding the brain (meningitis) and widening of the blood vessels (migraine, cluster headaches, tension headaches, carbon dioxide retention) or irritation of nerves surrounding the brain (tumors, inflammation) may lead to the sensation we call "headache."

Most headaches are intermittent and benign. Serious headaches are usually associated with abnormal sensation, weakness, neck stiffness, or nausea. They are often severe and may last for many minutes to hours. Most benign headaches, other than those related to caffeine withdrawal or alcohol intoxication, develop during the day, peak in the afternoon, subside in the evening, and are gone in the morning. Headaches that are present upon wakening should be viewed with suspicion, and if they occur frequently or over a period of time, should prompt medical attention. Headaches that develop as a result of diving are discussed in detail elsewhere.

It is unwise to dive with a headache, as it distracts the diver and also detracts from the pleasure of the experience. Additionally, the medication taken to suppress the headache may result in drowsiness and errors of judgement. The latter may be exacerbated by nitrogen narcosis. If medication other than acetaminophen (e.g., Tylenol®; also called paracetamol in Europe and Asia) is required to control a headache, it is strongly recommended not to dive until it has resolved.

MANIA

Mania (synonyms: bipolar disorder or manic-depressive disorder) is a type of mood disorder in which feelings, thoughts, behaviors, and perceptions are altered. It is characterized by episodes of agitation alternating with periods of depression. It may start in adolescence or appear for the first time in adults.

The diagnosis requires at least one episode of mania—an abnormal, often expansive and elevated mood lasting for at least 1 week—during which the individual may have a decreased need for sleep, racing thoughts, rapid and

183

often pressured speech, increased goal-directed activities or projects, hypersexuality, reckless behavior and risk taking, and "delusions of grandeur." These alternate with periods of depression in which self-esteem is reduced and the individual may teeter on the verge of suicide. Milder forms—called hypomania, with less "truly mad" thoughts—may also occur and do not require hospitalization. The overall incidence of mania is around 1% in adolescents. Twenty to thirty percent of all patients who develop mania do so before the age of 20.

The implications for diving are obvious: both elevations in mood and depression introduce risks of injury.

Treatment, usually in the form of lithium, does not guarantee absence of episodes. Confirmed mania is a contraindication to diving.

MENINGITIS

Meningitis is an inflammation of the membranes surrounding the brain, usually as a result of a bacterial infection. A particularly severe type of meningitis is associated with *meningococcus* bacteria, and individuals affected by it may die within hours of the onset of symptoms. These usually include headache, stiffness of the neck, and suppressed consciousness. It is common in underdeveloped countries and is associated with overcrowding. The two important aspects of meningitis are that (1) fever with neck stiffness should always prompt medical attention and (2) individuals who have suffered from meningitis may be at risk for developing epilepsy and should be cleared for diving by experienced diving physicians and a neurologist.

MOTOR NEURON DISEASES (MND)

Motor Neuron Diseases (MND) are a collective group of terminal illnesses in which the muscles become progressively weaker, ultimately leading to complete paralysis and death. One of the most common types of MND is called Amyotrophic Lateral Sclerosis (ALS), or Lou Gehrig disease for the famous baseball player who died of it.

Most people with ALS die within five years of the onset of symptoms. ALS does not affect a person's mental abilities, senses, intelligence, reasoning, memory, or personality. ALS is diagnosed in about 5,000 people each year in the United States. About 20,000 people are believed to have the condition at any time. It affects all ages, races, and ethnic groups. It is most common in men and in the age group 40–60 years. It has no cure and there is no means of reversing its effects. The paralysis usually affects the legs and gradually makes its way towards the head. The famous astronomer and physics genius Stephen Hawkins suffers from this disease and is now nearly completely paralyzed. Although it is unlikely that individuals affected by the disorder will volunteer for dive training, it may happen than certified divers attempt to continue diving during the early stages of the disease. The unpredictable progression of the illness prompts a recommendation against further diving, especially once the muscles of breathing and swallowing become affected.

MULTIPLE SCLEROSIS

Multiple sclerosis is an inflammatory condition of the central nervous system. Its exact cause is unknown, but it results in episodes of acute loss of muscle function, vision, speech, or coordination followed by full or partial recovery. These acute MS attacks result in a patchy loss of insulation around the nerve tracts in the brain and spinal cord. They may occur intermittently over months or years. Some individuals outlive their illness altogether, while others eventually succumb to the debilitating complications of the disease over a period of 15 to 35 years. MS is the most common debilitating illness amongst young adults. The incidence is 0.5–1.0 per 1,000 people, and the general population has a 0.2% life-time risk of acquiring MS. Approximately 25,000 new cases are diagnosed each year.

Hyperbaric oxygen therapy has been proposed as a promising treatment for the disease, but studies have failed to prove any long-term benefit. However, this has prompted some individuals to take up diving or even go as far as diving on oxygen. For a variety of reasons it is inadvisable for individuals with MS to dive. If they do, it should be under ideal conditions and in warm water with a buddy or buddies able to assist them depending on their level of disability. The underlying MS also poses the possible dilemma of differential diagnosis in case of decompression sickness. When in doubt, it is still advisable to treat for DCI.

PANIC DISORDERS

(See Psychological Aspects and Anxiety Disorders)

PARALYSIS

Paralysis is not a disease as such. Rather it is the description for loss of function in a limb, with or without a loss of sensation, as a result of an underlying illness or injury.

There are many causes for paralysis, including motor vehicle accidents with spinal fractures, infections like polio, multiple sclerosis (MS), stroke, birth injuries, and cerebral palsy.

The key considerations are (1) is the underlying condition stable or likely to deteriorate, and (2) to what extent will the individual's disability affect diving safety.

Progressive disorders like motor neuron disease and MS are usually considered contraindications to diving. On the other hand, individuals with chronic Guillian Barré paralysis or similar spinal cord injuries may be taught to dive successfully as long as they are able to perform all the necessary survival and equipment skills and have at least two trained buddies to assist them. Individuals with strokes may have an associated risk of cardiac disease, while individuals with brain damage may have associated epilepsy. Dive medical examination by an experienced diving physician is mandatory.

PHOBIAS
(See Anxiety Disorders)

SCHIZOPHRENIA
Schizophrenia is a relatively common psychiatric condition and is the archetypical form of madness. It is a chronic, severe, and disabling mental illness affecting men and women equally.

The origin of the term "schizophrenia" comes from the Greek word meaning "split mind." This is not an accurate description, as it appears to suggest a split-personality disorder—a completely separate illness. People with schizophrenia may present with (1) false personal beliefs (delusions) held with conviction, in spite of reason or evidence to the contrary, and without cultural context; (2) hallucinations, that is, perceptions of sound, sight, touch, smell, or taste in the absence of an actual external stimulus, such as hearing voices; (3) disorganized thoughts and behaviors; (4) disorganized speech; (5) catatonia (i.e., extreme muscular rigidity). The illness affects about 1% of the population—more than 2 million people in the US suffer from schizophrenia at any given time, and 100,000–200,000 people are diagnosed with the illness every year, usually between the ages of 17 and 35. Fifty percent of institutionalized people in mental hospitals have schizophrenia. Many of the remaining half are mentally disabled, unable to hold jobs and care for themselves; many are homeless. Some recover sufficiently to live a relatively independent life.

It is unlikely that persons with schizophrenia will take up diving, but it is most certainly a medical contraindication.

SPINAL SURGERY
Spinal surgery is usually the result of one of three medical problems: (1) trauma, (2) tumors, and (3) degeneration and collapse. All of these conditions threaten the integrity and function of the spinal cord and its associated nerve roots. Some forms also may be associated with pain.

There are theoretical concerns that spinal surgery may predispose individuals to decompression illness due to a disruption of the spinal architecture, but this risk has not been verified. A more important concern is that the heavy scuba equipment or diving from a bumpy, rocking boat may put a person with a "bad back" at risk of further injury. Divers with back injuries should be particularly careful about diving conditions and the type of diving they do. The use of pain medication also may introduce additional dangers. Back surgery for trauma or tumors also prompts consideration of the individual's subsequent disability. The same principles listed in the section on paralysis would then apply. It is wise to allow at least six months after back surgery before diving is reconsidered.

STROKE

Stroke is the colloquial name for the result of blockage or bleeding of a blood vessel in the brain.

With loss of circulation comes disruption of function, and the type and extent of the problem is determined by the area of the brain supplied by the affected blood vessel.

Common stroke symptoms include loss of vision, dizziness, sudden one-sided paralysis of an arm or leg, and acute loss of speech. Although associated with advanced age, strokes can affect young individuals as well. Stroke is the equivalent of a "heart attack" of the brain. It has been called a "brain attack" and requires prompt first aid action and transfer to an emergency medical facility. As with myocardial infarction, some types of stroke may be treated with clot busters and these may improve the chances of recovery significantly. Therefore, don't delay in getting a stroke victim to advanced medical care.

Stroke may be indistinguishable from arterial gas embolism. If the history of the dive does not suggest gas embolism, consider the possibility of a stroke. Recompression will not be harmful for a stroke victim and, in fact, hyperbaric oxygen has been used previously, although controversially, for the treatment of stroke. The only disadvantage may be that an individual eligible for receiving clot busters may miss the first three hours in which it may be given.

Individuals with previous strokes may wish to dive as a form of rehabilitation or to improve their physical fitness. The concern is that unconditioned exercise may provoke further strokes—or even a heart attack—and the individual may also have significant disability related to the stroke. In most cases, people who have had a previous stroke are discouraged from further diving. There are exceptions, but an experienced dive medical physician should carefully examine these.

SYNCOPE

Syncope is defined as a transient loss of consciousness or fainting due to a sudden, non-obstructive interruption in the circulation to the brain. This may be caused by a sudden widening of the arteries in the body, an irregular heartbeat, or dramatic slowing of heart rate. It excludes the diagnosis of seizures, coma, shock, or other states of altered consciousness.

Syncope is common and accounts for 3% of emergency department visits each year in the US and up to 6% of admissions. The multiple potential causes of fainting make it challenging to identify a single one. Often this cannot be found in spite of extensive (and expensive) testing. A cessation of circulation to the brain for as little as three to five seconds results in syncope. At least 3% of the population will have an episode of fainting within a 26-year period. Thirty percent will have more than one episode.

As in the case of seizures, the underlying cause and predictability of episodes form the basis of dive medical fitness and risk assessment. Irregular heart beat, severe low blood pressure, heart valve problems, or fainting when performing a Valsalva maneuver (i.e., ear clearing), constitute grounds for exclusion from diving. Again, the chief concern is the implications of loss of consciousness under water. If this cannot be assured with any certainty, diving becomes unacceptably hazardous.

RESPIRATORY

ASTHMA

Asthma is a lung disorder in which there is a tendency for the muscle surrounding the bronchi (breathing tubes) to contract excessively, causing narrowing, or bronchoconstriction. As a result, this causes increased breathing resistance, which can manifest as wheezing, chest "tightness," cough, or breathlessness. In asthmatics, bronchial constriction can be precipitated by exposure to allergens, noxious fumes, cold air, and exercise or respiratory infections such as a "cold." The increase in breathing resistance caused by bronchial narrowing may be compounded by the accumulation of mucus within the airways.

There are basically two issues that make scuba diving risky for asthmatics. First, there is an obligatory reduction in breathing capacity due to the effects of immersion and an increase in breathing resistance caused by the higher gas density at depth.[17] Given the reduction in an asthmatic's breathing capacity, there may not be sufficient reserve to accommodate the required increase demanded by exertion.

Second, the narrowing of the bronchi and excessive mucus production of asthmatics can inhibit exhalation of air during ascent, and could predispose the diver to pulmonary barotraumas, leading to pneumothorax, pneumo-mediastinum, and/or arterial gas embolism.

---

17. For example, at 2 atm (33 fsw/10 msw) under water, the maximum breathing capacity of a normal scuba diver is only 70% of the surface value. At 100 fsw (31 msw) under water, this reduction is approximately 50%.

Active, uncontrolled, exercise- cold- and emotionally-induced asthmatics should not dive. In addition, asthmatics requiring intermittent "rescue or reliever" medication should not dive. Some feel that asthmatics should not dive if they have needed a therapeutic bronchodilator in the last 48 hours or have had any other chest symptoms.

It is important to note that asthma severity can wax and wane. Symptoms may worsen for 4–6 weeks after a "cold" or during certain seasons (for example, in response to high levels of pollen in the air). Therefore, even if a person with asthma fulfills the criteria listed above, diving is not recommended unless the diver is free of respiratory symptoms before each dive. Mild to moderate asthmatics with normal screening spirometry whose asthma is controlled and does not deteriorate with exercise testing can be considered candidates for diving. If an asthmatic who has been cleared for diving has an attack, the individual should not dive until his airway function returns to normal.

The risk of diving is probably acceptable if the diving candidate with some asthmatic "history" demonstrates normal pulmonary function at rest and this does not deteriorate with strenuous exercise. The potential diver must, however, be made aware there appears to be a four-fold higher risk of DCI in asthmatics than in non-asthmatics, and the risk of a fatal accident also appears higher by an unspecified amount. Asthmatics adequately controlled on long-term inhaled steroids are thought to be able to dive.

BRONCHITIS (PULMONARY EMPHYSEMA)

Individuals with chronic bronchitis, chronic obstructive pulmonary disease (COPD), and pulmonary emphysema have chronically inflamed bronchi from irritants such as smoking, air pollution, or allergens. There is an increase in mucous production with lung damage and airflow restriction similar to what is seen in asthma. It causes shortness of breath, thick mucous production, and dilated, obstructed air sacs in the lungs.

The issue of whether a person with COPD should dive is very similar to the individual who has asthma. However, a person with scarred, obstructed lungs conceivably has a greater ongoing risk than an individual with healthy although temporarily obstructed lungs. The lungs of an individual with COPD never return to normal. Thus, the diver or diver candidate with COPD may have an increased theoretical risk of burst lung from rupture of obstructed small airways at all times.

From a practical point of view, by the time individuals with chronic lung diseases become symptomatic they are usually so short of breath that they are incapable of sustaining even the small exercise capacity necessary to dive. As a result, it is extremely rare to see a person with significant COPD volunteer for diving.

COPD is generally a disease that develops after decades of exposure to tobacco smoke, and is a disease of older individuals. This again makes it a rare encounter in diving medicine practice.

The biggest challenge is the seemingly normal individual who presents with poor lung function but is not asthmatic. Here a combination of medical history, x-rays, and response to bronchodilators assist in making the decision on risk and fitness.

CHEST INJURIES

Chest injuries occur as a result of accidental squashing or penetration of the chest cavity by foreign objects, e.g., motor vehicle accident injuries, fractured ribs, fractured ribs with pleural penetration, pneumothorax from sharp chest injuries, perforations from knives, bullets, needles (i.e., medically caused [iatrogenic], diagnostic, or therapeutic), etc. The relevance to diving is three-fold:

- Chest injuries may result in a breathing impairment that may preclude someone from diving because of impaired exercise tolerance. If a recent injury, a diver may be at risk for hypoxia, pulmonary barotrauma, and pneumothorax. The increased work of breathing gases that are more dense at depth and the changes that take place with immersion should also be considered.

- If a pneumothorax (i.e., collapsed lung) occurs at depth, it is likely to expand during ascent according to Boyle's law. This could cause a fatal tension pneumothorax. The same may happen to a diver diving with an undiagnosed pneumothorax.

- Chest injuries may result in scar tissue that makes the lungs vulnerable to tearing and may result in arterial gas embolism, even without causing a pneumothorax. Previous injury with significant scarring and where the lungs stick to the chest wall can lead to air trapping and pulmonary barotrauma with resultant pneumothorax, subcutaneous emphysema, and possibly arterial gas embolism.

Accordingly, before diving consent is given, careful evaluation should rule out any pleural adhesions, air trapping, or pulmonary blisters specialized testing, possibly including computer tomography (CAT scan) of the chest and by sophisticated pulmonary function studies (See Collapsed Lung, page 194).

CHEST SURGERY

Operations on the chest are performed for diseases of the lungs, trachea, esophagus, diaphragm, chest wall, and mediastinum. Sometimes the chest cavity is not entered and the surgery is performed in the space between the cavities that hold the lungs. This is important to the diver, because this kind of surgery does not leave adhesions between the surfaces of the chest wall and the covering of the lungs. The latter might place the diver at risk for pulmonary barotrauma. Similarly, surgical approaches can be made by going downward through the neck and upward through the abdomen.

Hazards to the diver after chest surgery may include one or all of the following:

- Recuperation (healed). Has the incision healed sufficiently so that there is no risk of infection or wound separation? The healing process varies considerably with each individual, but complete healing usually takes place in about two weeks.

- Rehabilitation. Even where the incision has healed completely, there is a period of time when the diver remains in a condition of decreased strength due to the enforced bed rest and decreased activity surrounding the operation. Depending on the type of surgery, rapidity of healing, and intensity of a rehabilitation program, a period of six to eight weeks might be required for return of the physical strength needed to safely perform a dive, self rescue, or buddy rescue.

- Respiratory reserve. Operations on the lungs sometimes entail removal of an entire lung or just a portion of a lung. Depending upon the extent of the surgery, there might be a considerable reduction in the ability to oxygenate the individual at rest or during exercise. This factor needs to be determined by the use of pulmonary function studies as determined by the operation and the physicians involved. Normal or borderline pulmonary reserves on the surface could easily become insufficient at depth due to the increased work of breathing denser gases and due to the effects of immersion on the central circulation.

- Evidence of pleural adhesions, collapse of portions of the lung (atelectasis). If there is evidence of pleural adhesions, blisters, or air trapping as a result of the surgery, then the diver would be at risk for pulmonary barotrauma. This would be due to Boyle's law, that is, the marked increase in volume that takes place in an air-containing structure resulting in rupture. This results in the escape of air into the chest cavity or subcutaneous tissues, the collapse of the lung, or the entrance of air into the arterial circulation with the development of gas embolism to the heart and brain blood vessels. This can cause death or brain damage and requires immediate recompression in a hyperbaric chamber.

Whether or not a person may dive depends upon the surgeon/physician's input, the respiratory reserve, the presence of pleural adhesions or air trapping (as determined by spiral CT scans and helium loop studies), and a judgment as to the "need to dive." A new diver contemplating certification lessons might have a different "need to dive" from a divemaster or instructor who has to dive for a living.

COLDS AND FLU
The conditions called a 'cold' or the 'flu' are widespread maladies that affect all of us on a fairly regular basis. They are caused by viruses that produce significant symptoms of the upper and lower respiratory systems, thereby becoming important in the production of situations that are adverse to diving. "Flu," or influenza, can sometimes lead to more serious problems, like the lung disease pneumonia. A stuffy nose, sore throat, and sneezing are usually signs of a cold. Tiredness, fever, headache, and major aches and pains probably mean you have the flu. Coughing can be a sign of either a cold or the flu. But a bad cough usually points to the flu.

Because of the nasal congestion that usually occurs with both of these conditions, diving poses a problem with air containing structures such as the sinuses and middle ears. Blockage of the openings to the sinuses and to the Eustachian tubes can lead to damage to the inner lining of the sinuses and the middle ears, with possible rupture of the ear drums. In addition, hearing and balance can be damaged due to inner ear barotrauma. Also, diving with inflammation of the bronchi and pneumonitis due to influenza can lead to lung barotrauma, from air trapping, and all of the increased risks of diminished air exchange at depth, with resultant hypoxia.

Difficulty clearing the ears with diving is already one of the most frequent injuries. Diving with a cold or the flu almost ensures that there will be damage done to the sinuses, middle ears, and ear drums. Other adverse effects can include severe balance problems under water. It would be wise for a diver not to dive until all symptoms of the cold and flu are well past. Resuming activities too soon after the flu can lead to a recurrence of the illness with the development of pneumonia—vomiting, high fever, shaking chills, chest pain, or coughing with thick, yellow-green mucus. Prevention of colds is possible by avoidance of people with the illness, frequent hand washing, covering your mouth when sneezing and coughing, washing surfaces with disinfectant, and keeping your hands away from your eyes, nose, and mouth. Flu shots are sometimes effective for prevention later on in the course of an epidemic, but usually are based upon last year's predominant flu strain. This needs to be discussed with your physician.

COLLAPSED LUNG
(PNEUMOTHORAX AND ATELECTASIS)

A pneumothorax ("air in the chest") is commonly known as a collapsed lung. Normally, the outer surface of the lung sits next to the inner surface of the chest wall. Thin membranes called pleura cover both surfaces. A pneumothorax occurs when air escapes from the lungs or leaks through the chest wall and enters the space between the two membranes (pleural cavity). As air builds up, it causes the nearby lung to collapse. Most cases of pneumothorax result from an injury to the lungs or chest wall, caused by a penetrating injury, such as a knife or gunshot wound, blunt trauma with rib fracture and penetration, or medical procedures from sharp instruments.

When a collapsed lung occurs without any direct injury to the lung or chest, it is called a spontaneous pneumothorax. Often, this results from lung damage caused by diseases such as asthma, cystic fibrosis, and pneumonia. It is particularly common in emphysema, which causes air-filled sacs, called blebs, to form. A spontaneous pneumothorax also can develop in people who don't have any obvious lung disease, but who have an inherited tendency to develop blebs that can rupture and cause the lung to collapse.

Another type of collapsed lung called tension pneumothorax sometimes occurs when a growing air pocket causes increased pressure within the pleural cavity. This collapses the nearby lung and can push the heart and major blood vessels to the unaffected side of the chest. This movement, called a mediastinal shift, can cause a life-threatening drop in blood pressure. Tension pneumothorax most commonly occurs in people with penetrating chest injuries. It also occurs in people on ventilators or those who have undergone cardiopulmonary resuscitation. These injuries require emergency insertion of a needle to allow the air to escape.

Atelectasis is when a portion of the lung collapses from having a bronchus blocked due to mucous plugs or shallow breathing. The air in the lung is absorbed and the tissue becomes a solid, blood filled mass, unable to move air across the membranes, producing decreased oxygenation.

These conditions affect the diver in several ways. Blebs cause the diver to be at risk for burst lung or pulmonary barotrauma due to the pressure changes that take place with every dive. A pneumothorax at depth is particularly dangerous, since the diver has to ascend and the air in the chest cavity has to increase in size due to Boyle's law. This can lead to tension pneumothorax, cardiopulmonary failure, and death. Atelectasis can also cause hypoxia, pulmonary barotraumas, and the dire possibility of arterial gas embolism.

Once a pneumothorax has healed, there is usually no long-term effect on your health. However, up to 50% of people have another pneumothorax, especially within a few months of the first one. To decrease the risk of a pneumothorax occurring again, the person should stop smoking and avoid changes in air pressure, such as flying in an unpressurized aircraft and scuba diving. Any lung disease, procedure, or event that can result in air trapping is thought to be a contraindication to diving. That having been said, most diving medical people would say that spontaneous, traumatic, and post-surgical pneumothoraces are felt to be disqualifying, due to the almost certain presence of "air trapping," either from the underlying disease process or the surgical procedure. Once a person has a spontaneous pneumothorax, recurrences are likely. If one spontaneous pneumothorax has occurred, there is a 33% chance that another will occur within two to three years; 30% will have a recurrence after three years, and there is a 60% long term risk for another pneumothorax.

Traumatic and medical pneumothoraces vary in degree; those due to blunt or penetrating trauma usually leave lacerations of the lung surface, often with significant radiographic changes that indicate scarring and air trapping. Such individuals should not be allowed to dive. In the event of isolated injury without significant scarring or air trapping, such as is seen with ice pick trauma, clean knife penetration, subclavian line placement, chest needle injury, and some mediastinal surgery, diving should be permitted, pending proper radiological evaluation to rule out air trapping.

Another type of collapsed lung is called "spontaneous pneumothorax," because it occurs with only minimal provocation in every day life and is caused by some pathological abnormality of the covering of the lung or scarring from disease. Aircraft travel, straining at stool, blowing the nose, Valsalva maneuvers, and simply coughing can cause rupture of blebs on the lungs. Persons should not dive after having had spontaneous pneumothorax, unless the problem has been surgically corrected to the satisfaction of a diving physician.

When a lung collapses while diving, the air in the chest cavity is at the ambient pressure of the dive depth. Upon ascending, the air in the chest cavity expands, and further compresses the lung (tension pneumothorax). This is a life-threatening situation and is one of the main reasons that a history of spontaneous pneumothorax is an absolute contraindication to diving, since most divers and dive boats are not prepared to provide first aid to a diver with pneumothorax. One of the symptoms of a small pneumothorax is a voice change after a dive. This would raise a warning flag about further diving, as there might be a small pneumothorax, which in itself is not harmful, but which will cause a serious problem if the diver does another dive.

Surgical procedures called pleurodesis (scarring the lung surface) and pleurectomy (excision of the pleura, a thin covering of the lungs) are commonly performed for recurrent collapsed lungs. There is a recurrence rate of 8 percent following pleurodesis. Recurrence is rare following pleurectomy. Even if recurrence of collapsed lung does not occur, the underlying cystic lung disease of the other lung remains, with the inherent danger now being pulmonary barotrauma with air embolism. The following are absolute contraindications to diving:

- Diving within three months after any type of collapsed lung
- Spontaneous collapsed lung in beginners
- Expert divers with recurrent collapsed lung after pleurectomy

If a diver feels that he or she will continue to dive regardless of the risk, spiral CT scans of the lungs should be performed so as to detail the degree of risk involved. Best advice here would be not to dive until one has been cleared by the chest specialist.

NEAR DROWNING

Submersion accidents which lead to unconsciousness in waters colder than 70°F (21°C) occur with regularity. Oxygen needs are much reduced when the body is cold, therefore permanent brain damage from low oxygen states may not occur. A 60-minute cold water submersion victim has been fully resuscitated. Similar to the hypothermic victims above, these nearly drowned individuals appear cold to touch, blue, with no respiration or evident circulation, and their pupils are fixed and dilated.

The principal physiologic consequence of immersion injury is prolonged low oxygen level in the blood (hypoxemia). After initial gasping, and possible swallowing of water, immersion stimulates hyperventilation, followed by voluntary cessation of breathing and a variable degree and duration of laryngospasm. This leads to hypoxemia. Depending upon the degree of hypoxemia and resultant increase in CO_2, the diver may develop cardiac arrest and lack of blood to the central nervous system (CNS). Asphyxia leads to relaxation of the airway, which permits the lungs to fill with more water in many individuals ("wet drowning"). Approximately 10%–20% of individuals maintain tight laryngospasm until cardiac arrest occurs and inspiratory efforts have ceased. These victims do not aspirate any fluid ("dry drowning").

The target organ of submersion injury is the lung. Injury to other systems is largely secondary to hypoxia and increased CO_2. Fluid aspirated into the lungs produces pulmonary vasoconstriction and increased blood pressure.

Some factors relating to surviving cold water near-drowning include age of the victim, especially young children, length of submersion up to 40 minutes, water temperature (the colder the better), CPR, water quality, the presence of other injuries, and how soon resuscitation is performed.

It's important to remember that cold water near-drowning is more survivable than previously thought. Resuscitations after as long as one hour of submersion have occurred. Cold water may be protective to some body systems as oxygen needs are markedly reduced.

Signs and symptoms of cold water near-drowning include cough producing a clear to frothy red sputum, blue skin color, shortness of breath, confusion or coma, absence of breathing, and signs of cardiac arrest.

Early management of the diver with cold water near-drowning is accomplished by removal from the water, avoidance of the Heimlich maneuver to clear the water from the lungs (it may cause vomiting and aspiration), induction of the ABCs of resuscitation, oxygen, remove wet and restrictive clothing, and initiate transport to the nearest medical facility. It should be noted that this is a diving accident and that a recompression chamber may be necessary, since DCS or air embolism may have initiated the near-drowning in the first place.

Return to diving after a near drowning episode should be allowed as soon as the physician is satisfied that there is adequate exchange of air, the diver is well oxygenated with normal pulmonary functions, and that there is no evidence of lung or pleural scarring that might lead to pulmonary barotrauma.

PNEUMONIA

Pneumonia is an inflammation of the lungs caused by an infection. Many different organisms can cause it, including bacteria, viruses, and fungi. In divers it can be caused by breathing micronized salt water (salt water aspiration syndrome), near drowning, and aspiration of pathogens from poorly cleaned equipment. Since pneumonia is a common illness that affects millions of people each year in the United States, the illness may have been initiated before diving and become evident with the respiratory stress placed on a diver. Pneumonia can range from mild to severe, and can occasionally be fatal. The type of organism, age, and underlying health have a great deal to do with the outcome of the illness.

The main symptoms of pneumonia include productive cough, bloody sputum, fever with shaking chills, chest pain worsened by deep breathing or coughing, rapid, shallow breathing, and shortness of breath.

If you have pneumonia, a good physician can make the diagnosis by listening to the breath sounds and by tapping on the chest. Crackles are heard when listening to your chest with a stethoscope. Other abnormal breathing sounds may also be heard through the stethoscope or via percussion (tapping on your chest wall).

Other tests that may show the presence of pneumonia include chest x-ray, bacterial study of the sputum, blood counts and arterial blood gases, chest CT, pulmonary perfusion/function studies, and study of pleural fluid drawn out of the chest with a needle.

Diving with pneumonia could have several adverse effects, mainly associated with the decreased oxygenation that occurs due to the areas of lung tissue that are not being aerated. Add to this the effects of immersion (blood moving centrally into the lungs) and increased work of breathing air of increased density, and it is clear that the diver would soon become hypoxic and acidotic from carbon dioxide retention.

In addition, pneumonia causes obstruction of bronchi and alveoli, adding another risk for pulmonary barotrauma on ascent, with the possibility of pneumothorax, subcutaneous emphysema, or arterial gas embolism.

The diver who has been diagnosed and treated successfully for pneumonia must adhere to the recommendations of the physician managing the case according to the severity of the infection and course of the illness. Return to diving is usually accomplished after complete recovery from the effects of the infection and x-ray and laboratory evidence shows clearing of the pneumonia and absence of significant scarring of the lungs.

PULMONARY BAROTRAUMA

Pulmonary barotrauma indicates injury to the lung due to the effects of pressure. This can occur on the surface, as in the use of an anesthetic intubation or endotracheal tube with positive pressure breathing. It can occur in aircraft travel, in susceptible individuals with blisters or blebs of thinned out pleurae and, for our purposes, it occurs in individuals who ascend from depth (high pressure) to the surface (low pressure) while holding their breath or not breathing adequately for some reason. The reason for this is Boyle's law, which states that given a constant temperature and quantity, the volume of an ideal gas varies inversely with the pressure.

Thus, as a diver ascends, spaces in the lung increase in size unless there is a release of air by breathing. If there is a pathological reason why this cannot take place, as with asthma, or lung blebs (or blisters on the lung), then there will be such a pressure buildup that there is a "blowout" of the tissues, with resultant collapse of the lung and escape of air into the surrounding tissues. Or some of the air gets into minute pulmonary venous blood vessels and is pumped through the heart into the blood supply of the heart and brain.

A typical occurrence would be the diver at the surface, raised out of the water, yelling, becoming comatose, convulsing, and requiring rescue. If treated properly with the head low position, oxygen by mask, and quick recompression, there is rapid response and usually complete recovery from the injury. Other things that can happen include confusion, vertigo, and cardiopulmonary arrest.

Other clinical manifestations include the sudden onset of paralysis, focal weakness, focal hypesthesia (decrease in reaction to stimulation), visual field defect, blindness, headache, and cranial nerve defects. The operative word here is "sudden." Nearly all of these symptoms can also be caused by neurological decompression sickness. Less common manifestations are chest pain and bloody, frothy sputum.

Mediastinal and subcutaneous emphysema, due to bubbling in the tissues, cause substernal pain, subcutaneous crepitus (a crunching feeling), a definite x-ray appearance, and occasionally circulatory embarrassment (rare).

Pneumothorax (collapsed lung) occurs when the pleura membrane overlying the lung is ruptured by the air pressure and the lung collapses. When this occurs there is pain, decreased respiration on the affected side, changes to stethoscope sounds, and percussion on physical exam with typical x-ray findings. If the opening is large, a tension pneumothorax can occur, gradually enlarging with each breath and as the diver ascends, requiring tube decompression of the chest before treatment with the compression chamber.

Prevention
There is the potential risk of pulmonary overpressure accidents on every compressed gas dive regardless of depth and time. Prevention of pulmonary overpressure accidents starts with a good diving physical exam to ensure no history of pulmonary pathology which would prevent free pressure equilibration of all parts of the lungs as well as psychological evaluation of a propensity to panic. The scuba instructor has in his hands the final prevention by teaching the dangers of breath-holding.

All of these things can happen when two precipitating factors occur:

1. Breath-holding ascent
2. Local air trapping

A breath-holding ascent occurs in association with panic, buddy-breathing, and acute laryngospasm from a breath of sea water. Local air trapping is the result of bronchospasm (asthma), mucous plugs (post-bronchitis), blebs (blisters on the surface of the lung), air-containing pulmonary cavities (as in scarring from TB), and very often no reason whatsoever.

Treatment
Treatment of these three entities varies from the simple bed rest, oxygen, and observation for the emphysema to immediate resuscitation while in transport and compression to 6 ATA for the arterial gas embolism. A chest tube is standard care for pneumothorax with a good neurological exam to rule out cerebral embolism.

Compression takes precedence over treatment of the pneumothorax. Frequently, attendants must also treat coexistent near-drowning, using an endotracheal tube, 100% oxygen, and IV fluids and dexamethasone.

Return to diving would be quite variable, depending upon the underlying condition, residual disability from the accident, the needs of the diver to dive, and a host of intangibles.

PULMONARY EMBOLISM (See also Deep Vein Thrombosis)
Pulmonary embolus is a blockage of an artery in the lungs by fat, air, tumor tissue, or blood clot. Pulmonary emboli are caused by clots from the venous circulation, from the right side of the heart, from tumors that have invaded the circulatory system, or from other sources such as amniotic fluid, air, fat, bone marrow, and foreign substances. Most are caused by deep vein thrombosis (DVT) of the lower extremities, and many resolve on their own. A pulmonary embolism affects as many as 5 out of 10,000 people in the U.S. each year, and sudden death can occur as a result of pulmonary embolism. The risk factors include prolonged bed rest or inactivity, oral contraceptive use, surgery, child birth, cancer, stroke, heart attack, heart surgery, and fractures of the hips or femur.

Some of the symptoms of a pulmonary embolus include sudden cough with bloody sputum, shortness of breath at rest or with exertion, splinting of ribs with breathing (i.e., bending over or holding the chest), fainting, dizziness, chest pain, sweating, anxiety, rapid breathing, and rapid heart rate (tachycardia).

Emergency treatment and hospitalization are necessary. Definitive treatment consists of dissolving the clot. Anticoagulant therapy is preventive by inhibiting further clot formation.

Thrombolytic therapy (clot-dissolving medication) includes streptokinase, urokinase, or TPA. Anticoagulation therapy (clot-preventing medication) consists of heparin by intravenous infusion initially, then oral Warfarin (Coumadin), or subcutaneous heparin may be started concurrently. Oxygen therapy is required to maintain normal oxygen concentrations until the acute injury to the lungs has resolved. There is a high death rate if left untreated.

Dangers to the diver are the result of the diminished functional lung capacity due to the loss of oxygenation from the blocked portion of the lung. This results in hypoxia and diminished physical capabilities. Should a new or further thrombosis occur while diving, there would be a diagnostic dilemma as to whether this were a diving injury or the embolus. In addition, diving while taking anticoagulants is thought to be dangerous because of the increased risk of hemorrhage from barotrauma to the sinuses, ears, and lungs, and possibly to spinal cord injury, should that occur with a decompression accident.

Diving may be resumed upon complete recovery from the effects of the embolus and cessation of anticoagulants. If there is a genetic predisposition for increased clotting, the person should be warned of the risks for air travel with prolonged periods of sitting with posterior leg compression as a cause of deep vein thrombosis (DVT). There is no evidence that diving *per se* causes DVT.

SMOKING

Most of the risks of smoking and diving are related to long term usage—the chronic obstructive pulmonary disease that smoking produces over many years. This obstruction is in the terminal airways and the emphysema (over-distension of lung tissue) that's caused can (and does) produce air-filled dilations that can markedly increase the chances of pulmonary barotrauma and arterial gas embolism. Smoking also causes an increase in bronchial mucous production with a concomitant paralysis of the cilia. Mucous plugs then become dangerous to the diver, setting the stage for air-filled sacs that lead to rupture upon ascent.

One other potential problem is the reduction in a smoker's oxygen saturation and increase in carbon dioxide retention. At depth, this could become a problem with the increased partial pressures of changing depths. There are few if any studies relating to CO (carbon monoxide) retention, but it might be a consideration in not smoking just before diving.

The effects of partial pressure on carbon monoxide concentration in recently inhaled cigarette smoke would be the same as if the carbon monoxide had come from some other source, such as the atmosphere or from oil lubricated compressors. However, carbon monoxide is immediately and quickly bound to the hemoglobin molecule, so very little of the gas is free in the blood stream.

Carbon monoxide binds with hemoglobin 220–290 times more efficiently than oxygen. The carbon monoxide level varies with the number of cigarettes you have already smoked that day, the length of time since your last cigarette, how the cigarette was smoked, and your level of activity on the day of the reading.

Typical end-of-day readings are as follows: 0–10 ppm of carbon monoxide for a non-smoker, 11–20 ppm of carbon monoxide for a light smoker, 21–100 ppm of carbon monoxide for a heavy smoker. To work out the approximate percentage of oxygen being replaced by carbon monoxide in your blood, divide your reading by six.

For example, 18 ppm of carbon monoxide divided by 6 = 3% of oxygen in your blood is being replaced by carbon monoxide. If you are a heavy smoker, up to 15% of your oxygen is possibly being replaced by carbon monoxide.

Most smokers also have nasal and sinus drainage problems. This markedly increases their chances of middle ear and sinus blocks and squeezes. There have been studies that have shown that stopping smoking prior to surgery actually increased the amount of mucous production for about a week. Taking this information to diving, one would have to say that if you are going to gain any benefit from stopping, then you need to have stopped at least one week in advance. If you can do this, then why not just stop forever?

The Nicotine Patch
The effects of nicotine on diving should not be any different with the patch than the effects of diving after smoking. The difference is the continued nicotine effect of the patch, compared to a smoker who dives after a nicotine load but also has a load of carbon monoxide with which to contend.

Pressure would have no effect as the drug is not in gaseous form. Another possibility is that the saltwater might increase the chance of a skin reaction to the patch—a side effect that already is fairly high.

TUBERCULOSIS, SARCOIDOSIS
Tuberculosis (TB) is a chronic bacterial infection. It is spread through the air and usually infects the lungs, although other organs are sometimes involved. Most persons that are infected with *Mycobacterium tuberculosis* harbor the bacterium without symptoms but many develop active TB disease. Each year, eight million people worldwide develop active TB and three million die.

Between two to eight weeks after being infected with *M. tuberculosis*, a person's immune system responds to the TB germ by walling off infected cells. From then on the body maintains a standoff with the infection, sometimes for years.

Most people undergo complete healing of their initial infection, and the bacteria eventually die off. A positive TB skin test, and old scars on a chest x-ray, may provide the only evidence of the infection.

However, it is this healing/walling off process that causes problems with divers. These tubercles and granulomas produce areas of lung collapse, terminal airway disease, and alveolar obstruction (air trapping and altered air flow with resultant increased risk for pulmonary barotraumas), "burst lung," pneumothorax, mediastinal and subcutaneous emphysema, and arterial gas embolism.

Allowing diving would depend upon the stage of the disease, extent of healing, presence or absence of air trapping (as evidenced by spiral CT scans or helium loop studies), and the physical conditioning of the diver.

Sarcoidosis is a systemic chronic granulomatous disease that commonly affects the lungs. It is similar to tuberculosis, with the main difference being the absence of granulomas. Pulmonary infiltrates would place the diver in jeopardy of pulmonary barotrauma. However, the illness has spontaneous remissions and diving can be allowed pending normal pulmonary studies.

UPPER RESPIRATORY INFECTION

Infections and allergies affecting the pharynx, tonsils, nose and throat, sinuses, and ears produce the most frequently seen problems facing all sports divers. The congestion associated with these maladies causes blockage of the air-containing sinuses and middle ears, leading to difficulties in clearing (equalizing) the air pressures in these structures. Damage is done to the linings of the sinuses and middle ears, resulting in more swelling, hemorrhage, and serum exudation. The ear drums are damaged or ruptured with possible hearing loss and the inner ears can be damaged due to strenuous attempts at clearing with use of the Valsalva maneuver, leading to round or oval window blowout and perilymph fistula with severe hearing and balance problems.

The diver should not dive while in the exudative phase of an upper respiratory infection and should wait until the runny nose and congestion are well cleared by antibiotics. Barotrauma can cause spread of localized infections into other nearby areas and into the lungs. Bacterial infections should have been treated and cleared by a physician to avoid these risks. Pseudoephedrine can be helpful with congestion, but there is always the risk that it might wear off during the dive and cause a reverse squeeze on ascent.

OTHER

AGE (THE "CHRONOLOGICALLY CHALLENGED" DIVER)

Recreational diving is, today, a mass phenomenon. It appeals to all ages and genders and the combination of availability of training and aggressive campaigning has extended its participants to the extremes of age.

However, even though our fetal life takes place in a liquid environment, once we take our first breath, water becomes deadly, and to return means to run the risk of drowning every time we do. To survive—let alone enjoy—the experience, we need certain intellectual and physical properties, some of which may be inconsistent with some stages of human development:

- The very young are still developing in body size, strength, and stamina. They lack some of the mental awareness and maturity, all of which are necessary to use the equipment effectively and to learn and apply the specialized procedures allowing us to outwit a watery grave.

- The very old may have lost strength, stamina, general health. They, too, may lack the physical and mental fitness required to survive under water.

Between these two extremes, however, age as such plays a less significant role. It is really a matter of state of health, level of fitness, mental maturity, and awareness that determines fitness. "Biological age" is more important than "chronological age."

The "Old" Diver

What is the relevance of aging to the diver? Well, the entire world population is aging. General state of health and life-expectancy in civilized areas are on the increase. Elders tend more and more to engage in physically challenging activities, frequently after retirement, involving extensive traveling and numerous sporting activities, some of them "extreme." Many divers in their 70s and 80s continue to dive, even to great depths, apparently with safety. It would therefore be wrong to apply age as the single determinant of diving fitness. There is no upper limit based purely on "chronological age." If the necessary physical and medical standards are met, there is no objective reason why an older individual should be precluded from diving. The question, however, is what are those standards? Several parameters are known to decrease with age: lung function, exercise tolerance, and hearing, to name but a few. What are the real issues?

Diving injury and accident statistics suggest that cardiac disease is the single most important precipitating cause of diving fatalities in divers over the age of 40. Accordingly, there is merit in defining cardiac fitness criteria. There are a number of asymptomatic conditions, like certain cancers, that may present with catastrophic bleeding or bowel obstruction, but these are probably no more likely to occur under water than a fatal marine life injury! Let us briefly consider the big issues.

Ischemic Heart Disease

Although coronary artery disease may start at an early age, it usually becomes apparent when the coronary circulation can no longer ensure sufficient blood flow in response to an increased work load. This only happens once the coronary arteries are 75% occluded. With maximal exercise the demand for blood flow to the heart also peaks and a mismatch between supply and demand may become evident. This may be asymptomatic or result in pain (i.e., angina), a disturbance in electrical activity (i.e., erratic beating or ventricular fibrillation) or severe breathlessness due to accumulation of fluid in the lung as the heart fails (i.e., pulmonary edema).

Ventricular fibrillation can result in sudden death. Stress and cold usually are aggravating factors, worsening the lack of blood to the heart muscles (myocardial ischemia) by making the coronaries contract further.

Studies at rest may not demonstrate a problem and a diver may remain asymptomatic even with moderate exercise. Maximal exercise testing with electrocardiographic and blood pressure monitoring (EKG stress test) are required to identify coronary risk in divers over 40. These tests, while not infallible, are non-invasive and relevant to diving, and recommended for the older diver.

Hypertension

Hypertension, or high blood pressure, is one of the most common medical conditions seen today in the diving and general adult population. Normal blood pressure is generally accepted to be a systolic pressure below 120 and a

205

diastolic pressure below 80 mm Hg, depending on age. Basically, two different sets of complications face a person with hypertension, short-term and long-term. Short-term complications are generally due to extremely high blood pressure. The most significant is the risk of a stroke due to rupture of blood vessels in the brain (called a cerebrovascular accident). Long-term detrimental effects are more common. They include coronary artery disease, kidney disease, congestive heart failure, eye problems, and cerebrovascular disease. As long as the individual's blood pressure is under control, the main concerns should be the side effects of medication(s) and evidence of end-organ damage. Divers who have demonstrated adequate control of blood pressure with no significant decrease in performance in the water due to the side effects of drugs should be able to dive safely. Regular physical examinations and appropriate screening for the long-term consequences of hypertension such as coronary artery disease are necessary. Mild hypertension may be controlled with diet and exercise. However, medication is often necessary. Any diver with long-standing high blood pressure should be monitored for secondary effects on the heart and kidneys.

Many drugs are used to treat hypertension, with varying side effects. Some individuals need to change medications when a particular drug appears to be, or becomes, ineffective. Others might require more than one drug to keep the blood pressure under control. Classes of drugs known as beta-blockers tend to cause a decrease in maximum exercise tolerance and may also have some effect on the airways. ACE (angiotension converting enzyme) inhibitors or the newer ACE-receptor inhibitors are the preferred class of drugs for treating hypertensive divers. A persistent cough is a possible side effect.

Calcium channel blockers are another choice, but lightheadedness when going from a sitting or supine position to standing may be a significant side effect.

Diuretics (drugs to reduce body water by increased urination) are also frequently used to treat hypertension. This requires careful attention to hydration and electrolyte status and is not the ideal choice for divers.

In general, most anti-hypertensive medications are compatible with diving as long as the side effects experienced by the diver are minimal and their performance in the water is not significantly compromised.

Increased Airway Resistance
The work of breathing is normally increased while scuba diving due to the increased gas density, the reduction of lung volumes, and bronchial calibre due to hydrostatic pressure effects and the additional respiratory resistance from breathing through a regulator.

Smoking can add to this if complicated by any degree of chronic bronchitis and emphysema (chronic destruction of lung tissue), even without recognized dysfunction. These phenomena and alterations, which are more frequent and evident with increasing age, especially in smokers, increase the risk of air trapping, lung barotraumas, and air embolism. Periodic chest x-rays and regular spirometric assessments (lung function test) will assist in identifying individuals at risk, although, as with cardio-vascular assessments, a negative result is not an absolute guarantee of perfect lung function. It may not be sufficient to identify local lung areas with problems of increased airway resistance.

Physical Condition and Stamina
Aging implies a reduced agility and capacity to deal with exercise, even if this is largely the consequence of the vicious circle: "sedentary life—lack of exercise— reduced exercise capacity – sedentary life." Regular exercise will be beneficial for the elderly in all respects, and will also improve performance and safety during diving. There is no logical reason why a healthy and reasonably fit individual cannot keep diving even in his or her 80s!

Children and Diving
The issue of children and diving is an emotional one, with little significant scientific evidence. Currently the American scuba training agencies have agreed on age limits of 8–12 years, while the new junior program of CMAS sets the minimum age limit at eight years. Medically speaking, there have been several authors pointing to the potential risk of bubbles impairing bone growth if the growth cartilage is affected. This is the reason for the relatively strict depth limits imposed by CMAS (< 30 fsw/10 msw). Although this particular issue has never been scientifically demonstrated, and it is very unlikely that it will ever be so, the concern is significant enough to curb any debate!

Some diving medicine experts have suggested body size limits (145 cm and 40 kg approximately), but this would preclude some small frame adults. As a consequence, it also has been suggested that a reasonable limit could be by reaching 90% of the estimated growth for that person, but even this is subject to interpretation. The major concern, and there is almost universal consensus about this even amongst the proponents of younger aged diving, relates to emotional maturity and the possibility of emotional breakdown and panic in stressful conditions. There are also concerns about parental pressure forcing children into the sport prematurely and whether or not a child is able to understand and accept the risks related to the activity.

Medical Concerns

- Children are not just small-frame adults. They function differently, think differently, act (and react) differently
- Children's small frame and limited strength may be incompatible with diving gear, which is essentially designed for adults, both for size and weight, and for the modality of use
- The ability to equalize the middle ear and the sinuses is often impaired in children due to the smaller ear anatomy. As a result barotrauma is more frequent in children than in adults
- In children, the proportions between body surface, mass, and metabolic rate predispose them to rapid "chilling"
- Children dehydrate faster than adults, especially when sweating
- Children are frequently subject to juvenile asthma and to juvenile cerebral irritation conditions (juvenile seizures)
- The long bones of children have open epiphyses (growth cartilage) and these are theoretically susceptible to damage due to the local development of decompression gas bubbles
- Children may not have reached sufficient mental maturation to cope with stress situations. Their risk perception may be inadequate, as well as their capacity for risk assessment and emergency management decisions. In such circumstances the behavior of children is frequently (if not always) unpredictable, which may result in uncontrolled ascent, pulmonary barotraumas, and drowning

In conclusion, many diving physicians, as well as diving instructors, believe that children younger than eight (minimum)—twelve (preferable)—years should not scuba dive for psychological rather than physical reasons.

If the ultimate decision is for a child to be trained, diving instructors who are familiar with the education of children report that the primary difference is not so much the skills that are taught, but in the approach to the rules and how to respect them. This is better achieved in a "play mode." For children, "play" behavior is frequently tough, strict, and unforgiving (complete with rewards and punishment). Children apply such behavior to themselves, and this may help overcome immature or oppositional behavior. This is a matter where there is no absolute truth, and where common sense and extreme caution should always apply.

ALCOHOL

Alcohol and diving are not compatible. The analogy to the effects of alcohol and the ability to drive a vehicle is pertinent. In addition, it is reputed that every 50 feet dived on compressed air is equivalent also to the effects of one unit of alcohol (traditionally "one martini") due to nitrogen narcosis. Nitrogen narcosis therefore will be enhanced by drinking alcohol, and, due to the accompanying dehydration, there may also be an increased risk of decompression sickness.

Although the diver may not feel impaired after a few drinks, studies indicate decrements in reaction time, concentration, ability to process information, judgment, and psychomotor ability, and this can lead to diving accidents. It takes time for alcohol to be metabolized and its effects to wear off. Yet it is not uncommon for some divers to believe that drinking beer rather than hard liquor is perfectly safe before a dive, during the surface interval, and after surfacing. Some have shown significantly degraded performance at blood alcohol levels of only 0.04%, or about half the levels commonly restricting driving of 0.08%. It was reported that a 180 lb (82 kg) man who drank two pints (375 mL) of beer in one hour on an empty stomach is at significantly greater risk of injury. For these reasons, the restrictions of alcohol use when driving apply equally to diving.

DIABETES

Historically, the diving medicine community has maintained a very conservative position on diabetes, primarily due to concerns about glucose-related loss of consciousness and disease-related impairment of fitness and exercise capacity. In fact, until recently, the nearly universal approach to diabetes has been to ban all persons with insulin-requiring forms of diabetes mellitus (IRDM) from diving. In addition, all types of diabetes in which there is some loss of physical fitness or evidence of damage to body organs were considered contraindications to diving. Dissent from this view has grown over the last 20 years. Recognizing that a substantial number of divers are diving successfully with diabetes—either openly or surreptitiously—many have felt that the time has come to acknowledge this fact and reexamine the position concerning diabetes and diving. The data available at this time support the position that at least some individuals with diabetes might reasonably be allowed to dive.

Two key factors must be understood: (1) At the DAN workshop only recreational diving was considered.[18] Issues concerning professional diving require future, separate deliberations; and (2) any general recommendations must be seen as guidelines that should be individualized and tailored to the specific needs and the condition of the individual in question.

It is also realized that other appropriate and justifiable procedures may exist and that interest groups must have the flexibility to use the guidelines that best serve the needs of the divers in question. The recommendations of the DAN/UHMS workshop are summarized in Table 3.

---

18. A workshop, jointly sponsored by the Undersea and Hyperbaric Medical Society (UHMS) and the Divers Alert Network (DAN), was held on June 19th, 2005 in Las Vegas, Nevada, USA, to review the existing data and determine if a consensus standard could be developed to address diabetes and recreational diving. Approximately 50 individuals from a range of nations, mostly clinicians and researchers, participated in the discussions.

Table 3. Guidelines for Recreational Diving with Diabetes—Summary Form

Selection and Surveillance

- Age ≥18 years (≥16 years if in special training program)
- Delay diving after start/change in medication
  - 3 months with oral hypoglycemic agents (OHA)
  - 1 year after initiation of insulin therapy
- No episodes of hypoglycemia or hyperglycemia requiring intervention from a third party for at least one year
- No history of hypoglycemia unawareness
- HbA_{1c} ≤9% no more than one month prior to initial assessment and at each annual review
  - values >9% indicate the need for further evaluation and possible modification of therapy
- No significant secondary complications from diabetes
- Physician/diabetologist should carry out annual review and determine that diver has good understanding of disease and effect of exercise
  - in consultation with an expert in diving medicine, as required
- Evaluation for silent ischemia for candidates >40 years of age
  - after initial evaluation, periodic surveillance for silent ischemia can be in accordance with accepted local/national guidelines for the evaluation of diabetes
- Candidate documents intent to follow protocol for divers with diabetes and to cease diving and seek medical review for any adverse events during diving possibly related to diabetes

Scope of Diving

- Diving should be planned to avoid
  - depths > 100 fsw (30 msw)
  - durations > 60 min
  - compulsory decompression stops
  - overhead environments (e.g., cave, wreck penetration)
  - situations that may exacerbate hypoglycemia (e.g., prolonged cold and arduous dives)
- Dive buddy/leader informed of diver's condition and steps to follow in case of problem
- Dive buddy should not have diabetes

Glucose Management on the Day of Diving

- General self-assessment of fitness to dive
- Blood glucose (BG)≥150 mg·dL⁻¹ (8.3 mmol·L⁻¹), stable or rising, before entering the water
  - complete a minimum of three pre-dive BG tests to evaluate trends
    - 60 min, 30 min, and immediately prior to diving
- Delay dive if BG
  - <150 mg·dL⁻¹ (8.3 mmol·L⁻¹)
  - >300 mg·dL⁻¹ (16.7 mmol·L⁻¹)
- Rescue medications
  - carry readily accessible oral glucose during all dives
  - have parenteral glucagon available at the surface
- If hypoglycemia noticed underwater, the diver should surface (with buddy), establish positive bouyancy, ingest glucose, and leave the water
- Check blood sugar frequently for 12–15 hours after diving
- Ensure adequate hydration on days of diving
- Log all dives (include BG test results and all information pertinent to diabetes management)

These guidelines are preliminary and obviously represent a work in progress. As experience is gained, some of them may be expanded or modified. (See Dear et al., 2005.)

DRUGS AND DIVING

Of all the questions diving physicians get, those related to the use of therapeutic drugs are the most common. In a way this is fortunate because divers:

- Are correctly concerned about the possible risks of diving while on medication, as this indicates an illness or health problem
- Are not necessarily able to evaluate the risks related to the drug or—often more importantly—the reason for taking it

As a rule of thumb, a prescription drug (i.e., drugs requiring an assessment and prescription by a physician) should also prompt assessment by a diving physician. In particular, priority attention should be given to the condition being treated and the effects and side-effects of the drug. Any of these may be contraindications to diving.

Looking at drugs on their own—that is, without consideration for the physical condition or ailment for which they have been prescribed—there are relatively few that would disqualify someone from diving. The predominant concerns relate to medication affecting mental processes and alertness (e.g., sedatives, antidepressants, anti-motion sickness medications, certain antihistamine drugs, certain anti-malaria drugs like mefloquine, anti-anxiety medication, etc.) as well as those that affect the individual's response to exercise (e.g., beta blockers).

Fitness to dive should be individualized for prescription medication. If in doubt, obtain expert advice through DAN or a diving physician. Self-medication with over-the-counter (OTC) non-prescription drugs is not without risk either.[19]

OTCs are medications classified as being safe for the short-term treatment of ailments that can be self-diagnosed. Many products combine two or more active agents to relieve a variety of simultaneous symptoms (as is frequently the case with cold and allergy medications) where one may be safe and the other not.

For those averse to regular medicines, homeopathic and herbal remedies may appear more attractive. However, these also have side-effects that should be considered.

---

19. Individuals react differently to medication. When trying a new drug, remember to first test it in an environment where undesired side effects would not be a problem. Only after excluding undesirable effects may it be assumed to be relatively safe to use while diving. This is particularly true for sedating drugs or those advising against operating dangerous machinery or driving while using them. This would apply equally to scuba diving which is also, in a sense, operating potentially dangerous machinery.

The most commonly used OTCs with respect to recreational divers are:

- Antihistamines
- Decongestants
- Anti-motion sickness preparations
- Analgesics and anti-inflammatory drugs

Antihistamines(Allergies, Allergic Rhinitis, Hay Fever, etc.)
Between 10% and 15% of the world population is sensitized to allergens present in the air, such as dust, pollen, and molds. The result is an "allergic response" manifesting itself as allergies affecting the nose and eyes (allergic rhinitis, conjunctivitis), or as seasonal allergies and hay fever, with possible occasional asthma-like symptoms, largely due to the release of a substance called histamine.[20]

Antihistamines act by blocking the effects of histamine. Although they can modify an allergic response, they frequently cause side effects. These may include drowsiness and sedation, dry mouth, blurred vision, urinary retention, and increased heart rate.

Drowsiness is particularly important for divers. It is a consequence of the effects of the drug on the central nervous system and the brain and can be enhanced by nitrogen narcosis. A drowsy diver is at greater risk of accident and injury.

Another one of the actions of antihistamines is to reduce secretions. Accordingly, dry mouth can be an undesired side effect, which can become particularly troublesome and disturbing when breathing dry air from a scuba regulator. They also cause thickening of mucus and are associated with reverse-block of the ears and sinuses. Correct pre-dive and inter-dive hydration (drinking water and non-alcoholic fluids before and between dives) can be of help, and saline mist sprays can help to tolerate possible side effects of nasal dryness.

---

20. Two of the major players in allergic reactions are "mast cells" and "eosinophils." These specialized white blood cells store "histamine" and various other mediators associated with the allergic and asthmatic responses. Mast cells abound in the skin, the bronchial tree of the lungs, and the intestines. During an allergic response, they release histamine and other active substances, which generate the allergic symptoms causing distress to so many. These may include congestion of the nasal mucosa with a "runny" nose, sneezing, itchiness, tearing from the eyes, cough, etc. Much of the treatment for allergies is aimed at stabilizing or reducing the number of mast cells and eosinophils.

New Generation Antihistamines

These drugs, such as loratidine (Claritin®), cetirizine (Zyrtec®) and fexofenadine (Allegra®), have very limited sedating properties and are considered relatively safe even when driving or maneuvering machines. As a (very general) rule of thumb, drugs that are safe for driving are usually safe for diving also—provided they are well tolerated. Other safe anti-allergy medication includes cromolyn sodium (Nasalcrom), which is available as an OTC product in some countries. Cromolyn sodium prevents the release of histamine. It is useful for certain types of seasonal rhinitis, sinusitis, and asthma when taken in advance.

Decongestants

Congestion of the membranes of the nose, throat, and sinuses is a common complication of allergies, colds, upper respiratory tract infections, and irritations. This can well ruin a dive or a diving holiday, since it may interfere with equalization of the middle ear and the sinuses, with resulting barotrauma.

The drugs used to treat congestion are usually related to epinephrine (also called adrenaline), a vasoconstrictive agent, i.e., it causes contraction and shrinking of blood vessels with a reduction in swelling of the mucosa—decongestion. Importantly, just like adrenaline, these drugs may cause elevations in heart rate and blood pressure. Their duration of action is usually short—3 to 5 hours—and this may wear off during a dive, with a possible rebound effect resulting in a reverse-block on ascent. Pseudoephedrine (Sudafed®) is a common ingredient in these OTC decongestants.

Some generalized side effects of these adrenaline-like drugs may be avoided by using topical sprays like Afrin®. However, the ingredients are still related to adrenaline, and side-effects may occur with overdosing. Some of these sprays are available in so-called slow-release or "retard" form, with an extended duration of action (8–12 hours).

None of these drugs should be used for prolonged periods (i.e., not more than 3–5 days at a time). Prolonged use frequently results in resistance to the effect of the drug and rebound congestion. Saline mist sprays may be an alternative and side-effect-free option. They can be used regularly and do not generate adaptation and failure of effect.

Anti-Motion Sickness Preparations (See Vomiting)

"Prevention is better than cure" holds true particularly for motion sickness. Once it occurs it is most resistant to treatment and it is better prevented before embarking on a boat trip.

Over the counter anti-emetics (anti-nausea and vomiting drugs) belong to the family of the antihistamines discussed earlier. However, the same properties that make them effective against nausea also make them sedating. An effective alternative to oral anti-motion sickness drugs is the scopolamine patch. The patch must be applied at least four hours prior to clean, thin skin, such as behind the ear. Immediately wash the hands to avoid contaminating the eye, which will result in light sensitivity and blurred vision as the pupil dilates. Scopolamine has the potential for serious side-effects, and, although uncommon, these should be recognized.[21]

Analgesics And Anti-Inflammatory Agents
Over the counter pain relievers generally belong to the following three categories: acetaminophen, salicylates (such as aspirin) and non-steroidal anti-inflammatory drugs (NSAIDs). They are all active against inflammation. Salycilates and NSAIDs inhibit the production of one of the chemicals that promote inflammation called prostaglandins, thereby relieving pain and reducing swelling. Acetaminophen can be also useful as a pain-reliever, but is not generally as effective in reducing inflammation as the other drugs.

Prostaglandins are also involved in protecting the stomach against ulceration, and the use of these inhibiting drugs may therefore have gastrointestinal ulceration as a result. Very high doses of aspirin can cause tinnitus (ringing ears) and may cause serious bleeding of the stomach.

More important than the medication is the reason for taking them. Often this is a contraindication to diving or enough reason to abort that specific dive.

Any injury, especially if painful and irrespective of medication, can affect independence under water. Furthermore, it may obscure or confuse the diagnosis of decompression sickness and interfere with the effects of nitrogen narcosis.

---

21. A recommendation by the US Navy Experimental Diving Unit in this respect is "to place the patch and wear it 24 hours on dry land and then be interviewed by...[a diving physician or other competent person]... to ensure there were no undesirable side effects before diving. The patch has then to be placed four hours before leaving shore, but once in place, it can be worn even while diving." One problem with the patch is that it may fall off without being noticed until motion sickness develops. After a specific controlled study, the US Navy concluded that modest hyperbaric exposures (i.e., recreational diving) would not increase the probability of side effects or adversely affect performance within the normal scuba diving depth range. However, it remains a prescription drug and should be tested on dry land for at least 24 hours before diving, and then only if no side effects occurred. Curiously, scopolamine can sometimes cause dilatation of the pupil (i.e., midriasis) of the eye, either because of absorption through the skin or by rubbing the eye with contaminated fingers. The midriasis is generally unilateral and can cause much anxiety in medical or paramedical circles where a unilateral dilated pupil is considered evidence of serious brain disease. It is therefore bound to prompt unnecessary emergency actions unless suspected. In an individual who is otherwise well but happens to have a unilateral midriasis, it is wise to question about or check for the presence of a scopolamine patch. If this is the cause, the patch should be removed until the pupil has recovered and it may then be applied to the other side of the head, usually behind the ear. If the problem reoccurs, further use should be abandoned.

In Summary:

Before using any drug during any dive:

- Test it beforehand on dry land and under controlled conditions
- Be assured that it does not cause undesired and potentially dangerous side effects
- Talk to your doctor about it, consult a diving medicine specialist, or ask Divers Alert Network (DAN), particularly if it induces any level of sedation or even minor drowsiness.

Remember that no active drug is totally innocuous, even if it is marketed as an OTC. In general, "drugs and diving don't mix." Missing a day's diving is better than spoiling an entire trip or putting yourself and your buddy at risk.

EXERCISE

Today everybody is advised to exercise in order to maintain vigorous health and many have a very active daily exercise program. However, there are concerns that exercise may increase the risk for decompression sickness, so how should divers balance these two issues: fitness maintenance vs. risk of decompression sickness?

Pre-dive Exercise

It is generally advised that you should wait six hours after exercising before diving. Exercise is believed to produce micronuclei (i.e., possibly extremely small bubbles) due to the shearing of tissues and agitation of blood related to vigorous movement. Micronuclei may grow into bubbles or serve as seeding agents, facilitating the production of bubbles. Decompression sickness (DCS) appears to be related to the presence of these micronuclei, so the presence of a greater number may increase the risk. Fortunately, micronuclei tend to disappear with time, and nearly 98% will be gone within six hours—hence the recommendation. Good advice also is not to be so vigorous and cut down the amount of exercise. Recently, there has been a very interesting preliminary research finding that exercise 24 hours before diving may actually help to prevent DCS. So it would appear that a wait of 6 to 24 hours is helpful and not likely to increase sensitivity to DCS. Attention should also be paid to hydration, as one does not want to start a dive dehydrated.

Post-dive Exercise

Again there is little definitive data. Exercise after diving has two potential complications:

- It may release extra gas trapped in muscles or elsewhere as exercise increases the blood flow. This may be sufficient to tip the scales and generate bubbles of sufficient size and quantity to cause DCS.

215

- It may also possibly increase the generation of micronuclei, which may again grow into bubbles from the retained gas still in the tissues.

So how long should you wait? Again, it is considered that waiting six 60-minute halftimes, i.e., six hours, should permit sufficient off-gassing so that any nuclei are unlikely to be a problem, and it may be advisable to moderate the degree of exercise even then.

Exercise While Diving
There are experimental data to support the contention that exercise during the descent or bottom phases of a dive may increase the incidence of DCS, possibly due to an increase in inert gas absorption. Thus, the underwater photographer who waits patiently for that great picture is less likely to get DCS than the diver who fins strongly everywhere throughout the dive. So keep exertion to the minimum required.

Exercise on Ascent
Again, there is good research data to support that light exercise during ascent or stop phases can decrease the risk of DCS by as much as 30%. It is considered that this is due to accelerating the removal of the gas responsible for DCS before experiencing a reduction in pressure that would permit the evolution of bubbles. So instead of hanging on the bar or buoy-line at the safety stop, fin gently around the bar or line for the duration of the stop and then make a slow leisurely return to the surface rather than a rapid swim to the ladder over the last 15–20 ft.

Note: higher intensity exercise may increase the risk of DCS by promoting micronuclei or bubble formation. Exercise during ascent or stop phases is definitely not a case of more is better!

FEMALE DIVERS
The equality of the sexes has recently been extended to diving. Today, nearly 30% of recreational divers are female. This has prompted greater interest and research on issues of female health and well-being in relation to diving.

The overall answer is that most differences are minor and of no real consequence or cause for concern. Therefore, the general guidelines of fitness to dive for men apply also to women.

Decompression Sickness
It was proposed in the past that since women in general have more adipose tissue, they may be at greater risk for decompression sickness (DCS). However, the results of altitude decompression have, at worst, suggested a 3%–4% increased risk for women. These results have not been confirmed in divers, and the issue remains controversial and inconclusive.

Breast Implants
Studies have been done exposing silicone, saline, and silicone/saline filled implants to increased pressures in a hyperbaric chamber. There was only a 1%–4% increase in size with decompression, no ruptures, and only a few small bubbles which disappeared with time. Research was not done with implants in situ (i.e., women with breast implants in place) and it is unlikely that inert gas uptake would be similar in implanted breasts. There have been no reports of any problems from the many recreational women divers diving today with breast implants. In summary, this appears to be a non-issue.

Pregnancy
Although there is no clear evidence of increased risk to the expectant mother or a greater number of birth defects in the children of diving mothers, the potential for harm does exist. There are differences in inert gas uptake so that the fetus is probably at greater risk. Accordingly, it is general medical advice that pregnant women should not dive. If a problem were to occur with the child after birth, diving could be blamed and the guilt would be significant. However, the risk is unverified and, should a woman be found to have been pregnant while diving, it is unnecessary to consider terminating the pregnancy.

Menstruation
There is conflicting evidence about the effect of oral contraceptives and decompression sickness. Some suggest an elevated risk, particularly while menstruating, while others suggest a reduced risk. The usual sage advice is to take it easy. This advice is particularly relevant to women who exhibit severe premenstrual symptoms. The suggestion that menstruation may provoke shark attacks is completely unfounded. Tampons are also safe for diving and do not cause "womb squeeze."

Breast Feeding
Although nitrogen or other gases may be absorbed by the body, including the breasts, it is relatively quickly given off on surfacing. There is no evidence that diving has any effect on breast tissue or breast milk.

Return to Diving After Giving Birth
The issue here is that the woman should have returned to her normal physical strength. After a normal delivery, it is wise to allow three to four weeks to allow for any pregnancy complications and post-delivery fatigue. After a cesarean delivery, it is wise to wait about eight weeks for wound healing and recovery of muscle strength and to enroll in an exercise conditioning program before resuming diving.

Breast Surgery, Hysterectomy, and Ovarian Tumors
Any surgery requires time to allow for wound healing and a return to normal strength and conditioning before having to deal with heavy diving equipment or heavy exercise. It is conventional wisdom to allow six to eight weeks after any surgery for recovery and the avoidance of infection. In the case of cancer requiring chemotherapy or irradiation, these should be considered independently. The deleterious effects (such as weakness, vomiting, etc.) of these treatments may preclude diving until several weeks after completion.

HANDICAPPED SCUBA DIVERS
It is very possible for divers with disabilities such as paralysis or even blindness to dive. However, specialized training, certification, and diving techniques are required. There are many associations and dive clubs dedicated to handicapped divers throughout the world.

The Handicapped Scuba Association (HSA), formed in the early 1980s in the USA, is comprised of over 3,000 underwater educators, handicapped divers, and members in 40 countries worldwide. Contact can be made for further advice from:

a. Handicapped Scuba Association
   1104 El Parado
   San Clemente, CA 92672-4637
   Telephone: 714-498-6128

b. National Instructors Association for Divers with Disabilities (NIADD)
   P.O. Box 112223
   Campbell, CA 95011-2223
   Telephone: 408-379-6536

c. An excellent book on this subject is available through Best Publishing
   Company titled *A Guide for Teaching Scuba to Diver's with Special Needs*
   www.bestpub.com
   Telephone: 800-468-1055

SEA SICKNESS
(See Motion Sickness – Diving Nuisances, Vomiting)

PART FOUR

REFERENCES

REFERENCES

Association of Diving Contractors. *ADC Consensus Standards for Commercial Diving Operations*. Association of Diving Contractors, Houston, TX.

Balestra, C, P Germonprè, A Marroni. 2003. Blood glucose variations in a diabetic diver using vigorous self-assessment and underwater intake. *DAN Europe Research Report 3-2003*. DAN Europe Foundation, Roseto Italy. www.daneurope.org, medical@daneurope.org

Bennett, PB, and DH Elliott, eds. 1993. *The Physiology and Medicine of Diving*, 4th edition. London, New York: Saunders.

Bove, A. 1995. Diabetics and diving. *SPUMS J* ; 26(2):106–7.

Bove, AA. 1996. Medical aspects of sport diving. *Med Sci Sports Exerc*; 28(5): 591–595.

Bove, AA. 2003. Fitness to dive. In Bennett and Elliott's *Physiology and Medicine of Diving*, 5th edition, pp 700-717. AO Brubakk and TS Neuman, eds. London, New York: Saunders.

Bove, AA. 2004. Bove and Davis, *Diving Medicine*. Philadelphia: Saunders.

Broome, JR, GA McNamee, AJ Dutka. 1994. Physical conditioning reduces the incidence of neurological DCI in pigs. *Undersea Hyperbar Med*; 21(suppl): 69.

Brown, M, J Jones, J Krohmer. 1992. Pseudoephedrine for the prevention of barotitis media: a controlled clinical trial in underwater divers. *Ann Em Med*; 21(7):849–52.

Butler, FK. 1995. Diving and hyperbaric ophthalmology. *Survey of Ophthalmology* 39:347–366.

Camporesi, EM. 1996. Diving and pregnancy. *Seminars in perinatology*, 20:292–302.

Carturan, D, A Boussuges, H Burnet, J Fondarai, B Gardette. 1999. Circulating venous bubbles in recreational diving: Relationships with age, weight, maximal oxygen uptake, and body fat percentage. *Int J Sports Med*; 20(6): 410–414.

Caruso, J, A Bove, D Uguccioni, J Ellis, J Dovenbarger, P Bennett. 2001. Recreational diving deaths associated with cardiovascular disease: Epidemiology and recommendations for pre-participation screening. *Undersea Hyper Med*; 28(sup):75–76.

Caruso, JL, DM Uguccioni, JA Dovenbarger, PB Bennett. 1997. Fatalities related to cardiovascular disease in the recreational diving population. *Undersea Hyperbar Med*; 24(suppl): 26.

Colvard, D, L Colvard. Examination of panic in 12,149 recreational scuba divers. 3725 National Dr #228, Raleigh, NC 27612.

Cooper, KH. 1977. *The Aerobics Way*. New York: Bantam Books.

Davis, JC. 1986. *Medical Examination of Scuba Divers*, Second Edition. San Antonio: Medical Seminars Inc.

Davis, M. 1987. Scopoderm and Diver Performance. *SPUMS J*; 17(1):23–24.

Dear G, NW Pollack, DM Uguccioni. 2005. Diabetes and recreational diving: Guidelines for the future. *Proceedings of the UHMS/DAN 2005 June 19 Workshop*. Durham, NC: Divers Alert Network.

Dembert, M, J Keith. 1986. Evaluating the potential pediatric scuba diver. *Am J Dis Child*; 140:1135–41.

Divers Alert Network. 1998–2003. Reports on decompression illness and diving fatalities. Multiple editions.

Dujic, Z, D Duplancic, I Marinovic-Terzic, D Bakovic, V Ivancev, Z Valic, D Eterovic, NM Petri, U Wisloff, AO Brubakk. 2004. Aerobic exercise before diving reduces venous gas bubble formation in humans. *J Physiol*; 555(3):637–642.

Edge, C. UK Sports Diving Medical Committee: Diving and diabetes. http://www.cru.uea.ac.uk/ukdiving/medicine/diabetes.htm

Edmonds, C. 1996. Scuba kids. *SPUMS J*; 26(3):154–57.

Elliott, DH, ed. 1994. Medical assessment of fitness to dive. *Proceedings International Conference, Edinburgh*. Flagstaff, AZ: Best Publishing Co.

Elliott, D, ed. 1995. Medical assessment of fitness to dive. *Biomedical Seminars*. Ewell, Surrey, England. ISBN 0-9525162.

Elliott, DH. 1996. Are asthmatics fit to dive? *Undersea and Hyperbaric Medical Society*, Kensington, Maryland.

Fife, WF, ed. 1987. Women in diving. *Proceedings 35th Undersea and Hyperbaric Medical Society Workshop*, Bethesda, MD. UHMS Publication No. 7 (WS-WD).

Francis, K, J Brasher. 1992. A height-adjusted step test for predicting maximal oxygen consumption in males. *J Sports Med Phys Fitness*; 32(3): 282–287.

Germonprè, P. 2000. Children and diving. Personal communication.

Germonpre, P, P Denoble, P Unger. 1998. Patent foramen ovale and decompression sickness in sports divers. *J Appl Physiol;* 84:1622–1626.

Harrison, JL. 1992. Drugs and diving. *Journal Florida Medical Assoc*. 79:165–167.

Health Canada. http://www.hc-sc.gc.ca.

Hickey, DD. 1984. Outline of medical standards for divers. *Undersea Biomed Res;* 11:407–432.

Hyatt, W and R Duncan, eds. 2003. *The DAN Guide to Dive Medical Frequently Asked Questions (FAQs)*. Durham, NC: Divers Alert Network.

Jackson, AS, SN Blair, MT Mahar, LT Wier, RM Ross, JE Stuteville. 1990. Prediction of functional aerobic capacity without exercise testing. *Med Sci Sports Exerc*; 22(6):863–870.

Kline, GM, JP Porcari, R Hintermeister, PS Freedson, A Ward, RF McCarron, J Ross, JM Rippe. 1987. Estimation of $VO_{2\,max}$ from a one mile track walk, gender, age, and body weight. *Med Sci Sports Exerc*; 19(3):253–259.

Kroos, B. 1997. Diving and drugs. *Immersed*; 2(4):15–20.

Levano, B. 1999. Taking drugs when you dive? *Alert Diver* Jan/Feb; 28–33.

Linaweaver, PG and J Vorosmarti. 1987. Fitness to dive. *Proceedings 34th Undersea and Hyperbaric Medicine Society Workshop*. Bethesda, MD. UHMS Publication No. 70 (WS-FD).

Marti, B, H Howald. 1990. Long-term effects of physical training on aerobic capacity: Controlled study of former elite athletes. *J Appl Physiol*; 69(4):1451–1459.

Martin, L. 1996. Smoking and diving—Is it really dangerous? *Skin Diver Magazine*, May:22.

McArdle, WD, FI Katch, GS Pechar, et al. 1972. Reliability and inter-relationships between maximal oxygen intake, physical work capacity, and step-test scores in college women. *Med Sci Sports*; 4:182–186.

Mebane, GY and NK McIver. 1993. Fitness to dive. In *The Physiology and Medicine of Diving*, 4th edition, pp 53–76. PB Bennett and DH Elliott, eds. London, New York: Saunders.

Millington, BJ. 1985. Physical standards for scuba divers. *Journal American Board of Family Practice*. 1:194–200.

Moon, RE, EM Camporesi, and JA Kisslo. 1989. Patent foramen ovale and decompression sickness in divers. *Lancet* I: 513–514.

Morgan, WP. 1995. Anxiety and panic in recreational scuba divers. *Sports Medicine* 20:398–421.

Neuman, TS, AA Bove, and RD Connor. 1994. Asthma and diving. *Ann Allergy* 73:344–350.

Neuman, TS and AO Brubakk. 2003. Bennett and Elliott's *Physiology and Medicine of Diving*. 5th edition. London, New York: Saunders.

Nord, D. 1996. Over the counter drugs and diving. *Alert Diver* May/June: 39–42.

Park, YH, J Iwamoto, F Tajima, K Miki, YS Park, K Shiraki. 1988. Effect of pressure on thermal insulation in humans wearing wet-suits. *J Appl Physiol*; 64: 1916–1922.

Parker, J. 2002. *The Sports Diving Medical*, Second Edition. Melbourne, AU: JL Publications. ABN 39059509474.

Paton, S. 1996. Fitness and the older diver. *SPUMS J*; 26(4):266–72.

Physical activity and health: A report of the surgeon general. http://www.cdc.gov/nccdphp/sgr/sgr.htm.

Rehman, H. 1999. Age and the cardiovascular system. *Hosp Med*; 60(9):645–49.

Ronning, P, G Bolstad. 1998. Does physical fitness influence the rate of nitrogen elimination in man? *XXIV Annual Meeting of the EUBS.* 117. Stockholm, Sweden.

Rosen, MJ, JD Sorkin, AP Goldberg, JM Hagberg, LI Katzel. 1998. Predictors of age-associated decline in maximal aerobic capacity: A comparison of four statistical models. *J Appl Physiol*; 84(6): 2163–2170.

Rudge, FW. 1990. Relationship of menstrual history to altitude chamber decompression sickness. *Aviation, Space, and Environmental Medicine.* July:657–659.

Taylor, MB. 1997. Women in diving. In *Diving Medicine.* AA Bove, ed. p 89–107. Philadelphia: Saunders.

Uguccioni, D, J Dovenbarger. 1996. The diabetes question. *Alert Diver* Jan/Feb:21–23.

Vann, RD, P Denoble, DM Uguccioni, JJ Freiberger, W Reed, J Dovenbarger, J Caruso, R Duncan, W Hyatt. 2003. Report on decompression illness, diving fatalities and Project Dive Exploration, 2003 Edition: DAN's Annual Review of Recreational Scuba Diving Injuries and Fatalities Based on 2001 Data. 130 pp. Durham, NC: Divers Alert Network.

Walker, R. 2002. Medical standards for recreational divers, etc. In *Diving and Subaquatic Medicine*, 4th edition, Chapters 53–61, pp 533–614. C Edmonds, C Lowry, J Pennefather, and R Walker, eds. London and New York: Arnold.

Weller, IM, SG Thomas, PN Corey, MH Cox. 1992. Selection of a maximal test protocol to validate the Canadian Aerobic Fitness Test. *Can J Sport Sci*; 17(2): 114–119.

Wendling, J, R Ehrsam, P Knessl, P Nussberger, A Uske. 2001. Medical assessment of fitness to dive. International Edition. Hyperbaric Editions, CH 2502 Biel. ISBN 3-95222284

Westerfield, R, ed. 1997. *The Best of Alert Diver.* Flagstaff, AZ : Best Publishing Co.

Wisloff, U, AO Brubakk. 2001. Aerobic endurance training reduces bubble formation and increases survival in rat exposed to hyperbaric pressure. *J Physiol*; 537(Pt. 2): 607–611.

Zwingelberg, K, M Knight, J Biles. 1987. Decompression sickness in women divers. *Undersea Biomed Res;* 14:311–317.

PART FIVE

ACRONYMS
AND
ABBREVIATIONS

ACRONYMS AND ABBREVIATIONS

ACE	Angiotension converting enzyme
ADD	Attention deficit disorder
ADHD	Attention deficit/hyperactivity disorder
AED	Automatic external defibrillator
AGE	Arterial gas embolism
AIDS	Acquired immune deficiency syndrome
ALS	Amyotrophic lateral sclerosis (Lou Gehrig's disease)
ATA	Atmospheres absolute
BC	Buoyancy compensator
BG	Blood glucose
BMI	Body mass index
BPPV	Benign paroxysmal positional vertigo
BTV	Beance tubaire voluntaire
CAD	Coronary artery disease
CAT	Computer aided tomography
CHD	Coronary heart disease
CLL	Chronic lymphocytic leukemia
CMAS	Confederation Mondiale de Activites Subaquatiques
CNS	Central nervous system
CO	Carbon monoxide
CO_2	Carbon dioxide
COPD	Chronic obstructive pulmonary disease
CPR	Cardio-pulmonary resuscitation
CT	Computer aided tomography
DAN	Diver's Alert Network
dB	Decibel(s)
DCI	Decompression illness
DCS	Decompression sickness
dL	deci-liter(s)
DVT	Deep vein thrombosis
ECHM	European Committee for Hyperbaric Medicine
EKG	Electro-cardiogram
ENT	Ear, nose, and throat
FEV_1	Forced expiratory volume in one second
FFW	Feet of fresh water
FITT	Frequency, intensity, time, and type (of exercise)
FSW	Feet of sea water

GERD	Gastro-esophageal reflux disease
HDL	High-density lipoprotein ("good" cholesterol)
HIV	Human immune-deficiency virus
HOA	Hypoxia of ascent
HPNS	High pressure nervous syndrome
HR_{max}	Maximal heart rate
HRR	Heart rate reserve
IBD	Inflammatory bowl disease
ICT	Immuno Chromatographic Test
IDA	International Diving Assistance
IMCA	International Marine Contractor's Association
INR	International Normalized Ratio
IRDM	Insulin-requiring diabetes mellitus
KCAL	Kilocalorie
kg	Kilogram
LASIK	Laser-in-situ keratomileusis
LBM	Lean body mass
LDL	Low-density lipoprotein ("bad" cholesterol)
LH	Latent hypoxia
LOCU	Loss of consciousness underwater
MDD	Major depressive disorder
MET	Metabolic equivalent
mg	milligram(s)
ml	milliliter(s)
mm Hg	Millimeters of mercury
MND	Motor neuron disease
MRI	Magnetic resonance imaging
MS	Multiple sclerosis
MSW	Meters of sea water
N_2	Nitrogen
N_2O	Nitrous oxide
NIADD	National Instructors Association for Divers with Disabilities
NOAA	National Oceanic and Atmospheric Administration
NSAID	Non-steroidal anti-inflammatory drug
O_2	Oxygen
OHA	Oral hypoglycemic agent(s)
OTC	Over the counter
PADI	Professional Association of Diving Instructors
PE	Polyethylene or pressure equalization (tubes)
PFO	Patent foramen ovale
PFT	Pulmonary function test
PO_2	Partial pressure of oxygen
PPM	Parts per million

PRK	Photorefractive keratectomy
PSI	Pounds per square inch
PTSD	Post-traumatic stress disorder
RGP	Rigid gas permeable (contact lenses)
RK	Radial keratotomy
SAUHMA	Southern African Undersea and Hyperbaric Medical Association
SLE	Systemic lupus erythematosis
SLS	Sodium lauryl sulphate
SPF	Sunscreen protection factor
SPUMS	South Pacific Underwater Medicine Society
SWB	Shallow water blackout
TB	Tuberculosis
TM	Tympanic membrane (ear drum)
TMJ	Temporal-mandibular joint
TPA	Tissue Plasminogen Activator
UHMS	Undersea and Hyperbaric Medicine Society
USCG	United States Coast Guard
USN	United States Navy
$VO_{2\,max}$	A measure of aerobic capacity

PART SIX

INDEX

INDEX

P

R

S

T

U

V